SWISS RAILWAYS
CHEMINS DE FER SUISSES

LOCOMOTIVES AND RAILCARS
MATERIEL MOTEUR

FIRST EDITION/PREMIERE EDITION

The complete guide to all Locomotives and Railcars of the Railways of Switzerland

Le guide complet de tout le Materiel Moteur des Chemins de Fer Suisses

Chris Appleby & Paul Russenberger

Translation by/Traduction par
M. et Mme D. Haydock

Published by /Publié par/ Platform 5 Publishing Ltd., Lydgate House, Lydgate Lane, Sheffield S10 5FH, England.

Printed in England by/ Imprimé en Angleterre par/ Icon Impressions, Bacup, Lancs, OL13 9AF and BDC Printing Services, Slack Lane, Derby.

ISBN 1 872524 09-5

During the 'Rhätische Bahn 100' celebrations, 'Baby Crocodile' Class Ge6/6 I No. 414 crosses the Wiesen Viaduct between Filisur and Davos on 25/06/89. The coaches are the four metre gauge Pullmans built for the MOB 'Golden Mountain Pullman' which only ran during the summer of 1931. *C.P. Boocock*

Lors les célébrations du centenaire des chemins de fer Rhétiques, le «Bébé Crocodile» 414 de la série Ge6/6 I traverse le viaduc de Wiesen entre Filisur et Davos. Il remorque quatre voitures Pullman qui furent construites pour le «Golden Mountain Pullman» du MOB et qui n'ont circulé que pendant l'été de 1931. 25/06/89. *C.P. Boocock*

CONTENTS/TABLE DES MATIERES

INTRODUCTION

Unlike the rest of Europe, a large proportion of the Swiss railway system is privately-owned by nearly 60 separate companies varying in length from 381 km down to just 294 metres! This book contains full details of all locomotives and railcars of the Swiss Federal railways, the Bern Lötschberg Simplon Railway Group and the Rhätische Bahn, together with information on the stock of the numerous private railways.

LANGUAGE

Switzerland is a country with four official languages. The most widely spoken is German, with a large French-speaking area in the west of the country and Italian being spoken in the areas south of the Gotthard and Bernina passes. The fourth language, Romantsch, is spoken in parts of Canton Graubunden in the south-east. The national timetable uses all languages as appropriate to each table; this system has been adopted in this publication for place names. it should be noted that such towns are bilingual, Biel/Bienne (German/French) being the best-known example.

The official use of three languages in the areas where the Federal Railways operate requires it to display an official name in each of the three languages:

German:	Schweizerische Bundesbahnen	SBB
French:	Chemins de Fer Fédéraux	CFF
Italian:	Ferrovie Federali Svizzere	FFS

The Romantsch – Viafers Federalas Svizras (VFF) – appears only in the timetable, which also has an introduction in English.

Swiss Federal Locomotives and coaches are either lettered "SBB CFF FFS" on both sides or "SBB CFF" on one side and "SBB FFS" on the other. Their controls are labelled in German, French and Italian.

In the English section of this publication, the initials "SBB" are used throughout.

TICKETS

Apart from the ordinary single and return tickets (the cost of a return being less than twice the single fare for journeys of about 40 km), numerous concessions are available, usually through the purchase of "passes" or "cards".

The Swiss Pass gives unlimited travel on most major railways, boats, the transport systems of 24 cities and most postbuses together with a reduction on many privately-owned funiculars and mountain railways. The current prices are : four days – £72 second class, £108 first class, 8 days – £88 second, £128 first, 15 days – £104 second, £152 first and 1 month – £144 second, £208 first.

The Swiss Card provides a transfer from the point of entry into Switzerland to the holder's destination and back and a 50% reduction on other tickets purchased. It is valid for 1 month and costs £44 second class and £56 first. In fact, the first and last days are effectively rover tickets, giving the enthusiast opportunities limited only by the timetable, his or her ingenuity and stamina. The Swiss Transfer Ticket is similar but omits the 50% reduction, costing £32 second class and £48 first.

Regional Passes can be obtained covering 8 different areas. The length of validity (7 days or 15 days) and class of tarvel available varies according to the area. Day, family and half-fare cards are also available and the latter two can be used to obtain a reduction on the cost of regional passes.

The prices quoted are correct at February 1991. Full details of all these tickets and other facilites are available from:

Swiss National Tourist Office, Swiss Centre, New Coventry Street, London, W1V 8BB, England.

CLASSIFICATION OF SWISS MOTIVE POWER

All Swiss railways use a standard classification system for their motive power. It should be noted that separate systems are used for locos and railcars; hence it is possible for a loco and a railcar to have the same classification.

PREFIX LETTERS (Locomotives)

R Max speed more than 110 km/h
A Max speed 85 to 110 km/h
B Max speed 70 to 80 km/h
C Max speed 60 to 65 km/h
D Max speed 45 to 55 km/h
E Shunting loco
G Narrow gauge loco
H Rack fitted loco (combined with above if rack & adhesion)
O Open wagon body
T Tractor
X Departmental vehicle (some of these are ex-railcars)

PREFIX LETTERS (Railcars)

Note: Further prefixed by R if max speed is more than 110 km/h.

A 1st class accommodation
B 2nd class accommodation
D Baggage compartment
S Saloon vehicle
Z Postal compartment

SUFFIX LETTERS (All motive power)

a Battery powered
e Electric powered
em Electric & diesel powered (i.e. an electro-diesel)
h Rack fitted (only used with railcars & tractors); if this precedes the a, e or m then the unit is pure rack; if it follows, the unit is rack & adhesion
m Diesel or petrol powered
r Restaurant vehicle
rot Rotary snowplough
t (only used with X in the form of Xt) Self propelled departmental vehicle, but not a loco (e.g. a self propelled crane or snowplough)

NUMBERS

These indicate the number of powered and total number of axles, e.g.
4/4 = all 4 axles powered (e.g. BoBo)
3/6 = 6 axles of which 3 are powered (e.g. 2Co1)

SUB-CLASS INDICES

To differentiate between classes with otherwise similar classifications, small Roman numbers are used, e.g. Re4/4 I, Re4/4 II, etc.

All the above are combined as required to give full classifications, e.g.

Ae6/6 CoCo electric loco, max speed 85–110 km/h
Be4/6 1BB1 electric loco, max speed 70–80 km/h
ABDe4/4 BoBo electric railcar, 1st, 2nd & baggage accommodation

ACKNOWLEDGENTS

We would like to thank all who have helped with the preparation of this book, especially Messrs. B. Garvin and R. Awde, various members of the Locomotive Club of Great Britain, various officials and staff of the SBB, all who submitted photographs and Mr. G. Hurst for the provision of maps.

In addition to much research by the authors, the following references have been consulted:

Die Elektrischen und Diesel Triebfahrzeuge Schweizerische Eisenbahnen (C. Jeanmaire).
Lokomotiven und Triebwagen der Schweizer Bahnen Band I–IV (P. Willen).
World Electric Locomotives (K. Harris).
Magazines: Eisenbahn Amateur, LCGB Bulletin, Modern Tramway.

INTRODUCTION

Contrairement aux autres pays d'Europe, une grande proportion du réseau ferroviare suisse appartient à une des presque 60 compagnies privées qui exploitent des réseaux allant de 381 km à seulement 284 metres! Ce livre contient des détails complets de toutes les locomotives et automotrices des Chemins de Fer Suisses (CFF), la compagnie Bern Lötschberg Simplon (BLS) et les Chemins de Fer Rhetiques (RhB). Une liste complète et quelques détails sont donnés pour le matériel moteur des autres chemins de fer privés.

LANGUES

La Suisse a quatre langues officielles; l'allemand est la langue la plus répandue. Le franȩis est parlé dans une grande partie de l'ouest du pays. L'italien est utilisé au sud des cols de St Gothard et de Bernina. La quatrième langue est le romanche qui est utilisé dans des parties du canton de Grisons. L'indicateur officiel suisse utilise la langue appropriée pour chaque tableau horaire. Dans la traduction française nous avons utilisé des noms de villes là où c'etait possible. Il existe plusieurs villes bilingues, dont Biel/Bienne est l'exemple le plus connu.

Ces quatre langues sont utilisées dans l'indicateur suisse et il existe quatre noms différents pour les Chemins de Fer Fédéraux Suisses :

Allemand – Schweitzerische Bundesbahn – SBB
Franȩis – Chemins de Fer Fédéraux Suisses – CFF
Italien – Ferrovie Fderali Svizzere – FFS
Romanche – Viafers Federalas Svizras – VFF

La version romanche n'est utilisée que très rarement et n'est pas marquée sur le matériel.

Le matériel moteur des chemins de fer fédéraux suisses porte soit le sigle «SBB CFF FFS» sur les deux côtés, soit «SBB CFF» sur un côté et «SBB FFS» sur l'autre. Les appareils de commande sont marqués en allemand, français et italien.

Pour éviter toute confusion, nous avons utilisé les lettres CFF dans ce livre.

BILLETS

Mis à part les billets aller et aller-retour habituels (un aller-retour coûte moins cher que deux allers sur les parcours de plus de 40 km) de nombreuses reductions sont possibles grâce à l'achat de "pass" ou de "cartes"

Le "Swiss Pass" est un ticket libre circulation pour les étrangers. Il est valable sur tout le réseau CFF et sur la plupart des réseaux privés (sur la plupart des lignes de montagne à crémaillère, il donne une réduction sur le prix du voyage), les bus des PTT, les bateaux des lacs et les services urbains de transports en commun de 24 grandes villes. Il existe pour des périodes de 4 jours (710 FF), 8 jours (860 FF), 15 jours (1020 FF) ou 1 mois (1410 FF). Ces prix sont pour le billet de deuxième classe et sont valables pendant 1991; les tickets pour la première classe sont environ 50% plus cher.

Les "Regional-Pass" sont des tickets libre circulation pour 8 régions de la Suisse. La validité varie selon la région choisie. Il existe beaucoup d'autres forfaits et de reductions. De plus amples renseignements seront fournis par l'Office National Suisse de Tourisme, 11bis rue Scribe, 75009 Paris.

CLASSIFICATION DU MATERIEL MOTEUR SUISSE

Tous les chemins de fer suisses utilisent un système standard de classification de matériel moteur. Il existe deux systèmes différents pour les locomotives et les automotrices; il est donc possible qu'une locomotive et une automotrice aient la même classification.

PREFIXES (Locomotives)

R Vitesse max supérieure à 110 km/h
A Vitesse max entre 85 et 110 km/h
B Vitesse max entre 70 et 80 km/h
C Vitesse max entre 60 et 65 km/h
D Vitesse max entre 45 et 55 km/h
E Locomotive de manoeuvre
G Locomotive à voie étroite
T Locotracteur
H Locomotive à crémaillère (utilisé avec les préfixes ci-dessus si le matériel fonctionne aussi en adhérence)
O Wagon ouvert avec cabine de conduite
X Matériel de service (parfois une automotrice déclassée)

PREFIXES (Automotrices)

Nota: Le préfixe R est ajouté si la vitesse max dépasse 110 km/h.

A 1re classe
B 2me classe
D Compartiment à bagages
S Voiture à aménagement spécial pour charters
Z Compartiment postal

SUFFIXES (Tout matériel moteur)

a	Matériel à accumulateurs
e	Matériel électrique
em	Matériel "amphibie" – électro-diesel
h	Matériel à crémaillère (utilisé seulement pour des automotrices et locotracteurs); si ce suffixe précède le a, e ou le m, le matériel fonctionne seulement à crémaillère; si le suffixe suit l'autre lettre, le matériel fonctionne à crémaillère et en adhérence.
m	Matériel thermique
r	Voiture restaurant
rot	Chasse-neige rotatif
t	(utilisé seulement avec X pour la classification Xt) Matériel de service autopropulsé, autre qu'une locomotive (par exemple, une grue autopropulsée ou un chasse-neige)

NUMEROS

Ceux-ci indiquent le nombre d'essieux moteurs et le nombre total d'essieux, par exemple: 4/4 tous les 4 essieux à moteur, par exemple BoBo 3/6 6 essieux dont 3 à moteur, par exemple 2Co1

INDICE DE SOUS SERIE

Afin de différencier les séries avec la même classification, des petits chiffres romains sont ajoutés, par exemple Re4/4^{I}, Re4/4^{II}, etc. Tous les préfixes et suffixes sont combinés pour donner la classification, par exemple:

Ae6/6	locomotive électrique CoCo, vitesse max 85–110 km/h.
Be4/6	locomotive électrique 1BB1, vitesse max 70–80 km/h.
ABDe4/4	automotrice électrique BoBo, 1re et 2me classes, compartiment à bagages.

REMERCIEMENTS

Nous tenons à remercier tous ce qui ont aidé à la preparation de ce livre, particulièrement M. B. Garvin et M. R. Awde, les membres du Locomotive Club of Great Britain, ainsi que de nombreux officiels et personels des CFF, toutes les personnes ayant contribué aux photos ainsi que M. G. Hurst pour les cartes.

Mise à par nos recherches personelles, nous avons consulté les livres suivants:

Die Elektrischen und Diesel Triebfahrzeuge Schweizerische Eisenbahnen (C. Jeanmaire).
Lokomotiven und Triebwagen der Schweizer Bahnen Band I–IV (P. Willen).
World Electric Locomotives (K. Harris).
Les revues: Eisenbahn Amateur, LCGB Bulletin, Modern Tramway.

BUILDERS/CONSTRUCTEURS

The following builder codes are used in this publication:
(All are in Switzerland, unless stated otherwise)

Les codes suivants sont utilisés pour les contructeurs:
(Tous sont en Suisse, sauf indication contraire)

ABB	ASEA Brown Boveri, Baden & Zürich Oerliken.
ACEC	Ateliers de Constructions Electriques de Charleroi, Belgium.
ACMV	Ateliers de Constructions Mécaniques SA, Vevey.
AEG	Allgemeine Elektrizitäts Gesellschaft, Berlin, Germany.
ALIOTH	Elektrizitätsgesellschaft Alioth, Münchenstein.
ASPER	Viktor Asper AG Maschinenbau, Küsnacht.
BBC	AG Brown Boveri & Cie, Baden.
BBC (M)	Brown Boveri & Cie, Mannheim, Germany.
BEIL	Martin Beilhack Maschinenfabrik, Rosenheim, Germany.
BIBUS	Bibus Hydraulik AG, Zumikon.
BL	Anciens Etablissements Brissonneau & Lotz, Creil, France.
BREDA	SA Ernesto Breda, Milano, Italy.
BÜH	Bühler SA, Officine Meccaniche, Taverne.
BÜS	Büssing Fahrzeug und Motorenbau, Braunschweig, Germany.
CAT	Caterpillar, Peoria, Illinois, USA.
CEG	Chemins de Fer Electriques de la Gruyère (predecessor of/prédécesseur de/ GFM).
CEM	Cie Electro Méchanique, Le Havre, France.
CET	Carminati e Toselli, Milano, Italy.
CFD	Chemins de Fer Départmenteaux, Montmirail, France.
CGV	Compagnie Générale de Villefranche sur Saone, France.
CMR	Constructions Mécaniques SA, Renens.
CUM	Cummins Engine Corporation, Columbus, Indiana, USA.
DBZ	Daimler Benz AG, Stuttgart, Germany.
DIEMA	Diepholzer Maschinenfabrik (Fr. Schöttler GmbH), Diepholz, Germany.
DMG	Daimler Motoren Gesellschaft, Stuttgart, Germany.
DZ	Klöckner Humboldt Deutz AG, Köln, Germany.
FFA	Flug und Fahrzeugwerke AG, Altenrhein.
FORD	Ford Motor Company, Detroit, Michigan, USA.
FUCHS	H. Fuchs Waggonfabrik AG, Heidelberg, Germany.
GANG	Gangloff Carrosserie AG, Bern.
Gm	Gmeinder & Co GmbH, Maschinenfabrik Mosbach, Germany.
GM	General Motors AG, Biel.
GSEG	Gewerkschaft Schalker-Eisenhütte, Gelsenkirchen, Germany.
HEN	Henschel Werke AG, Kassel, Germany (now/maintenant/ Thyssen Henschel).
HESS	Hess AG, Carrosserien, Bellach SO.
HÜR	H. Hürlimann Tractorenwerke, Wil SG.
IEG	Compagnie de l'Industrie Electrique, Genève.
JMR	J. Meyer AG, Rheinfelden.
JUNG	Arn. Jung Lokomotivfabrik GmbH, Jungenthal bei Kirchberg an der Sieg, Germany.
KM	Krauss Maffei AG, München, Germany.
KRON	L. Kronenberger & Söhne, Luzern.
KRUPP	Fried Krupp Maschi nenfabriken, Essen, Germany.
LISTER	R & A Lister & Co Ltd., Dursley, Glos., UK.
LMG	Lübecker Maschinenbau AG, Werk Dorstfeld, Germany.
LÜTHI	Eduard Lüthi, Worb.
MAK	Maschinenbau Kiel GmbH, Kiel, Germany.
MAN	Maschinenfabrik Augsburg-Nürnberg AG, Germany.
MAYBACH	Maybach Motorenbau, Friedrichshafen, Germany.
MB	Mercedes Benz, Berlin Marienfeld, Germany.
MFO	Maschinenfabrik Oerlikon, Zürich Oerlikon (now part of/maintenant une partie de/ BBC).
MOY	Gaston Moyse, La Corneuve, France.
MTU	Motoren und Turbinen Union GmbH, Friedrichshafen, Germany.
MWM	Motoren Werke Mannheim, Germany.
NEN	Martin Nencki AG, Fahrzeugbau und Hydraulik, Langenthal.

OK	Orenstein & Koppel AG, Dortmund, Germany.
PER	Perkins Engines Ltd., Peterborough, UK.
PETER	Konrad Peter, Maschinenfabrik, Liestal.
PFING	Pfingstweid AG, Zürich.
PLEI	Paul Pleiger Maschinenfabrik, Blankenstein, Germany.
POY	Moteurs Poyaud, Surgères, France.
Puch	Puch Werke.
RACO	Robert Aebi & Co AG, Regensdorf.
RC	Regazzoni Costruzioni, Lugano.
REG	Officine Meccaniche Italiane Reggiane, Reggio d'Emilia, Italy.
REN	Régie Nationale des Usines Renault, Billancourt, France.
RIET	AG vormals J.J. Rieter, Wintherthur.
RING	F. Ringhoffer Werke AG, Waggon & Tenderfabrik, Smichow bei Prague, Czechoslovakia.
ROBEL	Robel Maschinenfabrik, München, Germany.
RUHR	Ruhrthaler Maschinenfabrik, Müllheim, Germany.
SAAS	SA des Ateliers de Sécheron, Genève (now part of/maintenant une partie de/ BBC)
SAU	AG Adolf Saurer, Arbon.
SCH	Christoph Schöttler Maschinenfabrik GmbH, Diepholz, Germany. (trade name 'Schöma'/raison sociale «Schöma»)
SCIN	Scintilla AG, Zuchwil.
SE	Siemens AG, Werk Erlangen, Germany.
SIG	Schweizerische Industriegesellschaft, Neuhausen am Rheinfall.
SLM	Schweizerische Lokomotiv und Maschinenfabrik, Winterthur.
SSW	Siemens Schuckert Werke, Berlin, Germany.
STAD	Ernst Stadler AG, Fahrzeugbau, Bussnang.
STECK	Ferdinand Steck, Maschinenfabrik, Bowil.
SWP	Schindler Waggon AG, Pratteln.
SWS	Schweizerische Wagons und Aufzügefabrik AG, Schlieren.
SZ	Gebrüder Sulzer AG, Winterthur.
TIBB	Technomasio Italiano Brown Boveri, Milano, Italy.
TUCH	Gebrüder Tuchschmid AG, Frauenfeld.
U23A	Uzinele 23 August, Bucuresti, Romania.
VBZ	Verkehrsbetriebe der Stadt Zürich (Zürich Tranways).
VM	Stabilimenti Meccanici VM SpA, Cento Ferrara, Italy.
VOITH	J.M. Voith GmbH, Heidenheim, Germany.
VR	von Rollsche Eisenwerke, Gelafingen.
VW	Volkswagenwerke, Wolfsburg, Germany.
WIND	Rheiner Maschinenfabrik Windhoff AG, Rheine, Germany.
ZÜR	Zürcher & Cie SA, St Aubin.

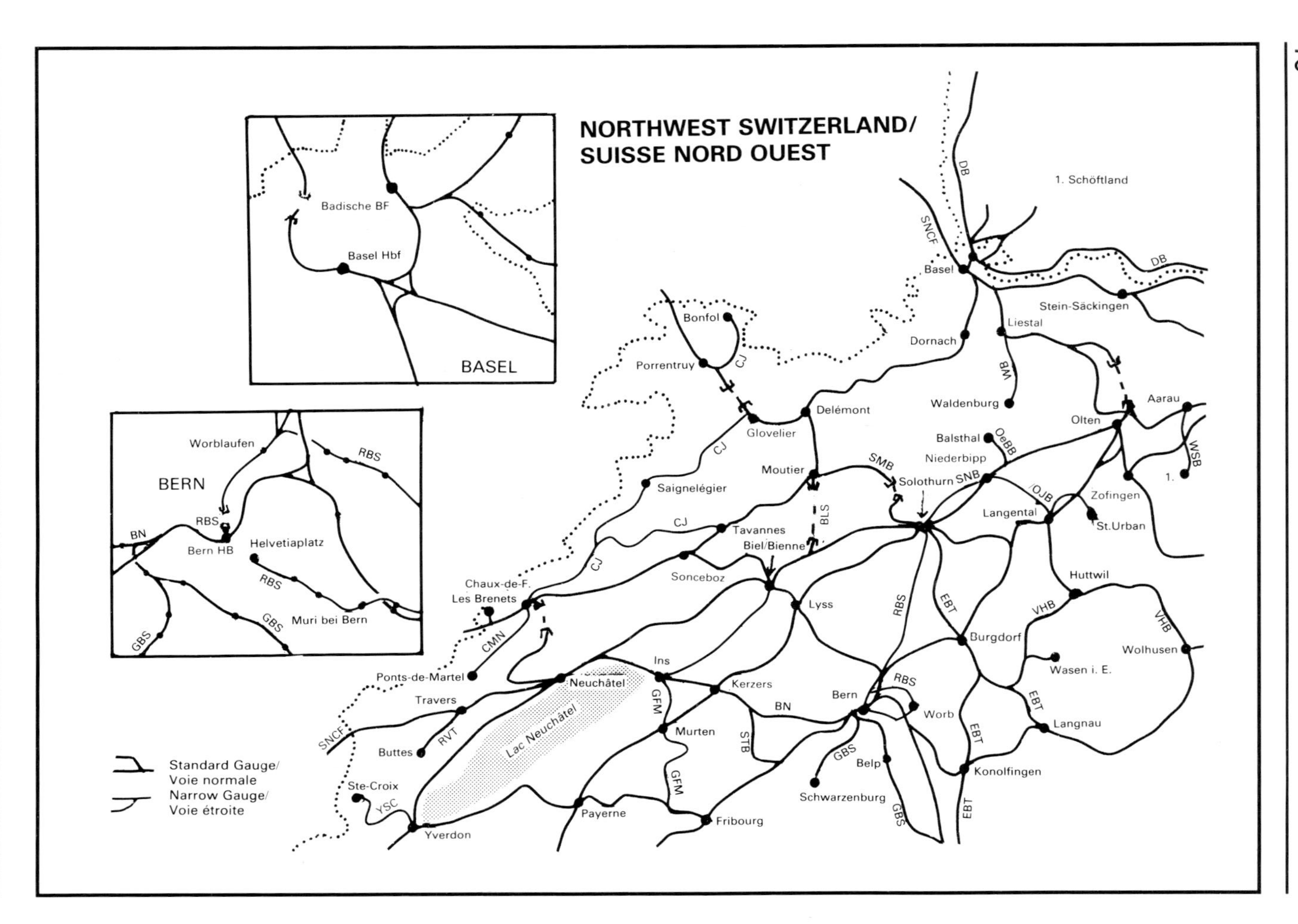

NORTHWEST SWITZERLAND/
SUISSE NORD OUEST
Badische BF
Basel Hbf
BASEL
Worblaufen
BERN
RBS
BN
Bern HB
Helvetiaplatz
Muri bei Bern
GBS
1. Schöftland
DB
SNCF
Basel
Stein-Säckingen
Liestal
Dornach
WB
Waldenburg
Aarau
Olten
WSB
1.
Zofingen
St.Urban
Bonfol
Porrentruy
CJ
Delémont
Glovelier
Balsthal
OeBB
Niederbipp
SMB
Solothurn
SNB
OJB
Langental
Moutier
Saignelégier
BLS
Tavannes
Biel/Bienne
Sonceboz
Chaux-de-F.
Les Brenets
Lyss
EBT
Burgdorf
Huttwil
VHB
Wolhusen
Wasen i. E.
Langnau
Konolfingen
CMN
Ponts-de-Martel
Ins
Neuchâtel
Kerzers
Bern
Worb
Travers
RVT
Buttes
Lac Neuchâtel
GFM
Murten
STB
Belp
Schwarzenburg
Standard Gauge/
Voie normale
Narrow Gauge/
Voie étroite
Ste-Croix
YSC
Yverdon
Payerne
Fribourg

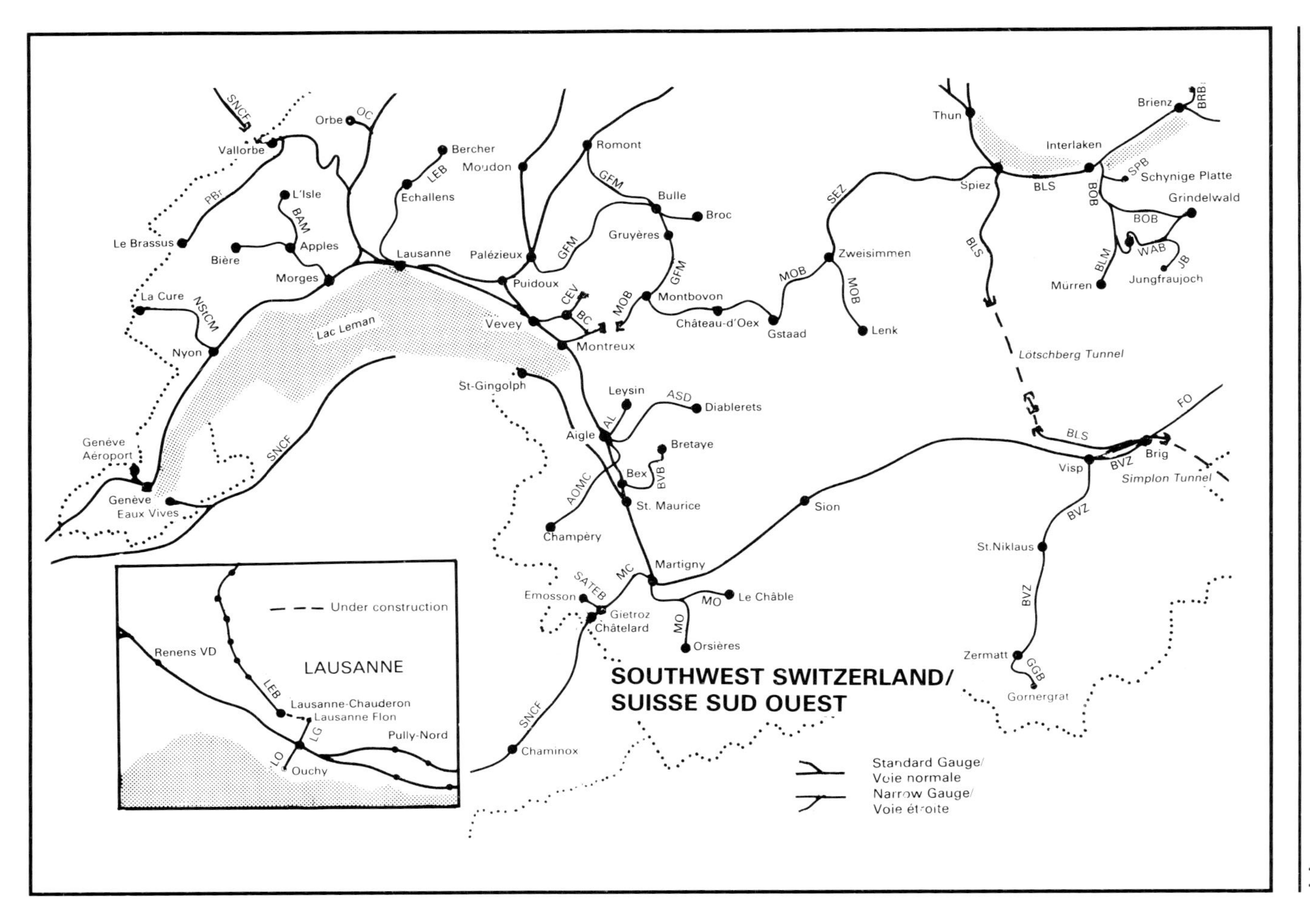
SNCF
Orbe
OC
Vallorbe
PBr
Le Brassus
L'Isle
BAM
Apples
Bière
Morges
La Cure
NStCM
Nyon
Lac Leman
Genève
Aéroport
Genève
Eaux Vives
SNCF
Bercher
LEB
Echallens
Lausanne
Moudon
Palézieux
Puidoux
Romont
GFM
Bulle
Broc
Gruyères
GFM
GFM
CEV
BC
Vevey
MOB
Montreux
Montbovon
Château-d'Oex
Gstaad
MOB
Zweisimmen
MOB
Lenk
SEZ
Thun
Spiez
BLS
Interlaken
Brienz
BRB
SPB
Schynige Platte
BOB
BOB
Grindelwald
WAB
JB
BLM
Mürren
Jungfraujoch
BLS
Lötschberg Tunnel
BLS
FO
Brig
Visp
BVZ
Simplon Tunnel
St-Gingolph
Leysin
ASD
Diablerets
AL
Aigle
Bretaye
Bex
BVB
AOMC
St. Maurice
Champéry
Sion
BVZ
St.Niklaus
BVZ
Zermatt
GGB
Gornergrat
Martigny
MC
SATEB
Emosson
Gietroz
Châtelard
MO
Le Châble
MO
Orsières
SNCF
Chaminox
SOUTHWEST SWITZERLAND/
SUISSE SUD OUEST
Standard Gauge/
Voie normale
Narrow Gauge/
Voie étroite
Under construction
LAUSANNE
Renens VD
LEB
Lausanne-Chauderon
Lausanne Flon
LG
LO
Ouchy
Pully-Nord

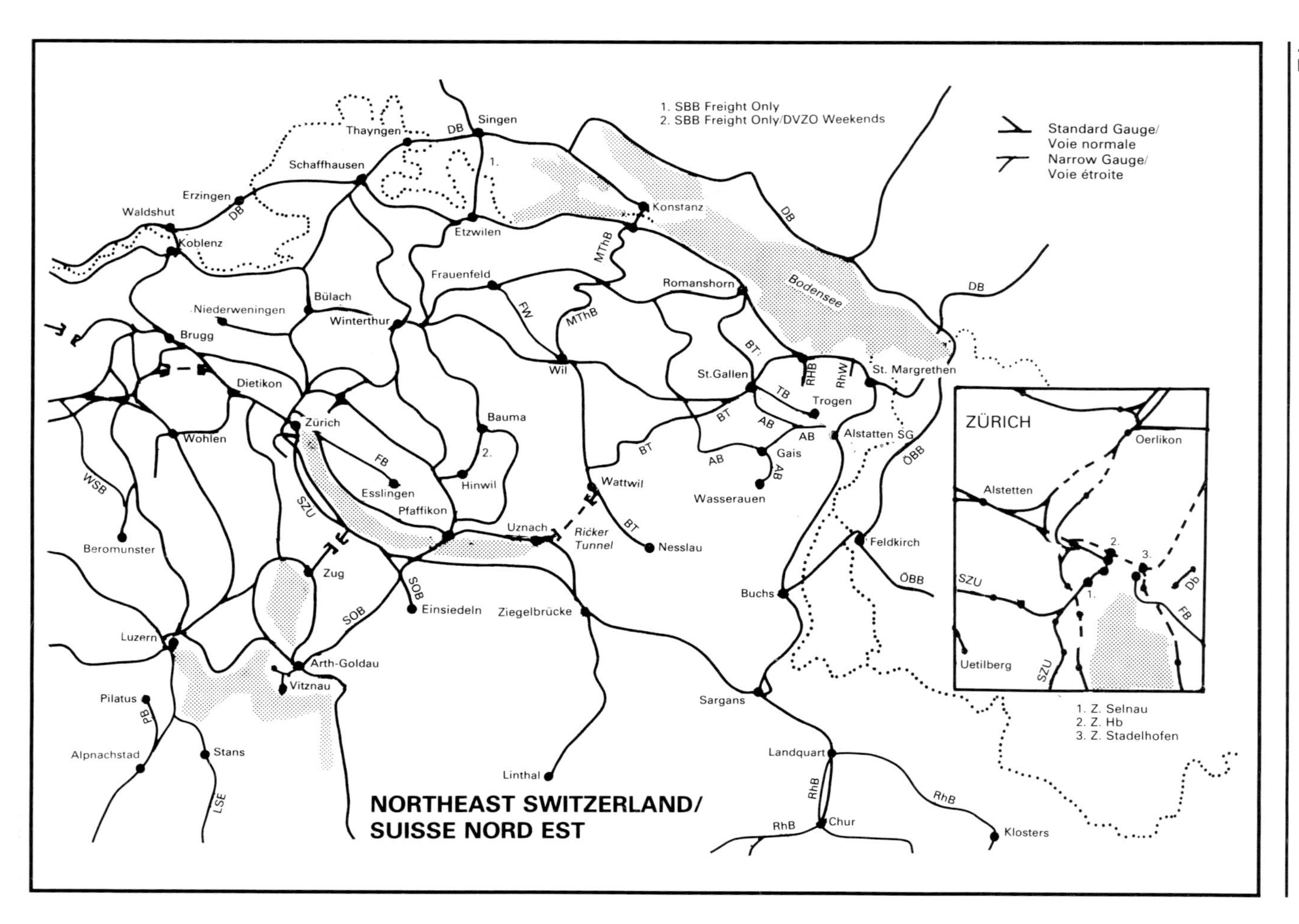

NORTHEAST SWITZERLAND/
SUISSE NORD EST
1. SBB Freight Only
2. SBB Freight Only/DVZO Weekends
Standard Gauge/
Voie normale
Narrow Gauge/
Voie étroite
ZÜRICH
Oerlikon
Alstetten
Uetilberg
SZU
Db
FB
1. Z. Selnau
2. Z. Hb
3. Z. Stadelhofen
Singen
Thayngen
Schaffhausen
Erzingen
Waldshut
Koblenz
Etzwilen
Konstanz
Bodensee
Romanshorn
Frauenfeld
Bülach
Niederweningen
Winterthur
Brugg
Dietikon
Zürich
Wohlen
Beromunster
Wil
Bauma
Hinwil
Esslingen
Pfaffikon
Uznach
Ricker Tunnel
Wattwil
Nesslau
St.Gallen
Trogen
Gais
Wasserauen
Alstatten SG
St. Margrethen
Feldkirch
Buchs
Zug
Einsiedeln
Ziegelbrücke
Linthal
Luzern
Arth-Goldau
Vitznau
Pilatus
Alpnachstad
Stans
Sargans
Landquart
Chur
Klosters
DB
MThB
FW
BT
TB
AB
RHB
RhW
ÖBB
SOB
WSB
PB
LSE
RhB

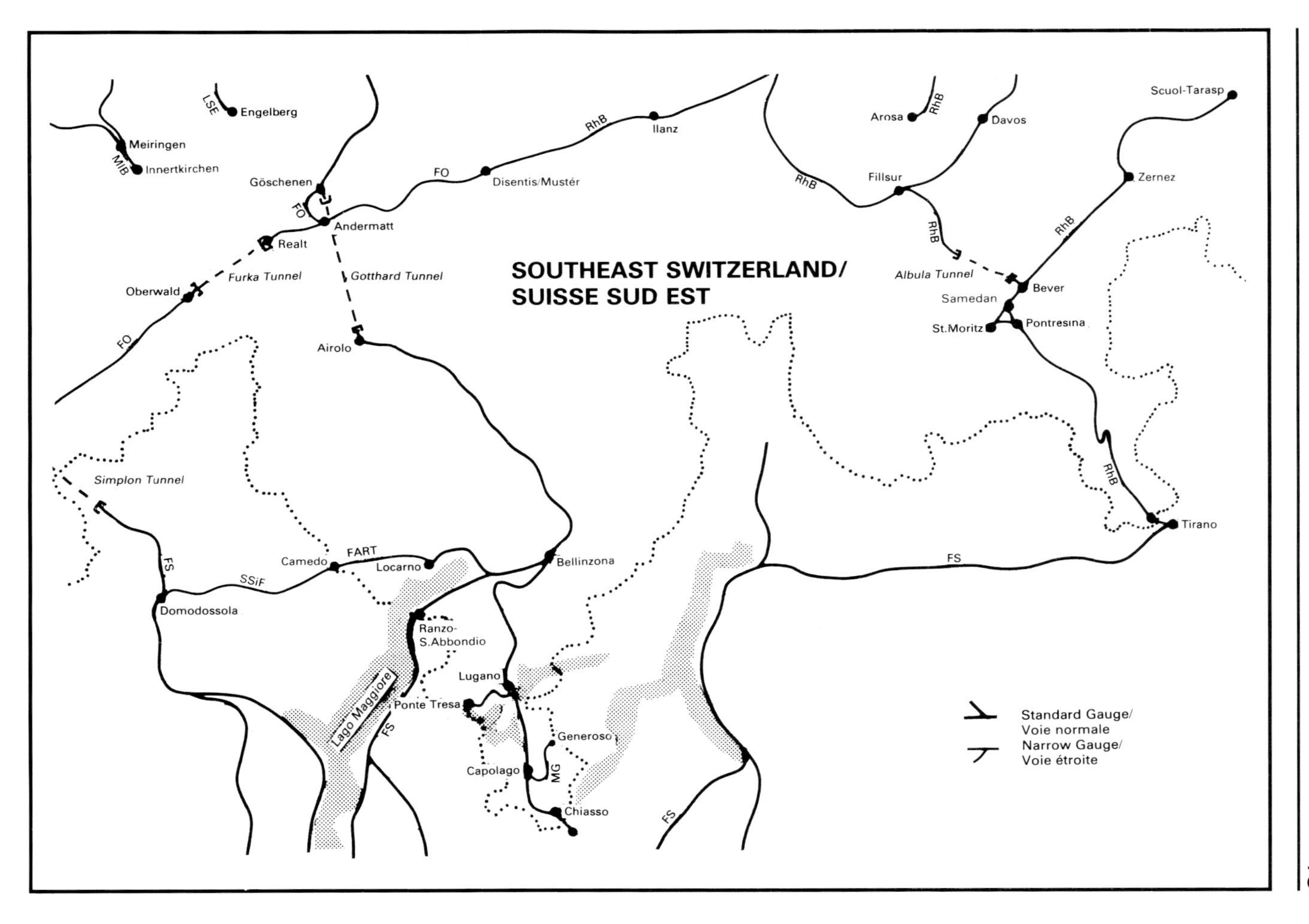
SOUTHEAST SWITZERLAND/
SUISSE SUD EST
LSE
Engelberg
Meiringen
MIB
Innertkirchen
Göschenen
FO
Andermatt
Realt
Oberwald
Furka Tunnel
Gotthard Tunnel
FO
FO
Disentis/Mustér
RhB
Ilanz
Airolo
Arosa
RhB
Davos
RhB
Fillsur
RhB
Albula Tunnel
Scuol-Tarasp
Zernez
RhB
Bever
Samedan
St.Moritz
Pontresina
RhB
Tirano
Simplon Tunnel
FS
Camedo
FART
Locarno
SSiF
Bellinzona
FS
Domodossola
Ranzo-
S.Abbondio
Lugano
Lago Maggiore
Ponte Tresa
FS
Generoso
Capolago
MG
Chiasso
FS
Standard Gauge/
Voie normale
Narrow Gauge/
Voie étroite

SWISS FEDERAL RAILWAYS

GENERAL

The SBB was formed in 1902 when most of the major private companies were nationalised, and a few other railways have been absorbed since. The SBB is now divided into 3 zones:
Zone I Lausanne – covers the south west.
Zone II Luzern – covers the Basel to Chiasso line and branches.
Zone III Zürich – covers the north and east.

NUMBERING SYSTEM

Steam locomotives were numbered below 10000, and consequently when main line electric locomotives first appeared, they were numbered 10001 upwards. However, when railcars, shunting tractors and later diesel locomotives were purchased, they each had their own separate numbering systems, railcars in fact being initially numbered in the carriage series. This resulted in many duplicated numbers, and to eliminate these much renumbering occurred during the 1950s and 1960s. Although this eliminated duplicated numbers (except the Brünig line – see below), the result was a non too logical system, particularly in the case of the 8xxx and 9xxx series tractors which were numbered in these blocks when vacant numbers in the earlier series were exhausted.

The Brünig narrow gauge stock was for many years numbered in its own separate series, and although the tractors and electric locomotives did not duplicate numbers in the standard gauge series, the older motor baggage vans clash with standard gauge tractors.

This number series is as follows:

1– 250	Electric tractors (traffic stock)
251– 399	Electro-diesel tractors (traffic stock)
401– 599	Diesel tractors (traffic stock)
601– 950	Diesel tractors (departmental stock)
901– 916	Electric railcars (Brünig Line)
951– 963	Electric tractors (departmental stock; all now withdrawn)
964– 979	Battery tractors (all are departmental)
980– 999	Diesel tractors (Brünig Line departmental stock)
1001– 1899	Electric railcars
1901– 1999	Electric locomotives (Brünig Line)
2001– 2999	Electric railcars
8001– 8399	Electric tractors (traffic stock)
8401– 8999	Diesel tractors (traffic stock)
9401– 9999	Diesel tractors (departmental stock)
10001–11999	Electric locomotives, max speed more than 80 km/h
12001–13999	Electric locomotives, max speed 70 to 80 km/h
14001–14999	Electric locomotives, max speed 60 to 65 km/h
15001–15999	Electric locomotives, max speed 45 to 55 km/h (all now withdrawn)
16001–16999	Electric shunting locomotives
17001–17999	Electro-diesel locomotives (being converted to diesels)
18001–18999	Diesel locomotives

Commencing in 1989, a new numbering system has been introduced for new classes. However, to date it has not been applied to existing classes, although all these have been allotted new class numbers. There is no indication of any intention to renumber existing stock. The new scheme consists of 7 digits, comprising a 3 digit class number, a 3 digit running number and a computer check digit. The system operates as follows:

1st Digit:
0 Steam Loco
1 Metre Gauge Loco (Brünig Line)
2 Tractor
3 Electric Loco (3 powered axles)
4 Electric Loco (4 powered axles)
5 Electric Railcar
6 Electric Loco (6 powered axles)
7 Departmental Stock (self-propelled, but not a loco–e.g. crane or tamper)

	8 Diesel Loco
	9 Electric Shunting Loco
2nd Digit:	0 Express Stock (Railcars only)
	1–6 Sub Class Index (Bogie Electric Locos)
	Type of Electric Railcar
	No. of Powered Axles (Diesel Locos)
	7–8 Not used
	9 Used in lieu of / on rigid frame electric locos
3rd Digit:	Used to differentiate between classes with identical 1st & 2nd digits. However, in some cases indicates the following:
	2–4; 2, 3, or 4 voltage loco or railcar
	No. of non-powered axles (rigid frame electric loco)

4th to 6th Digits: The last 3 digits of the old number.

Stock delivered with new numbers is detailed at the end of each section.

ELECTRIFICATION

The SBB is electrified on the 15 kV 16⅔ Hz system, the only exceptions being a few lines in border areas where the systems of neighbouring countries are used. All SBB electric stock can only operate on the above system unless stated otherwise.

SBB DEPOTS

Code	*Main Sheds*	*Sub-Sheds*
Zone 1 (Lausanne)		
BN	Bern	Fribourg
		Thun
BI	Biel/Bienne	Chaux de Fonds
		Delémont
		Neuchâtel
BR	Brig	-
GE	Genève	-
LS	Lausanne	Payerne
		St Maurice
		Vallorbe
Zone II (Luzern)		
BE	Bellinzona	Chiasso (a)
BS	Basel	Kleinhünigen
		Muttenz
CH	Chiasso (a)	-
ER	Erstfeld	-
LZ	Luzern (b)	Arth Goldau
		Beinwil
		Zug
MR	Meiringen	Luzern (n.g.) (b)
OL	Olten	Aarau
		Solothurn
Zone III (Zürich)		
RS	Rorschach	Buchs
		Chur
		Romanshorn
		Sargans
		St Gallen
WT	Winterthur	Schaffhausen (c)
		Wil
ZU	Zürich	Brugg
		Limmattal
		Rapperswil

(a) There are two depots in Chiasso; the main line depot is a sub-shed of Bellinzona, and a separate tractor depot has its own allocation.
(b) Separate standard and narrow gauge depots exist in Luzern; a few tractors are allocated to the n.g. shed.
(c) Winterthur depot will be reoplaced by a new depot at Oberwinterthur.

In addition to the above, many stations and other locations have small sheds housing one or more shunting tractors; often these belong to the permanent way or other engineer's departments.

SBB WORKSHOPS

Five workshops are responsible for the repair and overhaul of SBB motive power.

Bellinzona	Electric locos (Re4/4 II, Re4/4 III, Re6/6, Ae6/6). Electric railcars (Be4/6).
Biel	All diesel locos; also diesel engines from Tem
series tractors.	
Olten	All diesel tractors (this is the old works near the station; the new works some distance away is purely a carriage and wagon facility).
Yverdon	Electric locos (Re4/4 I, Re4/4 II). All electric shunters. All electric tractors (including electrical parts from Tem series). Electric railcars (BDe4/4 II, De4/4).
Zürich	Electric locos (Ae3/6 I, Ae4/7). Electric railcars (except BDe4/4 II, De4/4).

LIVERIES

Until 1984, most line electric locomotives and railcars were painted dark green, while diesels and shunters were reddish-brown. Since 1984, a red livery has been adopted for locomotives (except for the new 450 class), while new railcars are blue and cream. A number of non-standard liveries also exist, but several of these will disappear in the near future. The various liveries are shown in the lists using the following letter codes:

B Brown (the original electric loco livery, a few 'museum' locos have been restored to this livery).
D Dark Red (applied to new railcars in the late 1960s, only the RABDe12/12 class remains in this livery).
E Eurocity (2-tone grey; the former TEE railcars are now in this livery).
G Dark Green (the standard livery for most electric locomotives and railcars prior to 1984). All electric main-line locomotives and railcars are in this livery unless stated otherwise.
L Dark Green/Red ends (some railcars have red ends to improve visibility).
M Multi-Colour (Psychedelic!). There is only one railcar in this livery).
N NPZ (Neue Pendel Zug), blue and grey with red ends. The new livery for local trains.
O Orange/Grey ('Swiss Express') livery, applied to Mark III coaching stock and some Re4/4 II locos during the 1970s).
P Reddish-Brown. (The standard livery for shunters and tractors until 1984). All diesels, electric shunters & tractors are in this livery unless stated otherwise.
S S-Bahn (blue with red ends, applied only to the new 450 class for the Zürich S-Bahn services).
T Trans Europ Express (TEE). A few Re4/4 II remain in the red/cream TEE livery, although EE services to Switzerland have now ceased.
V Violet/Yellow (applied to the prototype RABDe8/16 class; neither the class nor the livery were perpetuated).
Y Yellow (a few tractors used as works pilots are in this livery).

LES CHEMINS DE FER FEDERAUX SUISSES

INTRODUCTION

Les CFF furent créés en 1902 par suite de la nationalisation de la plupart des principaux chemins de fer privés. Quelques autres compagnies ont été absorbées depuis. Les CFF sont divisés en 3 zones:

Zone I Lausanne – qui couvre le sud-est du pays.
Zone II Lucerne – qui couvre la ligne Bâle-Chiasso et ses branches.
Zone III Zurich – qui couvre le nord et l'est.

SYSTEME DE NUMEROTATION

Les machines à vapeur étaient numérotées jusqu'à 10000. Par conséquent, les premières machines électriques furent numérotées à partir de 10001. Cependant, les automotrices, locotracteurs et machines diesel acavtés plus tard avaient chacun leur propre système de numérotation. Les automotrices étaient d'abord numérotées dans la même série que les voitures remorquées. Pendant les années 50 et 60, beaucoup de matériel fut rénuméroté afin d'éliminer la duplication de numéros (sauf pour la ligne du Brünig, voir ci-dessous). Cependant, le nouveau système n'était pas très logique, surtout dans le cas des locotracteurs des séries 8000 et 9000, qui eurent ces numéros quand il n'y avait plus de numéros disponibles dans la série 401–950.

Le matériel à voie étroite de la ligne du Brünig eut pendant longtemps une série de numéros spéciaux. Bien que les numéros des locotracteurs et des locomotives électriques ne dupliquaient pas ceux du matériel à voie normale, ceux des anciens fourgons moteurs à bagages portent les mêmes numéros que les locotracteurs à voie normale.

Le système de numérotation se présente comme suit:

1– 250	Locotracteurs électriques de ligne
251– 399	Locotracteurs électro-diesel de ligne
401– 599	Locotracteurs diesel de ligne
601– 950	Locotracteurs diesel de service
901– 916	Locotracteurs électriques (ligne du Brünig)
951– 963	Locotracteurs électriques de service (tous radiés maintenant)
964– 979	Locotracteurs à accumulateurs (tous de service)
980– 999	Locotracteurs diesel (de service sur la ligne du Brünig)
1001– 1899	Automotrices électriques
1901– 1999	Locomotives électriques (ligne du Brünig)
2001– 2999	Automotrices électriques
8001– 8399	Locotracteurs électriques de ligne
8401– 8999	Locotracteurs diesel de ligne
9401– 9999	Locotracteurs diesel de service
10001–11999	Locomotives électriques, vitesse max supérieure à 80 km/h
12001–13999	Locomotives électriques, vitesse max 70 à 80 km/h
14001–14999	Locomotives électriques, vitesse max 60 à 65 km/h
15001–15999	Locomotives électriques, vitesse max 45 à 55 km/h (toutes radiées)
16001–16999	Locomotives de manoeuvre électriques
17001–17999	Locomotives électro-diesel (en train d'être transformées en diesel simple)
18001–18999	Locomotives diesel

En 1989, un nouveau système a été introduit pour les nouvelles séries. Bien qu'on ait affecté de nouveaux numéros aux séries déjà en service, celles-ci gardent leurs anciennes numérotations pour le moment. Le nouveau système est constitué de 7 chiffres – un numéro de classe de 3 chiffres, un numéro de série de 3 chiffres et une clé informatique. Le système se présente comme suit:

1re Chiffre: 0 Locomotive à vapeur
1 Locomotive à voie étroite
2 Locotracteur
3 Locomotive électrique (3 essieux à moteur)

4 Locomotive électrique (4 essieux à moteur)
5 Automotrice électrique
6 Locomotive électrique (6 essieux à moteur)
7 Machine de service (auto-propulsée, mais pas une locomotive, par exemple une grue ou un chasse-neige)
8 Locomotive diesel
9 Locomotive de manoeuvre électrique

2me Chiffre: 0 Matériel express (Automotrices seulement)
1 à 6 Indice de sous-série (Locomotives électriques à bogies)
Type d'automotrice électrique
Nombre d'essieux à moteur (locomotives diesel)
7 à 8 Non utilisés
9 Remplace le/pour les locomotives électriques aux essieux moteurs intégrés dans le châssis.

3me Chiffre: Utilisé pour différencier les séries ayant les mêmes 1er et 2me chiffre. Cependant, dans certains cas le chiffre indique:
2 à 4 Locomotive ou automotrice bi-, tri- ou quadri-courant ou nombre d'essieux porteurs
(sur les machines électriques aux essieux moteurs intégrés dans le chassis).

4me au 6me Chiffre: Les trois derniers chiffres de l'ancien numéro.

Le matériel livré avec les nouveaux numéros se trouve à la fin de chaque section du livre.

DEPOTS CFF

Code	*Dépôt principal*	*Sous-dépôts*
Zone 1 (Lausanne)		
BN	Berne	Fribourg
		Thoune
BI	Bienne	La Chaux de Fonds
		Delémont
		Neuchâtel
BR	Brigue	–
GE	Genève	–
LS	Lausanne	Payerne
		St Maurice
		Vallorbe
Zone II (Lucerne)		
BE	Bellinzone	Chiasso (a)
BS	Bâle	Kleinhünigen
		Muttenz
CH	Chiasso (a)	–
ER	Erstfeld	–
LZ	Lucerne (b)	Arth Goldau
		Beinwil
		Zoug
MR	Meiringen	Lucerne (voie étroite) (b)
OL	Olten	Aarau
		Soleure
Zone III (Zurich)		
RS	Rorschach	Buchs
		Coire
		Romanshorn
		Sargans
		St Gall
WT	Winterthour(c)	Schaffhouse
		Wil
ZU	Zurich	Brougg
		Limmattal
		Rapperswil

(a) Il existe deux dépôts à Chiasso; le dépôt principal dépend de Bellinzone; l'autre dépôt a sa propre affectation de locotracteurs.
(b) Il existe un dépôt à voie normale et un autre à voie étroite à Lucerne; quelques locotracteurs sont affectés au dépôt à voie étroite.
(c) Le dépôt de Winterthour sera bientôt remplacé par un nouveau dépôt à Oberwinterthour où seront affectés les trains du RER de Zurich.
En plus, beaucoup de gares et d'autres installations ont de petites remises pour un locotracteur ou plus; souvent, ces remises appartiennent au service de voie ou d'autres services auxiliaires.

ATELIERS CFF

Cinq ateliers sont responsables de la réparation et la révision du matériel CFF.

Bellinzone	Locomotives électriques (Re4/4^{II}, Re4/4^{III}, Re6/6, Ae6/6). Automotrices électriques (Be4/6).
Bienne	Toutes les locomotives diesel de ligne; aussi les moteurs diesel appartenant aux locotracteurs de la série Tem.
Olten	Tous les locotracteurs diesel (l'atelier se situe près de la gare; un nouvel atelier plus éloigné révise seulement le matériel voyageurs remorqué ainsi que les wagons de marchandises).
Yverdon	Locomotives électriques (Re4/4^{I}, Re4/4^{II}). Toutes les locomotives de manoeuvre électriques. Tous les locotracteurs électriques (plus les parties électriques de la série Tem). Automotrices électriques (BDe4/4^{II}, De4/4).
Zurich	Locomotives électriques (Ae3/6^{I}, Ae 4/7). Automotrices électriques (toutes sauf les BDe4/4^{II} et De4/4).

LIVREES CFF

Jusqu'à 1984, la plupart du matériel de ligne électrique était revêtu de vert foncé, tandis que les machines diesel et locotracteurs étaient de couleur brun-rouge. Depuis 1984, une livrée rouge a été adoptée pour toutes les locomotives (sauf pour la série 450), tandis que les automotrices nouvelles sont en bleu et gris clair. Il existe quelques livrées non-standard, mais plusieurs vont disparaître dans le procav avenir. Dans les listes, le numéro de chaque machine est suivi par une lettre indiquant la livrée portée:

B Marron (La livrée d'origine pour les machines électriques. Quelques locomotives dites «historiques» ont été repeintes dans cette livrée).
D Rouge foncé (Utilisée sur les nouvelles automotrices à la fin des années 60. Seules les RABDe12/12 portent toujours ces couleurs).
E Eurocity (Gris clair et foncé. Les anciennes automotrices TEE portent maintenant cette livrée).
G Vert foncé (La livrée standard pour la plupart du matériel électrique avant 1984). Toutes les machines électrique et automotrices portent cette livrée sauf indication contraire.
L Vert foncé/Rouge (Certaines automotrices ont des faces frontales rouges pour améliorer la visibilité).
M Multi-couleur (Psychédélique!) Il n'existe qu'une automotrice avec cette livrée.
N NPZ (Neue Pendel Zug) Bleu et gris clair/faces frontales rouges. La nouvelle livrée pour les trains «régionaux».
O Orange/Gris («Swiss Express») Appliquée sur les voitures Mark III et certaines machines Re4/4^{II} pendant les années 70.
P Brun-rouge (La livrée standard pour les machines de manoeuvre jusqu'à 1984). Toutes les machines diesel et machines de manoeuvre portent cette livrée sauf indication contraire.
S S-Bahn (Bleu foncé/faces frontales rouges. Utiliseé seulement pour la nouvelle série 450 sur le RER de Zurich).
T Trans Europ Express (TEE) Quelques Re4/4^{II} portent toujours la livrée TEE rouge/blanc cassé tandis que les services TEE ont cessé en Suisse.
V Violet/jaune (Utilisée sur les prototypes des RABDe8/16. Ni la série ni la livrée n'ont eu de successeurs).
Y Jaune (Certains locotracteurs utilisés dans les ateliers portent cette livrée).

ELECTRIFICATION ET ECARTEMENT

Presque tout le réseau CFF, sauf quelques lignes de marchandises et frontalières, est maintenant électrifié à 15 kV 16⅔ Hz. Le réseau est construit a l'écartement normal européen (1435 mm) sauf la ligne du Brünig, de Lucerne à interlaken, qui est à 1000 mm.

SHUNTING TRACTORS/LOCOTRACTEURS

The SBB operates a large number of tractors for light shunting duties. Those numbered between 1 and 599 and in the 8000 series belong to the traffic department and are mainly used in station goods yards where they are driven by station staff. Those numbered between 601 and 999 and in the 9000 series are in departmental use, the greatest number being allocated to the permanent way department, with others being used by the overhead line and signals departments and as depot and works pilots. In addition to the depot allocation, the station at which each tractor is based is shown since these change infrequently. Those shown as 'reserve' are used to cover for others under maintenance or in works.

The sub-classification of tractors is based on the rating; as a consequence, different classes of similar rating have the same classifications.

Les CFF ont un grand nombre de locotracteurs pour les manoeuvres légères. Ceux qui sont numérotés entre 1 et 599 et dans la série 8000 appartiennent au service transport et sont utilisés principalement dans les gares et conduits par le personnel des gares. Ceux qui sont numérotés de 601 à 999 et dans la série 9000 sont des machines de service. La plupart sont affectés au service de la voie, d'autres aux services de la caténaire et de la signalisation ou comme machines de manoeuvres dans les ateliers et les dépôts. Le dépôt d'affectation ainsi que la gare d'affectation sont indiqués puisque les affectations sont quasi-permanentes. Celles qui sont marqués «reserve» sont utilisés quand l'entretien des autres en dépôt ou en atelier est nécessaire. «... Works» = «Ateliers de ...».

La classification des locotracteurs en sous-séries est basée sur leur puissance; en consequence, les differenteds séries de puissance similaire ont la même classification.

CLASS/SERIE Te I — B

Nos. 15, 44 & 60 differ in having a canopy over the platform.
Les 15, 44 et 60 ont un auvent qui abrite la plate-forme.

Built/Date de mise en service: 1937–56.
Builder-Mech. Parts/Constructeur-Partie mécanique: SLM (SLM/Tuchschmid*).
Builder-Elec. Parts/Constructeur-Partie électrique: MFO.
Traction Motors: 1 single phase axle suspended with side rod drive.
Moteur de traction: 1 moteur à courant alternatif monophasé à collecteurs, suspendu sur l'essieu avec transmission par bielles.
One Hour Rating/Puissance horaire: 90 kW.
Maximum Tractive Effort/Effort de traction max.: 36 kN.
Driving Wheel Dia./Diamètre des roues motrices: 950 mm.
Weight/Masse: 13 tonnes.
Overall Length/Longeur hors tout: 5.620 m.
Max. Speed/Vitesse maximale: 60 km/h.

† Rebuilt from battery/electric tractors Tea 248–50.
† Transformés à partir des locotracteurs à accumulateurs Tea 248 à 50.

No.		*Dépôt*	*Station/Gare*
1		LS	La Sarraz
2		BR	*Reserve*
3		BR	Leuk
4		BN	*Reserve*
5		LS	Payerne
6		LS	Monthey
7		LS	*Reserve*
8		BI	Le Locle
9		BN	*Reserve*
10		BN	Gümligen
11	†	GE	Genève
12		LS	*Reserve*
13		BI	Sonceboz-Sombeval
15		OL	Murgenthal
16		LZ	*Reserve*
17		OL	Büren an der Aare
18		LZ	Küssnacht am Rigi
19		WT	Andelfingen
20		LZ	Entlebuch
21		OL	Oensingen
22		OL	*Reserve*
23		BE	*Reserve*
24		LZ	*Reserve*
25		BS	Gelterkinden
26		OL	*Reserve*
27		OL	Wangen an der Aare
28		BN	Hindelbank
29		OL	Mellingen
30		LZ	Schüpfheim
31		LZ	Signau
32		BS	*Reserve*
33		ZU	Siebnen-Wangen
34		WT	Winterthur
35		RS	*Reserve*

36		WT	Wald	48	*	WT	Bazenheid
37		ZU	*Reserve*	50	*	ZU	Mettmenstetten
38	†	WT	*Reserve*	51	*	WT	*Reserve*
39		ZU	Horgen	52	*	ZU	*Reserve*
41		RS	St Gallen Winkeln	53	*	RS	St Margrethen
42		ZU	Turgi	54	*	RS	Flawil
43	†	WT	Thalheim-Altikon	55	*	RS	*Reserve*
44	*	WT	Stein am Rhein	57	*	BI	Glovelier
45	*	WT	Winterthur Töss	58	*	BI	*Reserve*
46	*	WT	Winterthur	59	*	LS	Avenches
47	*	WT	Dielsdorf	60	*	BE	Magadino-Vira

CLASS/**SERIE** Te II　　B

Built/Date de mise en service: 1967–9.
Builder-Mech. Parts/Constructeur-Partie mécanique: SLM/Tuchschmid.
Builder-Elec. Parts/Constructeur-Partie électrique: MFO.
Traction Motors: 1 single phase axle suspended with side rod drive.
Moteur de traction: 1 moteur à courant alternatif monophasé à collecteurs, suspendu sur l'essieu avec transmission par bielles.
One Hour Rating/Puissance horaire: 120 kW.
Maximum Tractive Effort/Effort de traction max.: 33 kN.
Driving Wheel Dia./Diamètre des roues motrices: 950 mm.
Weight/Masse: 22 tonnes.
Overall Length/Longeur hors tout: 6.7 m.
Max. Speed/Vitesse maximale: 60 km/h.

61	LS	Montreux	80	RS	Uzwil
62	LS	*Reserve*	81	ZU	Baden
63	BN	Bern Bümpliz Süd	82	RS	Sulgen
64	GE	Versoix	83	WT	Uster
65	BI	Lyss	84	WT	Rüti
66	BI	Gorgier-St Aubin	85	ZU	Frick
67	BI	Tavannes	86	ZU	Rapperswil
68	BI	Le Landeron	87	ZU	Stäfa
69	LZ	*Reserve*	88	ZU	Weesen
70	OL	Läufelfingen	89	ZU	Uznach
71	BE	Rivera-Bironico	90	ZU	*Reserve*
72	LZ	Malters	91	RS	*Reserve*
73	OL	Muri	92	WT	Islikon
74	OL	Dottikon-Dintikon	93	RS	Erlen
75	CH	Maroggia-Melano	94	WT	Sirnach
76	LZ	Sins	95	ZU	Schwanden
77	RS	Kreuzlingen	96	WT	*Reserve*
78	RS	Obberriet	97	RS	Buchs
79	ZU	Reichenburg			

CLASS/**SERIE** Te III　　B

Built/Date de mise en service: 1941–9.
Builder-Mech. Parts/Constructeur-Partie mécanique: SLM.
Builder-Elec. Parts/Constructeur-Partie électrique: SAAS.
Traction Motors: 1 single phase axle suspended with side rod drive.
Moteur de traction: 1 moteur à courant alternatif monophasé à collecteurs, suspendu sur l'essieu avec transmission par bielles.
One Hour Rating/Puissance horaire: 250 kW.
Maximum Tractive Effort/Effort de traction max.: 72 kN.
Driving Wheel Dia./Diamètre des roues motrices: 1040 mm.
Weight/Masse: 28 tonnes.
Overall Length/Longeur hors tout: 6.6 m.
Max. Speed/Vitesse maximale: 60 km/h.

121	ZU	Wettingen	124	BS	Sissach
122	WT	Eglisau	125	LZ	Ebikon
123	LS	Moudon	126	LZ	Hochdorf

▼Class Te^{I} No. 51 at Horgen with a 4-wheel postal van on 04/04/86. *G.B. Wise*

▼▼Class Te^{II} No. 77 is station pilot at Kreuzlingen on 17/08/85. *E. Dunkling*

▲▲Le Te^{I} 51 à Horgen avec un fourgon postal à essieux. 04/04/86. *G.B. Wise*

▲Le Te^{II} 77 à Kreuzlingen. 17/08/85. *E. Dunkling*

127	OL	Nebikon	133	OL	Schönbuhl
128	LS	Bex	134	BI	Travers
129	BR	Visp	135	WT	Bauma
130	LS	Yverdon	136	ZU	Zürich Oerlikon
131	ZU	*Reserve*	138	WT	Weinfelden
132	OL	Othmarsingen			

CLASS/SERIE Te III — Bo

Built/Date de mise en service: 1965–6.
Builder-Mech. Parts/Constructeur-Partie mécanique: SLM.
Builder-Elec. Parts/Constructeur-Partie électrique: MFO.
Traction Motors: 2 single phase axle suspended.
Moteur de traction: 2 moteurs à courant alternatif monophasé à collecteurs, suspendu sur l'essieu.
One Hour Rating/Puissance horaire: 245 kW.
Maximum Tractive Effort/Effort de traction max.: 67 kN.
Driving Wheel Dia./Diamètre des roues motrices: 950 mm.
Weight/Masse: 28 tonnes.
Overall Length/Longeur hors tout: 6.64 m.
Max. Speed/Vitesse maximale: 60 km/h.

139	BE	Tenero	160	WT	Koblenz
140	LZ	*Reserve*	161	RS	Gossau
141	OL	*Reserve*	162	BN	Schüpfen
142	LZ	Konolfingen	163	BR	Gampel-Steg
143	LZ	Langnau	164	OL	Wohlen
144	WT	Rekingen	165	ZU	Glarus
145	RS	Heerbrugg	166	WT	Effretikon
146	LS	*Reserve*	167	BI	Porrentruy
147	BI	Kerzers	168	BI	Moutier
148	LS	Palézieux	169	BN	Düdingen
149	BR	Sierre	170	ZU	Thalwil
150	BN	Münsingen	171	ZU	Ziegelbrücke
151	LS	Murten	172	LS	Puidoux-Chexbres
152	BI	Münchenstein	173	LS	Martigny
153	ER	Brunnen	174	BE	Ambri-Piotta
154	ZU	*Reserve*	175	ZU	Stein-Säckingen
155	BI	*Reserve*	176	ER	Schwyz
156	BI	*Reserve*	177	WT	*Reserve*
157	LZ	Wolhusen	178	LS	Morges
158	ZU	Wädenswil	179	LS	Vevey
159	RS	St Gallen Winkeln			

CLASS/SERIE Te II — B

Built/Date de mise en service: 1927–39.
Builder-Mech. Parts/Constructeur-Partie mécanique: SLM.
Builder-Elec. Parts/Constructeur-Partie électrique: SAAS.
Traction Motors: 1 single phase frame mounted with gear train/side rod drive.
Moteur de traction: 1 moteur à courant alternatif monophasé à collecteurs, fixé sur le châssis avec train d'engrenages et bielles.
One Hour Rating/Puissance horaire: 140 kW (145 kW*).
Maximum Tractive Effort/Effort de traction max.: 51 kN (56 kN*).
Driving Wheel Dia./Diamètre des roues motrices: 1040 mm.
Weight/Masse: 26 tonnes (25 tonnes*).
Overall Length/Longeur hors tout: 6.5 m.
Max. Speed/Vitesse maximale: 60 km/h.

221	*	BS	Lausen	241	LZ	Baar
223	*	LS	*Reserve*	242	OL	*Reserve*
237		GE	Nyon	243	BI	St Imier
238		BS	Liestal	244	LS	Rolle
239		OL	Herzogenbuchsee	245	LS	Riddes
240		BE	Castione-Arbedo	246	WT	Elgg

CLASS/**SERIE** Tem I **B**

This class, and the following Tem II and Tem III classes are electric tractors fitted with a diesel engine to enable them to shunt non-electrified sidings.

Cette série et les séries Tem II et Tem III sont des locotracteurs «amphibies» – des machines électriques avec un moteur diesel afin de pouvoir manoeuvrer sur des faisceaux non-électrifiés.

Built/Date de mise en service: 1950–7.
Builder-Mech. Parts/Constructeur-Partie mécanique: Tuchschmid (SBB/CFF Yverdon *).
Builder-Elec. Parts/Constructeur-Partie électrique: BBC/MFO.
Traction Motors: 1 single phase axle suspended with side rod drive.
Moteur de traction: 1 moteur à courant alternatif monophasé à collecteurs, suspendu sur l'essieu avec transmission par bielles.
One Hour Rating/Puissance horaire: 90 kW (electric/électrique), 50 kW (diesel).
Weight/Masse: 15 tonnes.
Maximum Tractive Effort/Effort de traction max.: 36 kN (electric/électrique), 31 kN (diesel)
Driving Wheel Dia./Diamètre des roues motrices: 950 mm.
Overall Length/Longeur hors tout: 5.87 m.
Max. Speed/Vitesse maximale: 60 km/h.
Engine/Moteur: Saurer C615D 65 kW.

251		LS	Bouveret
252		BN	*Reserve*
253	*	WT	Märstetten
254	*	WT	*Reserve*
255		OL	Dulliken
256		OL	Aarburg Oftringen
258		BI	*Reserve*
259		BS	Aesch
260		OL	Niederbipp
261		WT	Pfäffikon
262		LS	*Reserve*
263		ZU	Unterterzen
265		RS	Amriswil
266		BE	Lugano
267		BE	Claro
268		WT	Bürglen
269		ZU	*Reserve*
270		RS	*Reserve*
271		RS	Walenstadt
272		LZ	Cham
273		OL	*Reserve*
274		BI	Le Locle-Col des Roc
275		BI	Les Verrières

CLASS/**SERIE** Tem III **B**

Built/Date de mise en service: 1967.
Builder-Mech. Parts/Constructeur-Partie mécanique: SLM/Tuchschmid.
Builder-Elec. Parts/Constructeur-Partie électrique: MFO.
Traction Motors: 1 single phase axle suspended with side rod drive.
Moteur de traction: 1 moteur à courant alternatif monophasé à collecteurs, suspendu sur l'essieu avec transmission par bielles.
One Hour Rating/Puissance horaire: 120 kW (electric/électrique), 60 kW (diesel).
Weight/Masse: 26 tonnes.
Maximum Tractive Effort/Effort de traction max.: 33 kN.
Driving Wheel Dia./Diamètre des roues motrices: 950 mm.
Engine/Moteur: Saurer C615D 85 kW.
Overall Length/Longeur hors tout: 6.7 m.
Max. Speed/Vitesse maximale: 60 km/h.

276	ZU	*Reserve*
277	RS	St Gallen St Fiden
278	ZU	Dübendorf
279	WT	*Reserve*
280	WT	Wetzikon
281	RS	Wattwil
282	WT	Feuerthalen
283	ZU	Zürich Wollishofen
284	ZU	*Reserve*
285	ZU	Döttingen-Klingnau
286	ZU	Lachen
287	ZU	Meilen
288	OL	Safenwil
289	OL	Aarau
290	OL	Dagmersellen
291	OL	Lenzburg
292	OL	Solothurn
293	ZU	Buchs-Dällikon
294	BE	Giubiasco
295	BI	Reconvilier
296	BI	Dornach-Arlesheim
297	BI	Colombier
298	GE	Genève

CLASS/SERIE Tem II — Bo

Built/Date de mise en service: 1954–62.
Builder-Mech. Parts/Constructeur-Partie mécanique: SLM (ACMV*).
Builder-Elec. Parts/Constructeur-Partie électrique: BBC/SAAS (SAAS *).
Traction Motors: 2 single phase axle suspended.
Moteurs de traction: 2 moteurs à courant alternatif monophasé à collecteurs, suspendus sur l'essieu.
One Hour Rating/Puissance horaire: 260 kW (electric/électrique), 95 kW (diesel).
Weight/Masse: 32 tonnes.
Maximum Tractive Effort/Effort de traction max.: 59 kN (electric/électrique), 64 kN (diesel)
Driving Wheel Dia./Diamètre des roues motrices: 1040 mm.
Overall Length/Longeur hors tout: 7.29 m, 7.04 m*, 7.35 m†.
Max. Speed/Vitesse maximale: 60 km/h.
Engine/Moteur: SLM 12BD11 145 kW, (Saurer CV1D 145 kW*).

321	*	BE	Cadenazzo
322	*	BE	Locarno
323	*	CH	Mendrisio
324		BN	Ostermundigen
325		RS	Horn
326		BI	*Reserve*
327		BS	Zwingen
328		BS	Laufen
329		BN	Schmitten
330		BI	Biel/Bienne Mett
331		OL	Langenthal
332		LZ	Zug
333		OL	*Reserve*
334		WT	Etzwilen
335		RS	*Reserve*
336		RS	Romanshorn
337		ZU	Pfäffikon
338		LS	Villeneuve
339		WT	*Reserve*
340		WT	Frauenfeld
341		WT	Laufenburg
342		RS	Salez-Sennwald
343		WT	Neuhausen
344	†	ZU	Wallisellen
345	†	ZU	*Reserve*
346	†	ZU	Zürich Tiefenbrunnen
347	†	ZU	Affoltern am Albis
348	†	RS	Kreuzlingen Hafen
349	†	OL	Suhr
350	†	LS	Estavayer-le-Lac
351	†	LS	*Reserve*
352	†	OL	Zofingen
353	†	OL	Aarau
354	†	BS	Rheinfelden
355	†	OL	*Reserve*
356	†	ZU	Glattbrugg
357	†	ZU	Bonstetten-Wettswil
358	†	LZ	Sursee
359	†	OL	Hunzenschwil
360	†	OL	Solothurn
361	†	OL	Olten
362	†	RS	St Gallen
363	†	WT	Dielsdorf
364	†	BR	Sion
365	†	LS	Bussigny

CLASS/SERIE Tm I (Tm *) — B

Built/Date de mise en service: 1957–65.
Builder/Constructeur: RACO (CMR †).
Engine/Moteur: SLM 6VD11 66 kW.
SLM 4VD111 44 kW (*).
Deutz F6L413 90 kW (b).
Deutz 87 kW (c).
VM 90 kW (d).
Transmission: Mechanical/Mécanique..
Maximum Tractive Effort/Effort de traction max.: kN.
Driving Wheel Dia./Diamètre des roues motrices: 600 mm.
Weight/Masse: 10 tonnes (13 tonnes b, c, d).
Overall Length/Longeur hors tout: 5.190 m.
Max. Speed/Vitesse maximale: 45 km/h (50 km/h *, c, d).

Originally all fitted with SLM engines, many of these tractors have been rebuilt with Deutz or VM engines since 1971.

Bien que dotés de moteurs SLM à l'origine, plusieurs machines on été modifiées avec des moteurs Deutz ou VM depuis 1971.

401	*	ER	Flüelen
402	*	ER	Brunnen
403	*	OL	Solothurn
407		ZU	*Reserve*
409		ZU	*Reserve*
410		ZU	*Reserve*

411		RS	*Reserve*	463	†c LZ	*Reserve*
412		ZU	*Reserve*	464	†c LZ	Sempach-Neuenkirch
413		OL	*Reserve*	465	†c LZ	Menziken
414		OL	*Reserve*	466	† WT	Kemptthal
415		OL	Dotzigen	467	†d RS	Alstätten
416		LS	Renens	468	†d WT	Hüntwangen-Wil
417	†	LS	Le Pont	469	c RS	Bischofszell Nord
418	†	LS	*Reserve*	470	b ZU	Netstal
419	†	BN	*Reserve*	471	b RS	Mels
421	†	BI	*Reserve*	472	c RS	Flums
422		BN	Wichtrach	473	b WT	*Reserve*
423		ZU	Eiken	474	d WT	Ramsen
424		RS	*Reserve*	475	b WT	Bubikon
425		OL	*Reserve*	476	c WT	Oberwintherthur
426		OL	*Reserve*	477	b RS	Ermatingen
427		OL	*Reserve*	478	c WT	Steckborn
428		OL	Leuzigen	479	RS	Arbon
429		WT	*Reserve*	480	d WT	Marthalen
430		RS	Romanshorn	481	b BE	Osogna-Crescia
431		WT	Müllheim-Wigoltingen	482	BE	*Reserve*
432		WT	Stammheim	483	c OL	Subingen
433		RS	Arnegg	484	c LZ	Eschenbach
434		WT	Bütschwil	485	OL	*Reserve*
435		RS	*Reserve*	486	c LZ	Steinhausen
436		WT	*Reserve*	487	d OL	Wildegg
437		WT	Aadorf	488	b BE	Lavorgo
438		ZU	*Reserve*	489	LS	Croy-Romainmôti
439	d	ZU	Näfels-Mollis	490	d LS	St Triphon
440		WT	Wil	491	c LS	Martigny
441	c	WT	Niederweningen	492	d BI	St Ursanne
442	c	ZU	Linthal	493	b BI	Aarberg
443		ZU	Uetikon	494	c LS	*Reserve*
444		ZU	Schmerikon	495	b BI	Biel/Bienne
445	b	WT	Winterthur Wülfingen	496	d BI	Boncourt
446	c	ZU	Rümlang	497	c BI	*Reserve*
447	c	RS	*Reserve*	498	d BI	Brügg
448		WT	Eschenz	499	b BE	Balerna
449	b	ZU	Nieder-Durnen	500	d OL	Lüsslingen
450	b	RS	Flums	501	ZU	Mühlehorn
451		WT	Kempten	502	WT	*Reserve*
452	c	BS	Lausen	503	b RS	Hauptwil
453	c	OL	Grenchen Süd	504	WT	*Reserve*
454	d	OL	Oberentfelden	505	b WT	Hüntwangen Wil
455	d	OL	Egerkingen	506	RS	Rheineck
456		OL	Wynigen	507	c BI	Les Hauts Geneveys
457	c	LZ	Gisikon-Root	508	c BI	*Reserve*
458		ZU	Horgen-Oberdorf	509	c BI	Court
459		OL	Rupperswil	510	† BI	Biel/Bienne
460		BS	Tecknau	511	†c BI	Courtelary
461	d	OL	Arch	512	†c GE	La Plaine
462	†d	OL	Wauwil	513	† ZU	*Reserve*

CLASS/SERIE Tm II — B

Built/Date de mise en service: 1950–68.
Builder/Constructeur: RACO.
Engine/Moteur: Saurer C615D 70 kW.
Transmission: Mechanical/Mécanique..
Maximum Tractive Effort/Effort de traction max.: kN.
Driving Wheel Dia./Diamètre des roues motrices: 600 mm.
Weight/Masse: 10 tonnes.
Overall Length/Longeur hors tout: 5.240 m.
Max. Speed/Vitesse maximale: 45 km/h.

These tractors have a cabin for 4 personnel, and a platform for carrying tools and materials.

Ces locotracteurs ont une cabine pour 4 personnes et une plate-forme pour le transport d'outils et de matériaux.
* Fitted for snowplough use./Modifié pour l'utilisation comme chasse-neige.

No.		Depot	Location
601			Yverdon Works
602		OL	Olten
603		BS	Basel
604		LZ	Luzern
605		OL	Solothurn
606		LZ	Zug
607	*	LZ	Konolfingen
608		ZU	Bridges Dept.
610		RS	Sargans
611		RS	Romanshorn
612		ZU	Zürich
613		ZU	Brugg
614	*	RS	Chur
615		ZU	Brugg
616	*	WT	Winterthur
617	*	WT	Wetzikon
618	*	WT	Wil
619		GE	Genève
620	*	BI	St Imier
621	*	BI	Neuchâtel
622	*	BI	Neuchâtel
623	*	OL	Solothurn
624		LZ	Luzern
625		ER	Erstfeld
626	*	LZ	Konolfingen
627		OL	Olten
628		BE	Bellinzona
629	*	LZ	Arth Goldau
630	*	ZU	Ziegelbrücke
631	*	ZU	Richterswil
632		ZU	Zürich
633		ZU	Zürich
634		RS	Gossau
635	*	ZU	Rapperswil
636		WT	Bülach
637	*	ZU	Rapperswil
638		ZU	Zürich
640	*	LS	Cossonay
641	*	BI	Delémont
642	*	RS	St Gallen
643		BN	Training Loco
644		LS	Lausanne
645	*	BI	St Imier
646	*	BR	Brig
647		BS	Muttenz
648		BE	Airolo
649		OL	Lenzburg
650		OL	Burgdorf
651		LZ	Luzern
652		OL	Aarau
653			Olten Works
654		BS	Basel
655		ER	Erstfeld
656		BE	Bellinzona
658		CH	Vedeggio
659		LZ	Luzern
660		BE	Airolo
661		ZU	Limmattal
662		WT	Wil
663		RS	Romanshorn
664		RS	Romanshorn
665		RS	Sargans
666		BI	Neuchâtel
667		BI	Biel/Bienne
669		GE	Genève
670		BN	Bern
671		BN	Thun
672		LS	Bussigny
673		CH	Giubiasco
674		LZ	Zug
675		LZ	Zug
676		BE	Faido
677		OL	Lenzburg
678		BS	Muttenz
679		BE	Airolo
680		WT	Frauenfeld
681		RS	St Gallen
682		ZU	Brugg
683		ZU	Zürich
684		ZU	Zürich
685		ZU	Rapperswil
686		BI	Biel/Bienne
687		GE	Genève
688		LS	Puidoux-Chexbres
689		BN	Kerzers
690		BR	Brig
691		BI	Neuchâtel
692		LS	Lausanne
693		GE	Genève
694		BS	Laufen
695		LS	Payerne
696		OL	Solothurn
697		LZ	Luzern
698		BS	Basel
699		LZ	Zug
700		BS	Muttenz
701		OL	Olten
702		ZU	Zürich
703		CH	Vedeggio
704		WT	Etzwilen
705		ZU	Brugg
706		ZU	Zürich
707		WT	Winterthur-Grüze
708		WT	Winterthur-Grüze
710	*	LS	Fribourg
711		LS	St Maurice
712		BI	Delémont
713		BN	Fribourg
714		BN	Fribourg
715		BE	Bellinzona
716		BS	Muttenz
717		OL	Solothurn
718		LZ	Arth Goldau
719		BN	Bern
720		BI	Biel/Bienne
721		LS	Bussigny

722	LS	Renens
724	LS	St Maurice
725	BE	Faido
726	LZ	Arth Goldau
727	OL	Burgdorf
728	OL	Dulliken
730	ER	Erstfeld
731	LS	Payerne
732	LS	St Maurice
733	BI	Biel/Bienne
734	LS	St Maurice
735	BN	Bern
736	BI	Neuchâtel
737	OL	Solothurn
738	OL	Olten
739	BS	Basel
740	LZ	Burgdorf
741	OL	Olten
742	ZU	Wallisellen
743	ZU	*Reserve*
744	ZU	*Reserve*
745	BI	Neuchâtel
746	BR	Sion
748	LS	Bussigny
749	LS	Bussigny
750	BR	Sion
751	LZ	Luzern
752	OL	Langenthal
753	LZ	Zug
754	ZU	Stein-Säckingen
755	RS	Sargans
756	ZU	Dietikon
757	ZU	Wetzikon
758	ZU	Zürich
759	BN	Fribourg
760	BR	Brig
761	LS	Lausanne
762	LS	Yverdon
763	LS	Yverdon
764	OL	Dulliken
765	OL	Olten
766	OL	Solothurn
767	BE	Rivera
768	OL	Dulliken
769	CH	Chiasso
770	LZ	Zug
771	BS	Muttenz
772	OL	Lenzburg
773	BI	Biel/Bienne
774	BI	Biel/Bienne
775	LS	Nyon
776	BI	Delémont
777	BI	Neuchâtel
778	BI	Biel/Bienne
779	BR	Sion
780	BN	Fribourg
781	LS	Kerzers
782	BN	Thun
783	BI	Biel/Bienne
784	OL	Dulliken
785	CH	Chiasso
786	BN	Bern
787	LZ	Bridges Dept
788	CH	Chiasso
789	LZ	Luzern
790	OL	Dulliken
791	LZ	Luzern
792	ZU	Zürich
793	ZU	Wallisellen
794	ZU	*Reserve*
795	ZU	Brugg
796	WT	Schaffhausen
797	RS	Gossau
798	ZU	Brugg
800	ZU	Zürich
801	WT	Etzwilen
802	ZU	Zürich Altstetten
803	ZU	Zürich
804	OL	Burgdorf
805	BE	Giubiasco
806	BN	Bern
807	LS	Lausanne
808	OL	Olten
809	GE	Genève Praille
810	ZU	Brugg
811	BI	Biel/Bienne
812	BI	Biel/Bienne
813		Biel/Bienne Works
814	ZU	Zürich
815	WT	Schaffhausen
816		Biel/Bienne Works
817	OL	Olten
818	OL	Olten
819	BR	Brig
820	LS	Puidoux-Chexbres
822	BI	Delémont
823	OL	Lenzburg
824	ZU	Zürich
825	ZU	Zürich
826	WT	Winterthur
827	CH	Chiasso
829	LZ	Sursee
830	LS	Lausanne
831	BN	Fribourg
832	BI	Kerzers
833	GE	Genève
834	BI	Neuchâtel
835	LS	Bussigny
836	BR	Brig
837	BN	Bern
838	BN	Bern
839	LS	Puidoux-chexbres
840	BS	Basel
841	LZ	Zug
842	BE	Bellinzona
843	ER	Erstfeld
844	CH	Chiasso
845	LZ	Luzern
846	BS	Liestal
847	OL	Langenthal
848	ZU	Zürich
849	ZU	Rapperswil
850	ZU	Brugg
851	ZU	Zürich
852	RS	Gossau
853	RS	Romanshorn

CLASS/SERIE Tm B

Five miscellaneous departmental tractors. 893–5 were originally numbered 404–6 in traffic stock. 896 is a similar tractor built new for departmental use. 900 is a unique design for shunting the traverser at Biel/Bienne Works.

Cinq locotracteurs variés de service. A l'origine, les 893 à 5 étaient numérotés 404 à 6. Le 896 est un locotracteur similaire mais construit à l'origine pour le service de la voie. Le 900 est un locotracteur de conception unique pour les manoeuvres sur le pont transbordeur des ateliers de Bienne.

Built/Date de mise en service: 1958 †, 1963 *.
Builder/Constructeur: RACO †, SBB/CFF Biel/Bienne *.
Engine/Moteur: SLM 4VD111 44 kW †, VW 22 kW *.
Transmission: Mechanical/Mécanique.
Driving Wheel Dia./Diamètre des roues motrices: 600 mm.
Weight/Masse: 10 tonnes†, 2.3 tonnes *.
Overall Length/Longeur hors tout: 5.19 m†, 2.00 m*.
Max. Speed/Vitesse maximale: 45 km/h†, 20 km/h*.

893	†	LS	Lausanne
894	†		Olten Works
895	†		Bellinzona Works
896	†	BE	Biasca
900	*		Biel/Bienne Works

CLASS/SERIE Tm III B

Diesel-electric tractors for use as shed and works pilots.
Locotracteurs diesel à transmission électrique pour les manoeuvres dans les ateliers et dépôts.

Built/Date de mise en service: 1958–66.
Builder-Mech. Parts/Constructeur-Partie mécanique: SLM.
Builder-Elec. Parts/Constructeur-Partie électrique: BBC.
Engine/Moteur: SLM 12BD11 145 kW.
Transmission: Electric.
Maximum Tractive Effort/Effort de traction max.: 92 kN.
Driving Wheel Dia./Diamètre des roues motrices: 950 mm.
Weight/Masse: 28 tonnes.
Overall Length/Longeur hors tout: 6.540 m.
Max. Speed/Vitesse maximale: 30 km/h.

901	BR	Brig
902	BS	Basel
903	RS	Chur Works
904		Bellinzona Works
905		Biel/Bienne Works
906		Yverdon Works
907		Zürich Works
908	ZU	Zürich
909	WT	Winterthur
910	RS	Rorschach
911	CH	Chiasso
912	BS	Basel
913	OL	Olten Works
914	LZ	Luzern
915	ER	Erstfeld
916	BE	Bellinzona
917		Zürich Works
918	LS	Lausanne
919	BN	Bern
920	GE	Genève
921	GE	Genève-Praille
922	LS	Lausanne-Terrasse
923	BI	Biel/Bienne
924	OL	*Reserve*

CLASS/SERIE Tm B

This tractor is fitted with exhaust filtration equipment for use on work inside tunnels.
Ce locotracteur est doté d'un système de filtrage des gaz d'échappement pour l'utilisation dans les tunnels.

Built/Date de mise en service: 1964.
Builder/Constructeur: Kronenberg.
Engine/Moteur: GM 62306–RD 170 kW.
Transmission: Hydro-mechanical/Hydromécanique.
Weight/Masse: 35 tonnes.

▼Class Te ^{IV} No. 8202 at Chavornay on 03/08/88. *G.B. Wise*

▼▼Class Tm ^{II} No. 9542 in red livery at Travers on 04/08/88. *G.B. Wise*

▲▲Le Te ^{IV} 8202 à Chavornay. 03/08/88. *G.B. Wise*

▲Le Tm ^{II} 9542 en livrée rouge à Travers. 04/08/88. *G.B. Wise*

Overall Length/Longeur hors tout: 7.520 m.
Max. Speed/Vitesse maximale: 35 km/h.

940 LZ Luzern

CLASS/SERIE Ta B

This assortment of battery tractors of eight widely differing designs are used as works pilots.

Cette serie est un assortiment de huit types différents de tracteurs qui sont utilisés dans les ateliers.

No. *No.*	*Date*	*Builder* *Constructeur*	*Hourly Rating* *Puissance*	*Weight* *Masse*	*Length* *Longeur*	*Max. Speed* *Vitesse Max*	*Location* *Affectation*
966	1987	Stadler	4 kW	7 t.	2.85 mm	10 km/h	Olten Works
967	1943	SBB Olten	3 kW	8 t.	3.40 mm	10 km/h	Olten Works
968	1977	SBB Yverdon	4 kW	6.5 t.	2.85 mm	10 km/h	Yverdon Works
969	1911	SBB Olten	4 kW	7 t.	3.30 mm	10 km/h	Yverdon Works
970	1924	SBB Olten	4 kW	7 t.	3.30 mm	10 km/h	Olten Works
971	1927	SBB Olten	4 kW	7 t.	3.30 mm	10 km/h	Olten Works
972	1914	SBB Olten	4 kW	7 t.	3.30 mm	10 km/h	Yverdon Works
974	1965	SBB Zürich	4 kW	6.5 t.	3.32 mm	10 km/h	Zürich Works
975	1971	Stadler	4 kW	6.5 t.	2.85 mm	10 km/h	Zürich Works
976	1971	Stadler	4 kW	6.5 t.	2.85 mm	10 km/h	Bellinzona Works
978	1913	AEG	145 kW	24 t.	8.40 mm	25 km/h	Bellinzona Works

Note: 1000–2185 are electric railcars. See page 35.
Note: 1000–2185 sont automotrices. Voir page 35.

CLASS/SERIE Te ^{IV} Bo

These tractors incorporate electrical equipment recovered from withdrawn De4/4 class railcars.
Certains équipements électriques récupérés des automotrices De4/4 sont incorporés dans ces tracteurs.

Built/Date de mise en service: 1980.
Builder-Mech. Parts/Constructeur-Partie mécanique: Tuchschmid.
Builder-Elec. Parts/Constructeur-Partie électrique: BBC.
Traction Motors: 2 single phase axle suspended.
Moteurs de traction: 2 moteurs à courant alternatif monophasé à collecteurs, suspendus sur l'essieu.
One Hour Rating/Puissance horaire: 480 kW.
Maximum Tractive Effort/Effort de traction max.:.
Driving Wheel Dia./Diamètre des roues motrices: .
Weight/Masse: 34 tonnes.
Overall Length/Longeur hors tout: 7.7 m.
Max. Speed/Vitesse maximale: 60 km/h.

8201 LS Chavornay
8202 LS Romont
8203 LS Aigle

CLASS/SERIE Tm ^{IV} B

In addition to the hydraulic transmission, these tractors have a 2 ratio gearbox giving a maximum shunting speed of 30 km/h.
En plus de la transmission hydraulique, ces locotracteurs ont une boîte de vitesses à deux réductions qui donne une vitesse maximale de 30 km/h pour les manoeuvres.

Built/Date de mise en service: 1970–8.
Builder/Constructeur: SLM.
Engine/Moteur: MAN R8V 16/18 280 kW.
Transmission: Hydraulic/Hydraulique.
Maximum Tractive Effort/Effort de traction max.: kN.
Driving Wheel Dia./Diamètre des roues motrices: 1040 mm.
Weight/Masse: 30 tonnes.
Overall Length/Longeur hors tout: 7.67 m.
Max. Speed/Vitesse maximale: 60 km/h.

8751	LS	St Prex	8774	OL	*Reserve*
8752	BE	Airolo	8775	OL	Oberbuchsiten
8753	LS	Cossonay	8776	ER	Göschenen
8754	CH	Chiasso	8777	OL	*Reserve*
8755	OL	Roggwil-Wynau	8778	BI	Reuchenette-Péry
8756	OL	Hägendorf	8779	BN	Thun
8757	BE	Biasca	8780	GE	*Reserve*
8758	RS	Bischofszell Nord	8781	BN	*Reserve*
8759	ZU	Regensdorf-Watt	8782	BI	Biel/Bienne
8760	ZU	Killwangen	8783	BI	Delémont
8761	ZU	Otelfingen	8784	BI	*Reserve*
8762	WT	Bülach	8785	ZU	Zürich Seebach
8763	ZU	Siggenthal-Würenlingen	8786	RS	Rorschach
8764	WT	Niederglatt	8787	WT	*Reserve*
8765	BS	Möhlin	8788	ZU	*Reserve*
8766	WT	Rielasingen	8789	OL	Rothrist
8767	ZU	Dietikon	8790	OL	*Reserve*
8768	WT	Hinwil	8791	BE	Taverne-Torricella
8769	ZU	Kloten	8792	OL	Wangen bei Olten
8770	BS	Kaiseraugst	8793	RS	*Reserve*
8771	RS	Landquart	8794	ZU	Schwerzenbach
8772	WT	*Reserve*	8795	ZU	*Reserve*
8773	BS	Frenkendorf-Füllinsdorf	8796	WT	Embrach-Rorbas

CLASS/SERIE Tm III — B

These tractors are fitted with a hydraulic platform for overhead line maintenance work.
Cette série est dotée d'une plate-forme hydraulique pour des travaux sur les caténaires.

Built/Date de mise en service: 1981–6.
Builder/Constructeur: RACO.
Engine/Moteur: Saurer D2K 165 kW.
Transmission: Hydraulic/Hydraulique.
Maximum Tractive Effort/Effort de traction max.: kN.
Driving Wheel Dia./Diamètre des roues motrices: mm.
Weight/Masse: 28 tonnes.
Overall Length/Longeur hors tout: 8.74 m.
Max. Speed/Vitesse maximale: 60 km/h.

9451	LS	Puidoux-Chexbres	9458	GE	Genève
9452	ER	Erstfeld	9459	BS	Basel
9453	ZU	Zürich	9460	OL	Dulliken
9454	ZU	Brugg	9461	LZ	Luzern
9455	WT	Winterthur Grüze	9462	BE	Airolo
9456	ZU	Rapperswil	9463	BE	Giubiasco
9457	BI	Delémont			

CLASS/SERIE Tm III — BoBo

Similar to the previous class, but fitted with a 3 tonne hydraulic crane and an open platform for use on permanent way work.
Semblable à la série précédente, mais dotés d'une grue hydraulique de 3 tonnes et d'une plate-forme ouverte pour les travaux de voie.

Built/Date de mise en service: 1976–88.
Builder/Constructeur: RACO.
Engine/Moteur: Saurer D2K 165 kW.
Transmission: Hydraulic/Hydraulique.
Maximum Tractive Effort/Effort de traction max.: .
Driving Wheel Dia./Diamètre des roues motrices: .
Weight/Masse: 24 tonnes.
Overall Length/Longeur hors tout: 8.74 m.
Max. Speed/Vitesse maximale: 60 km/h.

* Fitted for snowplough use./Modifié pour l'utilisation comme chasse-neige.

9501		BI	Biel/Bienne
9502		BR	Brig
9503		LS	St Maurice
9504		BS	Laufen
9505		LS	Yverdon
9506		BS	Basel
9507		BE	Faido
9508		OL	Solothurn
9509		LZ	Arth-Goldau
9510		BS	Liestal
9511		ZU	Brugg
9512		WT	Schaffhausen
9513		WT	Winterthur
9514		WT	Wil
9515		ZU	Rapperswil
9516		LS	Lausanne
9517		LZ	Luzern
9518		ZU	Zürich
9519		LZ	Luzern
9520		ZU	Zürich
9521		WT	Frauenfeld
9522		WT	Bülach
9523		ZU	Zürich
9524		LZ	Sursee
9525		BE	Bellinzona
9526		OL	Langenthal
9527		LZ	Hochdorf
9528		BS	Muttenz
9529		ER	Erstfeld
9530		LS	Puidoux-Chexbres
9531		LS	St Maurice
9532	*	LS	Payerne
9533	*	BI	Neuchâtel
9534	*	BI	St Imier
9535	*	LS	Cossonay
9536	*	ZU	Ziegelbrücke
9537	*	RS	St Gallen
9538	*	RS	Buchs
9539	*	WT	Wetzikon
9540	*	BS	Liestal
9541	*	LZ	Luzern
9542	*	BI	Neuchâtel
9543	*	ZU	Rapperswil
9551		GE	Genève
9552		BI	Biel/Bienne
9553		LZ	Luzern
9554		OL	Olten
9555		ZU	Wallisellen
9556		ZU	Pfäffikon
9557		WT	Bülach
9558		WT	Winterthur
9559		RS	Buchs
9560		WT	Wetzikon
9561		ZU	Zürich Altstetten
9562		BE	Airolo
9563		OL	Olten
9564		OL	Langenthal
9565		LZ	Zug
9566		CH	Chiasso
9567		GE	Nyon
9568		BR	Sion
9569		BI	Neuchâtel
9570		BN	Bern
9571		BN	Thun
9572		GE	Genève
9573		BI	Delémont
9574		LS	Lausanne
9575		BR	Brig
9576		BN	Fribourg
9577		ER	Erstfeld
9578		OL	Lenzburg
9579		BE	Rivera
9580		OL	Aarau
9581		BS	Muttenz
9582		ZU	Dietikon
9583		WT	Etzwilen
9584		RS	Romanshorn
9585		ZU	Richterswil
9586		ZU	Zürich
9587		ZU	Stein Säckingen
9588		RS	St Gallen
9589		RS	Chur
9590		OL	Olten
9591		BE	Bellinzona
9592		LZ	Arth Goldau
9593		OL	Langenthal
9594		LZ	Konolfingen
9595		LS	Nyon
9596		BN	Bern
9597		LS	Fribourg

CLASS/SERIE Tm IV — B

Identical with the 8751 series, these tractors are in departmental use.
Semblable à la série 8751 et avec les mêmes dimensions, ce sont des locotracteurs de service.

Built/Date de mise en service: 1971–7.
Builder/Constructeur: SLM.
Engine/Moteur: MAN R8V 16/18 280 kW.
Transmission: Hydraulic/Hydraulique.
Maximum Tractive Effort/Effort de traction max.: .
Driving Wheel Dia./Diamètre des roues motrices: 1040 mm.
Weight/Masse: 30 tonnes.
Overall Length/Longeur hors tout: 7.67 m.
Max. Speed/Vitesse maximale: 60 km/h.

* Purchased 1987 from SLM (was their works pilot).
* Acheté en 1987 de SLM (auparavant utilisé dans les ateliers SLM).

9651	WT	Wil
9652	ZU	Zürich
9653	WT	Schaffhausen
9654	BI	*Reserve*
9655	BE	Faido
9656	LZ	Arth-Goldau
9657	OL	Olten
9658	LS	Lausanne
9659	BR	*Reserve*
9660	BN	*Reserve*
9661	BI	*Reserve*
9662	ER	Erstfeld
9663	OL	Solothurn
9664	BE	Bellinzona
9665	RS	St Gallen
9666	ZU	Brugg
9667	ZU	Rapperswil
9668	ZU	Zürich
9669	ZU	Zürich
9670	BI	Neuchâtel
9671	LS	Lausanne
9672	BR	Sion
9673	LS	*Reserve*
9674	BI	Delémont
9675	BN	Bern
9676	BS	Muttenz
9677	BE	Airolo
9678	OL	Langenthal
9679	BE	Rivera
9680	LZ	Konolfingen
9681	WT	Winterthur
9682	ZU	Rapperswil
9683	ZU	Wallisellen
9684	ZU	Stein-Säckingen
9685	*	Olten Works

CLASS/SERIE 283 Bo

A second hand tractor purchased in 1989./Un locotracteur acheté d'occasion en 1989.

Built/Date de mise en service: 1973.
Builder/Constructeur: Gmeinder.
Engine/Moteur: MAN 650 kW.
Transmission: Electric/Electrique.
Maximum Tractive Effort/Effort de traction max.:
Driving Wheel Dia./Diamètre des roues motrices:
Weight/Masse: 23 tonnes.
Overall Length/Longeur hors tout: 7.63 m.
Max. Speed/Vitesse maximale: 60 km/h.

283 000-8 OL Solothurn

Te III Class No. 134 at Travers on 04/08/88. *G.B. Wise*

Le Te III 134 à Travers. 04/08/88. *G.B. Wise*

ELECTRIC RAILCARS/ AUTOMOTRICES ELECTRIQUES

Railcars are either made up of fixed formations, or are single motor coaches which may be coupled to randomly formed driving and intermediate trailer cars to make up push-pull trains. Apart from classes BDe4/4 II and RBDe4/4, they are double ended. Trailers are numbered in the carriage series. Under 'accommodation' are shown the number of 1st and 2nd class seats, followed by the number of toilets, e.g. 60/– 1T indicates 60 first class seats, no second class seats and one toilet.

Les automotrices sont soit des éléments indéformables soit des motrices qui sont couplées à un nombre variable de remorques pour former des rames réversibles. Mis à part les BDe4/4 II et les RBDe4/4, elles ont deux cabines de conduites. Les remorques sont numérotées dans la même série que les voitures remorquées. Dans «aménagement intérieur» on indique le nombre de places en 1re et 2me classe, suivi pare le nombre de toilettes, par exemple 60/– 1T indique 60 place en 1re, 0 en 2me et une toilette.

CLASS/SERIE RAe2/4

The last survivor of a number of lightweight, single units built during the 1930s, known as 'Red Arrows' because of their livery. This car is normally used on charter work.

La dernière survivante d'une classe d'automotrices simples légères qui fut construites pendant les années 30 et surnommées les «Flèches Rouges» à cause de leur livrée. Cette automotrice est normalement utilisée pour des trains charters.

Built/Date de mise en service: 1935.
Builder-Mech. Parts/Constructeur-Partie mécanique: SLM.
Builder-Elec. Parts/Constructeur-Partie électrique: BBC/MFO/SAAS.
Traction Motors: 2 single phase commutator type, fully suspended with BBC spring drive.
Moteurs de traction:2 moteurs à courant alternatif monophasé à collecteurs, entièrement suspendus avec transmission à ressorts BBC.
One Hour Rating/Puissance horaire: 400 kW.
Maximum Tractive Effort/Effort de traction max.: 25 kN.
Driving Wheel Dia./Diamètre des roues motrices: 900 mm.
Weight/Masse: 41 tonnes.
Overall Length/Longeur hors tout: 25.20 m.
Max. Speed/Vitesse maximale: 125 km/h.
Wheel Arrangement/Disposition des essieux: 2Bo.
Accommodation/Aménagement intérieur: 60/– 1T.
New Class No./Nouveau numéro de série: .

1001 BN |

CLASS/SERIE RABe

These 4-voltage six-car units were built for use on International TEE trains, and at one time could be seen as far afield as Brussels, Paris and Genova. All have now been refurbished for use on Eurocity services from Zürich, Genève & Lausanne to Milano. This has resulted in the installation of 2nd class seats in these once 1st class only units which are unusual in having separate toilet facilities for ladies and gentlemen.

Sets 1051–4 were built as 5-car units, and lengthened to 6 cars in 1967 when the 5th unit was delivered.

Ces automotrices quadri-courant de six caisses furent construites pour les trains internationaux TEE (1re classe uniquement), et furent auparavant utilisées jusqu'à Bruxelles, Paris et Gênes. Toutes ont été modernisées pour les services Eurocity de Zurich, Genève et Lausanne à Milan avec installation de sièges de 2me classe. Un aspect intéressant est l'existence de toilettes séparées pour hommes et femmes.

Les 1051 à 4 furent construites avec 5 caisses mais ont reçu une 6me voiture en 1967 au moment où la 1055 fut livrée.

All are mw fitted (for up to 2 sets in multiple)./Couplables en UM (deux éléments maximum).

Built/Date de mise en service: 1961–7.

Builder-Mech. Parts/Constructeur-Partie mécanique: SIG.
Builder-Elec. Parts/Constructeur-Partie électrique: MFO.
Traction Motors: 4 single phase commutator type, fully suspended with BBC spring drive.
Moteurs de traction:4 moteurs à courant alternatif monophasé à collecteurs, entièrement suspendus avec transmission à ressorts BBC.
One Hour Rating/Puissance horaire: 2345 kW.
Maximum Tractive Effort/Effort de traction max.: 157 kN.
Driving Wheel Dia./Diamètre des roues motrices: 1110 mm.
Wheel Arrangement/Disposition des essieux: 22+22+A1AA1A+22+22+22.
Accommodation: 42/– 2T + 42/– 2T + baggage/kitchen + –/39 15R + –/54 2T + –/54 2T.
Aménagement intérieur: 42/– 2T + 42/– 2T + fourgon/cuisine + –/39 15R + –/54 2T + –/54 2T.
Weight/Masse: 296 tonnes.
Overall Length/Longeur hors tout: 14.97 m.
Max. Speed/Vitesse maximale: 160 km/h.
System: 1500 V dc/3000 V dc, 15 kV 16⅔ Hz/25 kV 50 Hz.
New Class No./Nouveau numéro de série: 506.

1051 **E** ZU | 1052 **E** ZU | 1053 **E** ZU | 1054 **E** ZU | 1055 **E** ZU

CLASS/SERIE RABDe12/12

Three-car units built for Zürich suburban services. Originally there were 20 sets, but 6 coaches were written off in accidents in 1971, and others renumbered to fill the gaps. Used mainly on the Winterthur–Zürich–Meilen–Rapperswil service.

Although the single pantograph is mounted on the centre coach, the control gear and two transformers are on the outer coaches. Automatic speed and acceleration control and regenerative braking are fitted.

Eléments à 3 caisses construits pour les services de la banlieue de Zurich. A l'origine il existait 20 éléments mais 6 caisses furent radiées après des accidents en 1971 et les autres ont étés renumérotées. Utilisés principalement sur le service Winterthour–Zurich–Meilen–Rapperswil.

Bien que le pantographe soit monté sur la caisse centrale, l'équipement de puissance et les deux transformateurs sont installés dans les deux autres caisses. Dotées du contrôle automatique de la vitesse et de l'accélération, ainsi que du freinage à récupération.

mw fitted for up to 4 sets in multiple./Jusqu'à 4 éléments couplables en UM.

Built/Date de mise en service: 1965–7.
Builder-Mech. Parts/Constructeur-Partie mécanique: SWP/FFA.
Builder-Elec. Parts/Constructeur-Partie électrique: SAAS/BBC.
Traction Motors: 12 single phase commutator type, fully suspended with BBC spring drive.
Moteurs de traction:12 moteurs à courant alternatif monophasé à collecteurs, entièrement suspendus avec transmission à ressorts BBC.
One Hour Rating/Puissance horaire: 2475 kW.
Maximum Tractive Effort/Effort de traction max.: 239 kN.
Driving Wheel Dia./Diamètre des roues motrices: 850 mm.
Weight/Masse: 170 tonnes.
Overall Length/Longeur hors tout: 73.30 m.
Max. Speed/Vitesse maximale: 125 km/h.
Wheel Arrangement/Disposition des essieux: BoBo+BoBo+BoBo.
Accommodation/Aménagement intérieur: –/72 1T + 56/– 1T + –/72 1T.
New Class No./Nouveau numéro de série: 511.

1101 **D**	ZU	1105 **D**	ZU	1109 **D**	ZU	1113 **D**	ZU	1116 **D**	ZU
1102 **D**	ZU	1106 **D**	ZU	1110 **D**	ZU	1114 **D**	ZU	1117 **D**	ZU
1103 **D**	ZU	1107 **D**	ZU	1111 **D**	ZU	1115 **D**	ZU	1118 **D**	ZU
1104 **D**	ZU	1108 **D**	ZU	1112 **D**	ZU				

CLASS/SERIE BDe4/4 II

These two cars were built specially for the Genève–La Plaine service, since this line is electrified at 1500 V dc to enable SNCF trains to work into Genève. They cannot operate elsewhere. Gangwayed at the non-driving end.

Ces deux automotrices furent construites pour la ligne Genève–La Plaine qui est électrifiée en 1500 V continu pour les trains SNCF. Elles ne peuvent pas donc être utilisées ailleurs. Dotées d'une porte d'intercirculation à l'autre extremité de la cabine de conduite.

Built/Date de mise en service: 1956–7.
Builder-Mech. Parts/Constructeur-Partie mécanique: SWS.
Builder-Elec. Parts/Constructeur-Partie électrique: SAAS.
Traction Motors: 4 single phase commutator type, axle suspended.
Moteurs de traction: 4 moteurs à courant alternatif monophasé à collecteurs, suspendus sur les essieux.
One Hour Rating/Puissance horaire: 1105 kW.
Maximum Tractive Effort/Effort de traction max.: 108 kN.
Driving Wheel Dia./Diamètre des roues motrices: 910 mm.
Wheel Arrangement/Disposition des essieux: BoBo.
Weight/Masse: 49 tonnes.
Max. Speed/Vitesse maximale: 100 km/h.
System/Système: 1500 V dc/courant continu.
Accommodation/Aménagement intérieur: –/48 1T.
New Class No./Nouveau numéro de série: 533.

1301 GE	1302 GE

CLASS/SERIE RBe4/4

Originally built for longer distance push-pull workings, these motor coaches are now mainly used on the Zürich S-Bahn, and most have been formed into 4-coach push-pull sets. 1419 was written off in an accident in 1972. 1401–6 have been modified recently for working the Seetalbahn, a mainly roadside line from Luzern to Lenzberg.

Construites pour des trains sur de longues distances, ces automotrices sont maintenant utilisées principalement sur le RER de Zurich en rames réversibles de 4 caisses. La 1419 a été radiée après un accident en 1972. Les 1401 à 6 ont été modifiées récemment pour le Seetalbahn, une ligne qui suit largement la route entre Lucerne et Lenzbourg.

Built/Date de mise en service: 1959–60*, 1963–66.
Builder-Mech. Parts/Constructeur-Partie mécanique: SIG/SWS.
Builder-Elec. Parts/Constructeur-Partie électrique: BBC/MFO.
Traction Motors: 4 single phase, commutator type, fully suspended with BBC spring drive.
Moteurs de traction: 4 moteurs à courant alternatif monophasé à collecteurs, entièrement suspendus avec transmission à ressorts BBC.
One Hour Rating/Puissance horaire: 2030 kW.
Maximum Tractive Effort/Effort de traction max.: 188 kN.
Driving Wheel Dia./Diamètre des roues motrices: 1040 mm.
Weight/Masse: 68 tonnes (64 tonnes*).
Overall Length/Longeur hors tout: 22.90 m.
Overall Length/Longeur hors tout: 23.70 m.
Max. Speed/Vitesse maximale: 125 km/h.
Wheel Arrangement/Disposition des essieux: BoBo.
Accommodation/Aménagement intérieur: –/64 1T (–/60 1T§).
New Class No./Nouveau numéro de série: 524.

All are push-pull & mw fitted (can mw with Re4/4 II, Re4/4 III, Re4/4 IV & Re6/6 classes).
Toutes sont dotées de la reversibilité et sont couplables en UM entre elles et avec les Re4/4 II, RE4/4 III, Re4/4 IV et Re6/6.
† Rebuilt with thyristor control./Modifiée avec des thyristors.

1401 L * LZ	1417 † WT	1434 † WT	1450 † WT	1467 † WT
1402 L * LZ	1418 BI	1435 WT	1451 BI	1468 † WT
1403 L * LZ	1420 L † WT	1436 BI	1452 † WT	1469 † WT
1404 L * LZ	1421 † WT	1437 L † WT	1453 WT	1470 L † WT
1405 L * LZ	1422 †§ WT	1438 † WT	1455 L † WT	1471 † WT
1406 L * LZ	1423 † WT	1439 † WT	1456 L † WT	1472 † WT
1407 WT	1424 WT	1440 † WT	1457 † WT	1473 † WT
1408 † WT	1425 † WT	1441 L † WT	1458 WT	1474 † WT
1409 L † WT	1426 † WT	1442 † WT	1459 † WT	1475 † WT
1410 WT	1427 † WT	1443 WT	1460 † WT	1476 † WT
1411 † WT	1428 † WT	1444 † WT	1461 † WT	1477 WT
1412 WT	1429 † WT	1445 † WT	1462 † WT	1478 † WT
1413 † WT	1430 † WT	1446 † WT	1463 † WT	1479 † WT
1414 L WT	1431 WT	1447 † WT	1464 † WT	1480 † WT
1415 BI	1432 † WT	1448 † WT	1465 † WT	1481 † WT
1416 BI	1433 WT	1449 † WT	1466 † WT	1482 † WT

CLASS/SERIE Be4/6

These were the first Swiss push-pull railcars, originally built for the Zürich suburban services where they worked with 4-wheel trailers. Extensive modernisation took place between 1961 and 1966. Now being slowly withdrawn, the survivors are mainly used on staff trains.

Les premières automotrices réversibles en Suisse, construites à l'origine pour les services de banlieue de Zurich où elles furent utilisées avec des remorques à essieux. Elles furent profondément modernisées entre 1961 et 1966. Les survivantes sont en cours d'amortissement et sont utilisées principalement pour des trains de personnel.

Built/Date de mise en service: 1923–7.
Builder-Mech. Parts/Constructeur-Partie mécanique: SIG/SWS.
Builder-Elec. Parts/Constructeur-Partie électrique: SAAS.
Traction Motors: 4 single phase commutator type, axle suspended.
Moteurs de traction:4 moteurs à courant alternatif monophasé à collecteurs, suspendus sur les essieux.
One Hour Rating/Puissance horaire: 635 kW.
Maximum Tractive Effort/Effort de traction max.: 88 kN.
Driving Wheel Dia./Diamètre des roues motrices: 1040 mm.
Wheel Arrangement/Disposition des essieux: A1AA1A.
Weight/Masse: 72 tonnes.
Overall Length/Longeur hors tout: 20.00 m.
Max. Speed/Vitesse maximale: 90 km/h.
Pony Wheel Dia./Diamè des roues porteuses: 850 km.
Accommodation/Aménagement intérieur: –/56 1T.
New Class No./Nouveau numéro de série: 526.

Push-pull fitted./Dotées de la reversibilité.

1602	OL	1606	ZU	1608	ZU	1614	BS	1616	LS
1603	ZU	1607	OL	1613 M	LS	1615	LS		

CLASS/SERIE BDe4/4

These railcars, bearing a distinct resemblance to the Re4/4 I, are used on local and branch line services in the north and west of the country. Some have had the gangway at the luggage end removed.

Ces automotrices, qui ressemblent beaucoup aux Re4/4 I, sont utilisées sur des trains omnibus dans le nord et l'ouest du pays. Certaines ont vu leur porte d'intercirculation supprimée à l'extremité où se trouve le compartiment à bagages.

Built/Date de mise en service: 1952–5.
Builder-Mech. Parts/Constructeur-Partie mécanique: SLM/SWP.
Builder-Elec. Parts/Constructeur-Partie électrique: BBC/MFO/SAAS.
Traction Motors: 4 single phase commutator type, axle suspended.
Moteurs de traction:4 moteurs à courant alternatif monophasé à collecteurs, suspendus sur les essieux.
One Hour Rating/Puissance horaire: 1195 kW.
Maximum Tractive Effort/Effort de traction max.: 98 kN.
Driving Wheel Dia./Diamètre des roues motrices: 940 mm.
Weight/Masse: 57 tonnes.
Overall Length/Longeur hors tout: 22.70 m.
Max. Speed/Vitesse maximale: 110 km/h.
Wheel Arrangement/Disposition des essieux: BoBo.
Accommodation/Aménagement intérieur: –/40 1T.
New Class No./Nouveau numéro de série: 536.

Rheostatic brake and push-pull fitted./Dotées du freinage rhéostatique et de la reversabilité.
* Fitted for one person operation./Modifiée pour l'exploitation à un agent seul.

1621	LS	1627	LS	1633	OL	1640	WT	1646	WT
1622	* LS	1628	* OL	1634	OL	1641	WT	1647	WT
1623	* LS	1629	* OL	1635	OL	1642	WT	1648	WT
1624	* LS	1630	OL	1636	OL	1643	WT	1649	WT
1625	LS	1631	OL	1637	LS	1644	WT	1650	WT
1626	LS	1632	OL	1639	WT	1645	WT	1651	* LS

CLASS/SERIE De4/4

Once a class of 25 motor luggage vans originally built for use on local services. Eleven (1661–71) were rebuilt with new bodies in 1966–71 and used for many years on the Seetalbahn and Pont Brassus line, but have now been withdrawn. The last survivor, in unrebuilt condition, is now a museum car.

A l'origine une série de 25 fourgons automoteurs construits pour les services omnibus. Onze (1661 à 71) ont reçu de nouvelles caisses de 1966 à 71 et furent utilisés sur le Seetalbahn et la ligne de Pont Brassus jusqu'à leur amortissement. Le dernier survivant, dans son état d'origine, est maintenant une automotrice historique.

Built/Date de mise en service: 1928.
Builder-Mech. Parts/Constructeur-Partie mécanique: SIG/SWS.
Builder-Elec. Parts/Constructeur-Partie électrique: MFO.
Traction Motors: 4 single phase commutator type, axle suspended.
Moteurs de traction:4 moteurs à courant alternatif monophasé à collecteurs, suspendus sur les essieux.
One Hour Rating/Puissance horaire: 820 kW.
Maximum Tractive Effort/Effort de traction max.: 86 kN.
Driving Wheel Dia./Diamètre des roues motrices: 1040 mm.
Weight/Masse: 59 tonnes.
Overall Length/Longeur hors tout: 15.20 m.
Max. Speed/Vitesse maximale: 85 km/h.
Wheel Arrangement/Disposition des essieux: BoBo.
New Class No./Nouveau numéro de série: 546.

1679 G RS |

CLASS/SERIE RABDe8/16

Four-car, lightweight, thyristor controlled units built for Zürich suburban services. However, this design has not proved to be very successful, and no further examples have been built since the 4 prototypes. Since May 1990 they have been used on the Winterthur to Stein am Rhein service. They are gangwayed within set and nicknamed 'Chiquitas'.

Des éléments légers à 4 caisses avec thyristors qui furent construits pour les services de la banlieue de Zurich. Cependant, la série n'a pas eu le succès souhaité et les 4 prototypes ne connaitront pas de suite. Depuis mai 1990, elles sont utilisées sur le service entre Winterthour et Stein-am-Rhein. La classe est surnommée les «Chiquitas».
Built/Date de mise en service: 1976.
Builder-Mech. Parts/Constructeur-Partie mécanique: SIG/SWS/SWP.
Builder-Elec. Parts/Constructeur-Partie électrique: SAAS.
Traction Motors: 8 single phase, fully suspended with BBC spring drive.
Moteurs de traction:8 moteurs à courant alternatif monophasé à collecteurs, entièrement suspendus avec transmission à ressorts BBC.
One Hour Rating/Puissance horaire: 2280 kW.
Maximum Tractive Effort/Effort de traction max.: 187 kN.
Driving Wheel Dia./Diamètre des roues motrices: 850 mm.
Weight/Masse: (per set) 149 tonnes.
Overall Length/Longeur hors tout: 100.00 m.
Max. Speed/Vitesse maximale: 125 km/h.
Wheel Arrangement/Disposition des essieux: BoBo+22+22+BoBo.
Accommodation/Aménagement intérieur: –/72 1T + 54/– 1T + –/80 1T + –/72S.
New Class No./Nouveau numéro de série: 512.

mw fitted (for up to 2 sets in multiple)./Couplables en UM (2 éléments maximum).

2001 V ZU | 2002 V ZU | 2003 V ZU | 2004 V ZU |

CLASS/SERIE RBDe4/4

This new design for local services is formally known as the 'NPZ' – Neue Pendel Zug or 'new shuttle train' – and informally, though officially, as the 'Kolibri' or 'humming bird'. Four prototypes were delivered in 1984 with series production beginning in 1987. Units are still being delivered. They are equipped with solid state control. Operating in sets of varying length, with control and intermediate trailers, they can also multiple with other members of the class. Gangwayed at the non-driving end only.

2184/5 are operated by the SBB on behalf of the Chemin de Fer Pont Brassus and are lettered

"Vallée de Joux" for the Lausanne–Vallorbe–Le Brassus service.

Ces nouvelles automotrices sont officiellement nommées «NPZ» – Neue Pendel Zug ou nouveaux trains navettes, mais officieusement surnommées les «Colibris». Quatre prototypes furent livrés en 1984; la production en série a commencé en 1987 et se poursuit en ce moment. Elles sont équipées de thyristors. Le nombre de caisses peut être varié et les éléments sont couplables entre eux en UM.

Les 2184 et 85 sont exploités par les CFF pour le compte du Chemin de Fer Pont Brassus et sont marqués «Vallée de Joux» pour le service Lausanne–Vallorbe–Le Brassus.

Built/Date de mise en service: 1984* 1987–90.
Builder-Mech. Parts/Constructeur-Partie mécanique: FFA/SIG/SWP.
Builder-Elec. Parts/Constructeur-Partie électrique: BBC (ABB).
One Hour Rating/Puissance horaire: 1650 kW.
Maximum Tractive Effort/Effort de traction max.: 166 kN.
Driving Wheel Dia./Diamètre des roues motrices: 950 mm.
Weight/Masse: 70 tonnes.
Overall Length/Longeur hors tout: 25.00 m.
Max. Speed/Vitesse maximale: 140 km/h.
Wheel Arrangement/Disposition des essieux: BoBo.
Accommodation/Aménagement intérieur: –/65 1T.
New Class No./Nouveau numéro de série: 532.

2100	**N***	LS	Altstätten SG
2101	**N***	LS	Münsingen
2102	**N***	LS	Sempach-Neuenkirch
2103	**N***	LS	Frenkendorf-Füllinsdorf
2104	**N**	LS	Grandvaux
2105	**N**	LS	Untersiggenthal
2106	**N**	LS	Wünnewil-Flammatt
2107	**N**	LS	Rekingen AG
2108	**N**	LS	Buttes
2109	**N**	LS	Lachen
2110	**N**	LS	Jona
2111	**N**	LS	Aesch
2112	**N**	LS	Zwingen
2113	**N**	BI	Oberbuchsiten
2114	**N**	BI	Näfels-Mollis
2115	**N**	BI	Lausen
2116	**N**	BI	Dottikon-Dintikon-Villmergen
2117	**N**	BI	Bad Ragaz
2118	**N**	BI	Les Hauts Geneveys
2119	**N**	BI	Rivera-Bironico
2120	**N**	BI	Birsfelden
2121	**N**	BI	Entlebuch
2122	**N**	BI	Rothenburg
2123	**N**	BI	Ebikon
2124	**N**	BI	Bauma
2125	**N**	BI	Düdigen
2126	**N**	BI	Versoix
2127	**N**	BI	Tenero-Contra
2128	**N**	BI	Saint Ursanne
2129	**N**	BI	Saint Imier
2130	**N**	BI	Amriswil
2131	**N**	LZ	Rolle
2132	**N**	LZ	Birr-Lupfig
2133	**N**	LZ	Avenches
2134	**N**	LZ	Cressier NE
2135	**N**	LZ	Niederbipp
2136	**N**	LZ	Andelfingen
2137	**N**	LZ	Brügg BE
2138	**N**	LZ	Müchenbuchsee
2139	**N**	LZ	Steinhausen
2140	**N**	LZ	Tecknau
2141	**N**	LZ	Wassen
2142	**N**	LZ	Saint Gingolph
2143	**N**	LZ	Pully
2144	**N**	LZ	Twann
2145	**N**	LZ	Glovelier
2146	**N**	BE	Muralto
2147	**N**	BI	Les Eplatures
2148	**N**	BI	Frick
2149	**N**	BI	Reinach
2150	**N**	BI	La Neuveville
2151	**N**	BI	Egerkingen
2152	**N**	BI	Dagmersellen
2153	**N**	BI	Boncourt-Delle
2154	**N**	BI	Küssnacht am Rigi
2155	**N**	BI	Saint Blaise
2156	**N**	BI	Sins
2157	**N**	BI	Reconvilier
2158	**N**	BI	Saxon
2159	**N**	BI	Gurtnellen
2160	**N**	BI	Kaiseraugst
2161	**N**	BI	Sins
2162	**N**	BI	Deitingen
2163	**N**	BI	Giornico
2164	**N**	WT	
2165	**N**	WT	
2166	**N**	LZ	Schüpfheim
2167	**N**	WT	Moudon
2168	**N**	LZ	Gisikon Root
2169	**N**	WT	
2170	**N**	LZ	Trubschachen
2171	**N**	WT	
2172	**N**	LS	Vernayaz
2173	**N**	LS	Gland
2174	**N**	LS	Gorgier–St. Aubin
2175	**N**	WT	Grellingen
2176	**N**	LS	Orbe
2177	**N**	LS	Puidoux–Chexbres
2178	**N**		
2179	**N**		
2180	**N**		
2181	**N**		
2182	**N**		
2183	**N**		
2184	**N**	LS	
2185	**N**	LS	

ELECTRIC LOCOMOTIVES
LOCOMOTIVES ELECTRIQUES

CLASS/***SERIE*** Re4/4 I — BoBo

A development of the RFe4/4 motor luggage vans (now De4/4 of the SOB and SZU), the Re4/4 I was introduced to work lightweight expresses. It was the first production design to omit carrying wheels and to have a maximum speed of over 110 km/h. Various liveries have been carried, the most significant variation being TEE red and cream applied to 10033/34/46/50 in 1972; these have now reverted to standard livery.

Conçue comme une version des fourgons automoteurs RFe4/4 (devenus maintenant les De4/4 des SOB et SZU), la série Re4/4 I fut construite pour remorquer des express légers. C'était la première locomotive de série sans essieux porteurs et avec une vitesse maximale supérieure à 110 km/h. La série a porté plusieurs livrées, la plus significative étant rouge et blanc cassé TEE, utilisée sur 10033/34/46/50 en 1972. Celles-ci sont maintenant dans la livrée standard.

Built/*Date de mise en service*: 1946–48 p (1950–51 remainder/autres).
Builder-Mech. Parts/*Constructeur-Partie mécanique*: SLM.
Builder-Elec. Parts/*Constructeur-Partie électrique*: BBC/MFO/SAAS.
Traction Motors: 4 single phase commutator type, fully suspended with BBC spring drive.
***Moteurs de traction*:** 4 moteurs à courant alternatif monophasé à collecteurs, entièrement suspendus avec transmission à ressorts BBC.
One Hour Rating/*Puissance horaire*: 1854 (1830 p) kW.
Maximum Tractive Effort/*Effort de traction max.*: 137 kN.
Driving Wheel Dia./*Diamètre des roues motrices*: 1040 mm.
Weight/*Masse*: 57 tonnes.
Overall Length/*Longeur hors tout*: 14.90 m (14.70 m p).
Max. Speed/*Vitesse maximale*: 125 km/h.
New Class No./*Nouveau numéro de série*: 410.

p Fitted for push-pull working with regenerative braking and corridor connections.
p Dotées de la réversibilité, du freinage par récupération et de portes d'intercirculation.

10001 p BE	10011 p BE	10021 p LS	10031 RS	10041 LS
10002 p BE	10012 **R** p BE	10022 **R** p LS	10032 RS	10042 LS
10003 **R** p BE	10013 p BE	10023 **R** p LS	10033 **R** RS	10043 **R** LS
10004 **R** p BE	10014 **R** p BE	10024 p LS	10034 **R** RS	10044 **R** LS
10005 p BE	10015 p BE	10025 **R** p LS	10035 **R** LS	10045 **R** LS
10006 p BE	10016 p BE	10026 p LS	10036 **R** LS	10046 LS
10007 p BE	10017 **R** p BE	10027 **R** RS	10037 **R** LS	10047 LS
10008 **R** p BE	10018 p BE	10028 **R** RS	10038 **R** LS	10048 **R** LS
10009 **R** p BE	10019 p LS	10029 **R** RS	10039 LS	10049 **R** LS
10010 **R** p BE	10020 p LS	10030 **R** RS	10040 LS	10050 **R** LS

CLASS/***SERIE*** Re4/4 IV — BoBo

These four locos were built as prototypes for a new generation of traction with solid state power control and dc traction motors. The class will not go into series production, but have acted as a useful development facility. They are usually used on the Genève–Brig–Domodossola route, but have appeared elsewhere, usually on test trains. They also see use on the BLS. All carry the 'Bahn 2000' publicity livery.

Ces quatre locomotives sont des prototypes pour une nouvelle génération de matériel moteur à thyristors et moteurs à courant continu. Les machines n'ont pas été produites en série mais ont été utilisées comme bancs d'essais. En général, elles sont utilisées sur la ligne Genève–Brigue–Domodossola et sur le BLS, mais parfois sont apparues ailleurs en tête de trains d'essais. Toutes sont revêtues de la livrée publicitaire pour le projet «Bahn 2000».

Built/*Date de mise en service*: 1982.
Builder-Mech. Parts/*Constructeur-Partie mécanique*: SLM.
Builder-Elec. Parts/*Constructeur-Partie électrique*: BBC.
One Hour Rating/*Puissance horaire*: 4960 kW.
Maximum Tractive Effort/*Effort de traction max.*: 300 kN.
Driving Wheel Dia./*Diamètre des roues motrices*: 1260 mm.
Weight/*Masse*: 80 tonnes.

Overall Length/Longeur hors tout: 15.8 m.
Max. Speed/Vitesse maximale: 160 km/h.
New Class No./Nouveau numéro de série: 440.

All locos mw fitted (can work with Re4/4 II, Re4/4 III, Re6/6, & RBe4/4 classes).
Toutes sont couplables en unité multiple (UM) entre elles et avec les séries Re4/4 II, Re4/4 III, Re6/6 et RBe4/4.

10101 **R**	LS	Vallée de Joux	10103 **R**	LS	Luino
10102 **R**	LS	Ostermundigen	10104 **R**	LS	Walenstadt

CLASS/SERIE Ae3/5 — 1Co1

A museum loco, the last survivor of a class once totalling 26.

Une locomotive «historique», la dernière survivante d'une classe totalisant 26 unités auparavant.

Built/Date de mise en service: 1924.
Builder-Mech. Parts/Constructeur-Partie mécanique: SLM.
Builder-Elec. Parts/Constructeur-Partie électrique: SAAS.
Traction Motors: 6 single phase commutator type, body mounted with hollow axle drive.
Moteurs de traction: 6 moteurs à courant alternatif monophasé à collecteurs, fixés dans la caisse avec transmission Westinghouse-Sécheron à arbre creux.
One Hour Rating/Puissance horaire: 1340 kW.
Maximum Tractive Effort/Effort de traction max.: 137 kN.
Driving Wheel Dia./Diamètre des roues motrices: 1610 mm.
Pony Wheel Dia./Diamètre des roues porteuses: 950 mm.
Weight/Masse: 81 tonnes.
Overall Length/Longeur hors tout: 12.32 m.
Max. Speed/Vitesse maximale: 90 km/h.
New Class No./Nouveau numéro de série: 395.

10217 **G** BN

CLASS/SERIE Ae3/6 III — 2Co1

Another museum loco, this class being a lengthened version of the previous one, with a bogie at one end instead of a pony truck.

Une autre locomotive historique. Cette série était une plus longue version de la Ae3/5, avec une bogie au lieu d'un seul essieu porteur.

Built/Date de mise en service: 1926.
Builder-Mech. Parts/Constructeur-Partie mécanique: SLM.
Builder-Elec. Parts/Constructeur-Partie électrique: SAAS.
Traction Motors: 6 single phase commutator type, body mounted with hollow axle drive.
Moteurs de traction: 6 moteurs à courant alternatif monophasé à collecteurs, fixés dans la caisse avec transmission Westinghouse-Sécheron à arbre creux.
One Hour Rating/Puissance horaire: 1340 kW.
Maximum Tractive Effort/Effort de traction max.: 137 kN.
Driving Wheel Dia./Diamètre des roues motrices: 1610 mm.
Pony Wheel Dia./Diamètre des roues porteuses: 950 mm.
Weight/Masse: 89 tonnes.
Overall Length/Longeur hors tout: 13.76 m.
Max. Speed/Vitesse maximale: 90 km/h.
New Class No./Nouveau numéro de série: 396.

10264 **B** LS

CLASS/SERIE Ae3/6 II — 2C1

Yet another museum loco, this class differs from the other Ae3/6 series in having rod drive. Once a class of 60 locos, several others survive as heating units.

Encore une locomotive historique. Cette série se distingue des autres Ae3/6 par sa transmission par bielles. D'une série de 60 unités, certains exemplaires ont survécu pour des missions à poste fixe (préchauffage de rames vides).

Built/Date de mise en service: 1925.
Builder-Mech. Parts/Constructeur-Partie mécanique: SLM.

Builder-Elec. Parts/Constructeur-Partie électrique: MFO.
Traction Motors: 2 single phase commutator type, body mounted with jackshaft/side rod drive.
Moteurs de traction: 2 moteurs à courant alternatif monophasé à collecteurs, fixés dans la caisse avec transmission par faux-essieux et bielles.
One Hour Rating/Puissance horaire: 1490 kW.
Maximum Tractive Effort/Effort de traction max.: 147 kN.
Driving Wheel Dia./Diamètre des roues motrices: 1610 mm.
Pony Wheel Dia./Diamètre des roues porteuses: 950 mm.
Weight/Masse: 98 tonnes.
Overall Length/Longeur hors tout: 14.15 m.
Max. Speed/Vitesse maximale: 100 km/h.
New Class No./Nouveau numéro de série: 396.

10439 **B** OL

CLASS/SERIE Ae3/6 I — 2Co1

Once a class of 114 units, this was the most successful of several general purpose types introduced in the early years of electrification. The powered wheels are rigid with the frame and are each driven by a motor mounted above in the locomotive body through a 'Büchli' drive. This is carried in a circular casing outside the wheels on one side only, completely obscuring them on that side. The survivors are now used on light duties in the flatter areas, including some passenger work. Some are expected to remain in service at least until 1995.

Au début, cette classe comptait 114 unités et avait le plus de succès parmi plusieurs séries d'électriques pour le trafic mixte dans les premières années de l'électrification. Les essieux moteurs sont fixés au châssis et chacun est mû par un moteur positionné au-dessus de l'essieu avec une transmission «Buchli». Celle-ci est montée dans un carter circulaire sur l'extérieur des roues sur un côté seulement, derrière lequel la roue est complètement cachée. Les dernières machines encore en service sont utilisées pour des trains légers sur les lignes à profil facile, y compris quelques services voyageurs. Certaines seront en service jusqu'en 1995.

Built/Date de mise en service: 1924–9.
Builder-Mech. Parts/Constructeur-Partie mécanique: SLM.
Builder-Elec. Parts/Constructeur-Partie électrique: BBC (MFO 10690–10712).
Traction Motors: 3 single phase commutator type, frame mounted with BBC Büchli flexible drive.
Moteurs de traction: 3 moteurs à courant alternatif monophasé à collecteurs, fixé au châssis avec transmission Buchli.
One Hour Rating/Puissance horaire: 1560 kW.
Maximum Tractive Effort/Effort de traction max.: 147 kN.
Driving Wheel Dia./Diamètre des roues motrices: 1610 mm.
Pony Wheel Dia./Diamètre des roues porteuses: 950 mm.
Weight/Masse: 95.5 tonnes (93.8 tonnes 10690–10712).
Overall Length/Longeur hors tout: 14.70 m.
Max. Speed/Vitesse maximale: 110 km/h.
New Class No./Nouveau numéro de série: 396.

§ Museum Loco; used to haul the 'Bahn 2000' Exhibition Train.
§ Locomotive historique; utilisée pour remorquer le train exposition «Bahn 2000».

10637	RS	10649	RS	10664	RS	10690	OL	10700 **B** §	BN
10639	RS	10650	RS	10679	OL	10691	OL	10702	BN
10641	RS	10653	RS	10680	OL	10693	OL	10709	BN
10647	RS	10659	RS	10684	OL	10694	BN	10711	BN
10648	RS	10661	OL	10685	OL	10699	BN	10712	BN

CLASS/SERIE Ae4/7 — 2Do1

An enlargement of the Ae3/6 I class, this was for many years the most numerous type in Switzerland until exceeded by the Re4/4 II, and formed the mainstay of SBB mainline passenger power well into the 1960s. Although withdrawal is slowly taking place, the class is still used on secondary duties throughout the SBB, except for the Gotthard line, and some locos are expected to survive until 2004.

Se présentant comme une version plus grande des Ae3/6 I, c'était la série la plus nombreuse avant l'introduction des Re4/4 II. Les Ae4/7 prenaient en charge la plupart des express en Suisse jusqu'au milieu des années 60. L'amortissement de la classe est lente et doit se poursuivre jusqu'en 2004, mais ces machines sont toujours utilisées partout en Suisse (sauf sur la ligne du Gothard) sur des trains moins prestigeux.

Built/Date de mise en service: 1927–34.
Builder-Mech. Parts/Constructeur-Partie mécanique: SLM.
Builder-Elec. Parts/Constructeur-Partie électrique: BBC (MFO 10919–31/66–11002, SAAS m).
Traction Motors: 4 single phase commutator type, frame mounted with BBC Büchli flexible drive.
Moteurs de traction: 4 moteurs à courant alternatif monophasé à collecteurs, fixés au châssis avec transmission Buchli.
One Hour Rating/Puissance horaire: 2300 kW.
Maximum Tractive Effort/Effort de traction max.: 196 kN.
Driving Wheel Dia./Diamètre des roues motrices: 1610 mm.
Pony Wheel Dia./Diamètre des roues porteuses: 950 mm.
Weight/Masse: 118 tonnes (123 tonnes*).
Overall Length/Longeur hors tout: 16.76 m (17.10 m*).
Max. Speed/Vitesse maximale: 100 km/h.
New Class No./Nouveau numéro de série: 497.

m mw fitted/couplables en UM.

10901	RS	10926	RS	10949	m BN	10974	* LS	11004	OL
10902	RS	10927	RS	10950	m BN	10976	* LS	11005	BS
10903	RS	10928	RS	10951	m BN	10978	* LS	11007	BS
10904	RS	10929	RS	10952	BN	10979	* LS	11008	BS
10905	RS	10930	RS	10954	BN	10980	* LS	11009	m BN
10907	RS	10931	RS	10955	BN	10984	* LS	11010	m BN
10908	RS	10932	RS	10956	BN	10986	* LS	11012	m BN
10909	RS	10933	RS	10957	BN	10987	* LS	11014	m BN
10910	RS	10934	RS	10958	BN	10990	* LS	11015	m BN
10911	RS	10935	RS	10959	BN	10991	* OL	11016	m BN
10912	RS	10937	RS	10960	BN	10992	* OL	11017	m BN
10913	RS	10938	RS	10961	BN	10993	* OL	11018	RS
10914	RS	10939	m BN	10962	OL	10995	* OL	11019	RS
10915	RS	10941	m BN	10963	OL	10996	* OL	11020	RS
10916	RS	10942	m BN	10964	OL	10997	* OL	11021	RS
10919	RS	10943	m BN	10966	OL	10998	* OL	11022	RS
10920	RS	10944	m BN	10967	OL	10999	* OL	11023	RS
10921	RS	10945	m BN	10969	OL	11000	* OL	11024	RS
10922	RS	10946	m BN	10970	OL	11001	* OL	11025	RS
10923	RS	10947	m BN	10971	RS	11002	* OL	11026	RS
10925	RS	10948	m BN	10972	RS	11003	OL	11027	RS

CLASSES/SERIES Re4/4 II & Re4/4 III * BoBo

With 273 examples in service, this is now the standard SBB electric loco and is to be found throughout the system. The first six appeared in 1964 with series production beginning in 1967. The different lengths arise from variations in the body below the cabs. Those which have carried "Swiss Express" livery were fitted with automatic couplers, but have now reverted to standard. 11172, 11282 and 11312 were withdrawn following accidents.

Class Re4/4 III is a variation with a lower gear ratio for use on the Gotthard line. Three locos of this class (11351–3) have been sold to the Südostbahn

Avec 273 exemples en service, c'est la locomotive électrique standard des CFF. On les trouve sur toute le réseau. Les six premiers exemplaires furent construits en 1964 et la livraison des autres commença en 1967. Les différences de longuer proviement du fait des variations de la traverse. Les exemplaires qui ont porté la livrée «Swiss Express» ne portent plus les attelages automatiques. Les 11172, 11282 et 11312 furent radiées suite à des accidents.

La série Re4/4 III a un rapport d'engrenages différent pour la ligne du Gotthard. Les 11351–3 ont été vendues au Südostbahn

Built/Date de mise en service: 1964–85.
Builder-Mech. Parts/Constructeur-Partie mécanique: SLM.
Builder-Elec. Parts/Constructeur-Partie électrique: BBC/MFO/SAAS.
Traction Motors: 4 single phase commutator type, fully suspended with BBC spring drive.
Moteurs de traction: 4 moteurs à courant alternatif monophasé à collecteurs, entièrement suspendus avec transmission à ressorts BBC.
One Hour Rating/Puissance horaire: 4700 (4650*) kW.
Maximum Tractive Effort/Effort de traction max.: 255 (280*) kN.
Driving Wheel Dia./Diamètre des roues motrices: 1260 mm.
Weight/Masse: 80 tonnes.
Overall Length/Longeur hors tout: 14.80 –15.58 m.
Max. Speed/Vitesse maximale: 140 (125*) km/h.
New Class No./Nouveau numéro de série: 420/430*.

Pantographs/Pantographes:

11101–11155: One, double arm Swiss./Un à deux bras Suisses.
11195–11201: Two, single arm, one Swiss and one DB/ÖBB-type for through working to Lindau./Un pantographe unijambiste suisse et un pantographe unijambiste de type DB/ÖBB pour des trains jusqu'à Lindau.
Remainder/Autres: One single arm Swiss /Un pantographe unijambiste suisse.

There are many variations in length./Il y a plusieurs varietés de longeur.

11101–11106 (Prototypes)	14.80 m	(15.58 m a)
11107–11155 (1st production series)	14.90 m	(14.96 m b, 15.07 m c, 15.01 m d)
11156–11219, 11236–11238 (2nd production series)	15.41 m	(15.465 m e, 15.52 m f)
11220–11235, 11239–11254 (2nd prod. series, mod.)	15.51 m	
11255–11349, 11354–11397 (Final production series)	15.52 m	(15.41 m *)

All locos are push-pull and mw fitted and can multiple work with Classes Re4/4 ^{III}, Re4/4 ^{IV}, Re6/6 and RBe4/4.
Toutes sont dotées de la réversibilité et couplables en UM, entre elles et avec les séries Re4/4 ^{III}, Re4/4 ^{IV}, Re6/6 et RBe4/4.

No.		Depot	No.		Depot	No.		Depot	No.		Depot	No.		Depot
11101	**R**	ZU	11134	**R**	LZ	11167	**R**	BS	11201	**R**	ZU	11234		BN
11102		ZU	11135	**R**	LZ	11168		BS	11202		ZU	11235		BN
11103	**O** a	ZU	11136	**R**	LZ	11169	**R** f	BS	11203	**R**	ZU	11236		BN
11104	**R**	ZU	11137		LZ	11170	**R**	BS	11204		ZU	11237	**R**	BN
11105		ZU	11138	**R**	LZ	11171	**R**	BS	11205		ZU	11238		BN
11106	**O** a	ZU	11139	**R**	LZ	11173	**R**	BS	11206		ZU	11239	**R**	BN
11107	**R**	ZU	11140		LZ	11174		BS	11207		ZU	11240		BN
11108	**O** c	ZU	11141	**O**	LZ	11175	**R**	BS	11208		ZU	11241		BN
11109	**O** c	ZU	11142		LZ	11176	**R**	LS	11209	**R**	ZU	11242		BN
11110		ZU	11143	**R**	LZ	11177	**R**	LS	11210		ZU	11243		BN
11111	**R**	ZU	11144	**R**	LZ	11178	**R**	LS	11211		ZU	11244		BN
11112	**R** b	ZU	11145	**R**	LZ	11179	**R**	LS	11212		ZU	11245		BN
11113	**R** b	ZU	11146	**R**	LZ	11180	**R**	LS	11213	**R**	RS	11246		BN
11114	**R**	ZU	11147	**R**	LZ	11181	**R**	BN	11214		RS	11247		BN
11115	**R**	ZU	11148	**R**	LZ	11182	**R**	BN	11215		RS	11248		BN
11116	**R**	ZU	11149	**R**	LZ	11183	**R**	BN	11216		RS	11249	**T**	BN
11117		ZU	11150		LZ	11184	**R**	BN	11217		RS	11250	**T**	BN
11118	**R**	ZU	11151		BS	11185	**R**	BN	11218		RS	11251	**T**	BN
11119		ZU	11152		BS	11186	**R**	BN	11219		RS	11252	**T**	BN
11120	**R**	ZU	11153		BS	11187	**R**	BN	11220		RS	11253	**T**	BN
11121	**R**	ZU	11154		BS	11188	**R**	BN	11221		RS	11254		BN
11122	**R**	LZ	11155	d	BS	11189	**R**	BN	11222		RS	11255		BN
11123		LZ	11156		BS	11190	**R**	BN	11223	**R**	RS	11256		BN
11124	**R**	LZ	11157	e	BS	11191	**R**	BN	11224		RS	11257		BN
11125		LZ	11158		BS	11192	**R**	BN	11225		RS	11258		BN
11126	**R**	LZ	11159		BS	11193	**R**	BN	11226		RS	11259		BN
11127		LZ	11160		BS	11194	**R**	BN	11227		RS	11260		BN
11128		LZ	11161		BS	11195	**R**	ZU	11228		RS	11261		BN
11129	**R**	LZ	11162		BS	11196	**R**	ZU	11229		RS	11262		BN
11130		LZ	11163	**R**	BS	11197	**R**	ZU	11230	**R**	RS	11263		BN
11131		LZ	11164		BS	11198	**R**	ZU	11231		BN	11264		BN
11132	**R**	LZ	11165	**R**	BS	11199	**R**	ZU	11232		BN	11265	**R**	BN
11133	**O**	LZ	11166	f	BS	11200		ZU	11233		BN	11266		BN

11267	BN	11293	RS	11319	LS	11344	LS	11373	ZU
11268	BN	11294	RS	11320	LS	11345	LS	11374	ZU
11269	BN	11295	RS	11321	LS	11346	LS	11375	ZU
11270	BN	11296	RS	11322	LS	11347	LS	11376	ZU
11271	BN	11297	RS	11323	LS	11348	LS	11377 **R**	ZU
11272	BN	11298	RS	11324	LS	11349	LS	11378 **R**	ZU
11273	BN	11299	LZ	11325	LS	11354 *	ER	11379 **R**	ZU
11274	BN	11300	LZ	11326	LS	11355 *	ER	11380 **R**	ZU
11275	BN	11301	LZ	11327	LS	11356 **R** *	ER	11381 **R**	ZU
11276	RS	11302	LZ	11328	LS	11357 *	ER	11382 **R**	ZU
11277	RS	11303	LZ	11329	LS	11358 *	ER	11383 **R**	ZU
11278	RS	11304	LZ	11330	LS	11359 *	ER	11384 **R**	ZU
11279	RS	11305	LS	11331	LS	11360 **R** *	ER	11385 **R**	ZU
11280	RS	11306	LS	11332	LS	11361 **R** *	ER	11386 **R**	ZU
11281	RS	11307	LS	11333	LS	11362 *	ER	11387 **R**	ZU
11283	RS	11308	LS	11334	LS	11363 **R** *	ER	11388 **R**	ZU
11284	RS	11309	LS	11335	LS	11364 *	ER	11389 **R**	ZU
11285	RS	11310	LS	11336	LS	11365 *	ER	11390 **R**	ZU
11286	RS	11311	LS	11337	LS	11366 *	ER	11391 **R**	ZU
11287 **R**	RS	11313	LS	11338	LS	11367 **R** *	ER	11392 **R**	ZU
11288	RS	11314	LS	11339	LS	11368 *	ER	11393 **R**	ZU
11289	RS	11315 **R**	LS	11340	LS	11369 *	ER	11394 **R**	ZU
11290	RS	11316	LS	11341	LS	11370 *	ER	11395 **R**	ZU
11291	RS	11317	LS	11342	LS	11371	ZU	11396 **R**	ZU
11292	RS	11318	LS	11343 **R**	LS	11372	ZU	11397 **R**	ZU

Name/Nom: 11239 PORRENTRUY

CLASS/SERIE Ae6/6 CoCo

Built for general use on the Gotthard and Simplon lines, this class has been largely displaced to other routes. It was the first SBB type to receive names and emblems and to carry the White Cross on the ends. 11401–25 carry chrome decorations.

Bien que construite pour les lignes du Gothard et Simplon, cette série a été largement transférée sur d'autres lignes. Les Ae6/6 furent les premières machines CFF à être baptisées et à porter la croix blanche sur leurs faces frontales. 11401 à 25 ont des enjoliveurs en chrome.

Built/Date de mise en service: 1952–3*, 1955–66.
Builder-Mech. Parts/Constructeur-Partie mécanique: SLM.
Builder-Elec. Parts/Constructeur-Partie électrique: BBC/MFO.
Traction Motors: 6 single phase commutator type, fully suspended with BBC spring drive.
Moteurs de traction: 6 moteurs à courant alternatif monophasé à collecteurs, entièrement suspendus avec transmission à ressorts BBC.
One Hour Rating/Puissance horaire: 4300 kW.
Maximum Tractive Effort/Effort de traction max.: 392 kN (324 kN*).
Driving Wheel Dia./Diamètre des roues motrices: 1260 mm.
Weight/Masse: 128 tonnes (124 tonnes*).
Overall Length/Longeur hors tout: 18.40 m.
Max. Speed/Vitesse maximale: 125 km/h.
New Class No./Nouveau numéro de série: 610.

Some locos carry names in different languages on opposite sides.
Certaines machines portent des noms en langues différentes sur chaque côté.

11401 *	ZU	TICINO	11413	ER	SCHAFFHAUSEN
11402 **R** *	ZU	URI	11414	ER	BERN/BERNE
11403	ER	SCHWYZ	11415	ER	THURGAU
11404	ER	LUZERN	11416 **R**	ER	GLARUS
11405	ER	NIDWALDEN	11417 **R**	ER	FRIBOURG/FREIBURG
11406	ER	OBWALDEN	11418 **R**	ER	ST GALLEN
11407	ER	AAGAU	11419 **R**	ER	APPENZELL IRH
11408	ER	SOLOTHURN	11420 **R**	ER	APPENZELL A. RH
11409	ER	BASELLAND	11421	ER	GRISCHUN/GRAUBÜNDEN
11410 **R**	ER	BASEL-STADT	11422 **R**	ER	VAUD
11411	ER	ZUG	11423 **R**	ER	VALAIS/WALLIS
11412	ER	ZÜRICH	11424 **R**	ER	NEUCHÂTEL

11425 **R**	ER	GENÈVE
11426 **R**	ER	STADT ZÜRICH
11427	ER	STADT BERN
11428	ER	STADT LUZERN
11429 **R**	ER	ALTDORF
11430	ZU	GEMEINDE SCHWYZ
11431	ZU	SARNEN
11432	ZU	STANS
11433	ZU	GLARUS
11434	ZU	STADT ZUG
11435	ZU	FRIBOURG
11436	ZU	STADT SOLOTHURN
11437	ZU	STADT BASEL
11438	ZU	LIESTAL
11439	ZU	SCHAFFHAUSEN
11440	ZU	HERISAU
11441	ZU	APPENZELL
11442	ZU	ST GALLEN
11443	ZU	CHUR
11444	ZU	AARAU
11445	ZU	FRAUENFELD
11446	ZU	BELLINZONA
11447	ZU	LAUSANNE
11448	ZU	SION
11449	ZU	NEUCHÂTEL
11450	ZU	VILLE DE GENÈVE
11451	ZU	WINTERTHUR
11452	ZU	BADEN
11453	ZU	ARTH-GOLDAU
11454 **R**	ZU	YVERDON
11455	ZU	BIEL/BIENNE
11456	ZU	OLTEN
11457	ZU	ROMANSHORN
11458	ZU	RORSCHACH
11459	ZU	CHIASSO
11460	ZU	LUGANO
11461	ZU	LOCARNO
11462	ZU	BIASCA
11463	ZU	GÖSCHENEN
11464	ZU	ERSTFELD
11465	BI	OERLIKON
11466	BI	SURSEE
11467	BI	ZOFINGEN
11468	BI	LENZBURG
11469	BI	THALWIL
11470	BI	BRUGG
11471	BI	PRATTELN
11472	BI	BRIG
11473	BI	ST MAURICE
11474	BI	VEVEY
11475	BI	VALLORBE
11476	BI	LES VERRIÈRES
11477 **R**	BI	MARTIGNY
11478	BI	SIERRE
11479	BI	VISP
11480	BI	MONTREUX
11481	BI	LA CHAUX DE FONDS
11482	BI	DELÉMONT
11483	BI	JURA
11484	BI	ROMONT
11485	BI	THUN
11486	BI	BURGDORF
11487	BI	LANGENTHAL
11488	BI	MENDRISIO
11489	OL	AIROLO
11490	OL	ROTKREUZ
11491	OL	WOHLEN AG
11492	OL	EMMEN
11493	OL	SISSACH
11494	OL	SCHLIEREN
11495	OL	BÜLACH
11496	OL	STADT WIL
11497	OL	ST MARGRETHEN
11498	OL	BUCHS SG
11499	OL	SARGANS
11500	OL	LANDQUART
11501	OL	RENENS
11502	OL	NYON
11503	OL	PAYERNE
11504	OL	LE LOCLE
11505	BS	LYSS
11506	BS	GRENCHEN
11507	BS	WILDEGG
11508	BS	WETTINGEN
11509	BS	GOSSAU SG
11510	BS	RHEINFELDEN
11511	BS	DIETIKON
11512	BS	HORGEN
11513	BS	WALLISELLEN
11514	BS	WEINFELDEN
11515	BS	KREUZLINGEN
11516	BS	BAAR
11517	BS	BRUNNEN
11518	BS	FLÜELEN
11519	BS	GIUBIASCO
11520 **R**	BS	LANGNAU I. E

CLASS/SERIE Re6/6 — BoBoBo

Effectively an enlarged and uprated version of the Re4/4 II, this class was built to work on the mountain routes, but also appears elsewhere. The wheel arrangement was selected to provide a total adhesion weight similar to the Ae6/6, but with a better ability to run through curves, and to reduce weight transfer. Four prototypes were built, the first two having a hinged body with the axis of the hinge horizontal; the rigid body design was adopted for the production version.

En effet, une plus grande et plus longue version de la Re4/4 II, cette série a été conçue pour remorquer des trains sur les lignes de montagne, bien qu'elle soit également utilisée ailleurs. La disposition des essieux a été conçue pour donner une adhérence proche de celle des Ae6/6, mais avec un comportement amélioré dans les courbes et un moindre effort sur le rail. Il y avait 4 prototypes dont les deux premiers avaient une caisse articulée. Cependant, la caisse rigide fut retenue pour les machines de série.

Built/Date de mise en service: 1972*, 1975–80.
Builder-Mech. Parts/Constructeur-Partie mécanique: SLM.
Builder-Elec. Parts/Constructeur-Partie électrique: BBC/SAAS (BBC*).
Traction Motors: 6 single phase commutator type, fully suspended with BBC spring drive.
Moteurs de traction: 6 moteurs à courant alternatif monophasé à collecteurs, entièrement suspendus avec transmission à ressorts BBC.
One Hour Rating/Puissance horaire: 7850 kW.
Maximum Tractive Effort/Effort de traction max.: 398 kN (394 kN*).
Driving Wheel Dia./Diamètre des roues motrices: 1260 mm.
Weight/Masse: 120 tonnes.
Overall Length/Longeur hors tout: 19.31 m.
Max. Speed/Vitesse maximale: 140 km/h.
New Class No./Nouveau numéro de série: 620.

All locos are mw fitted (can mw with Re4/4^{II}, Re4/4^{III}, Re4/4^{IV}, RBe4/4 classes).
Toutes sont couplables en UM entre elles et avec les Re4/4^{II}, Re4/4^{III}, Re4/4^{IV} et RBe4/4.

No.		Depot	Name
11601	*	ER	WOLHUSEN
11602	*	ER	MORGES
11603	*	ER	WÄDENSWIL
11604	*	ER	FAIDO
11605		ER	USTER
11606		ER	TURGI
11607		ER	WATTWIL
11608		ER	WETZIKON
11609		ER	UZWIL
11610		ER	SPREITENBACH
11611	**R**	ER	RÜTI ZH
11612		ER	REGENSDORF
11613		ER	RAPPERSWIL
11614		ER	MEILEN
11615	**R**	ER	KLOTEN
11616		ER	ILLNAU-EFFRETIKON
11617		ER	HEERBRUGG
11618		ER	DÜBENDORF
11619		ER	ARBON
11620		ER	WANGEN BEI OLTEN
11621		ER	TAVERNE-TORRICELLA
11622		ER	SUHR
11623		ER	RUPPERSWIL
11624		ER	ROTHRIST
11625		ER	OENSINGEN
11626		ER	ZOLLIKOFEN
11627		ER	LUTERBACH-ATTISHOLZ
11628		ER	KONOLFINGEN
11629		BE	INTERLAKEN
11630		BE	HERZOGENBUCHSEE
11631		BE	DULLIKEN
11632		BE	DÄNIKEN
11633		BE	MURI AG
11634		BE	AARBURG-OFTRINGEN
11635		BE	MUTTENZ
11636	**R**	LS	VERNIER-MEYRIN
11637	**R**	LS	SONCEBOZ-SOMBEVAL
11639		LS	MURTEN
11640		BE	MÜNCHENSTEIN
11641		LS	MOUTIER
11642		LS	MONTHEY
11643		LS	LAUFEN
11644		LS	CORNAUX
11645		LS	COLOMBIER
11646		LS	BUSSIGNY
11647		LS	BEX
11648		LS	AIGLE
11649		LS	AARBERG
11650		LS	SCHÖNENWERD
11651		LS	DORNACH-ARLESHEIM
11652		BE	KERZERS
11653		BE	GÜMLINGEN
11654		BE	VILLENEUVE
11655		BE	COSSONAY
11656		BE	TRAVERS
11657		BE	ESTAVAYER-LE-LAC
11658		BE	AUVERNIER
11659		BE	CHAVORNAY
11660		BE	TAVANNES
11661		BE	GAMPEL-STEG
11662		BE	REUCHENETTE-PÉRY
11663		BE	EGLISAU
11664		BE	KÖNIZ
11665		BE	ZIEGELBRÜCKE
11666		BE	STEIN AM RHEIN
11667		BE	BODIO
11668		BE	STEIN-SÄCKINGEN
11669		BE	HÄGENDORF
11670		BE	AFFOLTERN AM ALBIS
11671		BE	OTHMARSINGEN
11672	**R**	BE	BALERNA
11673		BE	CHAM
11674	**R**	BE	MURGENTHAL
11675		BE	GELTERKINDEN
11676		BE	ZURZACH
11677		BE	NEUHAUSEN AM RHEINFALL
11678		BE	BASSERSDORF
11679		BE	CADENAZZO
11680		BE	MÖHLIN
11681		BE	IMMENSEE
11682		BE	PFÄFFIKON SZ
11683		BE	AMSTEG-SILENEN
11684		BE	UZNACH
11685		BE	SULGEN
11686		BE	HOCHDORF
11687		BE	BISCHOFSZELL
11688		BE	LINTHAL
11689		BE	GERRA-GAMBAROGNO

CLASS/SERIE Ae8/14 1AA1AA1+1AA1AA1

This museum loco is effectively two Ae4/7s permanently coupled with the wheels and electrical equipment rearranged. Regenerative braking is fitted. It was the first of three high power, twin units built for the Gotthard route between 1931 and 1940; experience showed smaller, single units to be more practical.

Cette locomotive historique est en effet deux Ae4/7 attelées en permanence mais avec une redistribution des essieux et de l'équipement électrique. Cette machine fut la première de trois locomotives de haute puissance à deux caisses qui furent construites pour la ligne du Gothard entre 1931 et 1940. L'expérience a montré que de plus petites locomotives à caisse unique étaient plus pratiques. Dotée du freinage à récupération.

Built/Date de mise en service: 1931.
Builder-Mech. Parts/Constructeur-Partie mécanique: SLM.
Builder-Elec. Parts/Constructeur-Partie électrique: BBC.
Traction Motors: 8 single phase commutator type, frame mounted with BBC Büchli flexible drive.
Moteurs de traction: 8 moteurs à courant alternatif monophasé à collecteurs, fixés au châssis avec transmission Buchli.
One Hour Rating/Puissance horaire: 4650 kW.
Maximum Tractive Effort/Effort de traction max.: 490 kN.
Driving Wheel Dia./Diamètre des roues motrices: 1610 mm.
Pony Wheel Dia./Diamètre des roues porteuses: 950 mm.
Weight/Masse: 240 tonnes.
Overall Length/Longeur hors tout: 34.00 m.
Max. Speed/Vitesse maximale: 100 km/h.
New Class No./Nouveau numéro de série: 498.

11801 **G** ER |

CLASS/SERIE Be4/6 1BB1

Another museum loco, the last survivor of a class of 40 built for passenger use when the Gotthard line was electrified. Each bogie carries two motors geared to a single layshaft connected to the driving wheels by coupling rods.

Encore une locomotive historique qui est la dernière survivante d'une série de 40 conçue pour remorquer des trains de voyageurs lors de l'électrification de la ligne du Gothard. Chaque bogie a deux moteurs actionnant un faux-essieu qui entraine les roues par des bielles.

Built/Date de mise en service: 1921.
Builder-Mech. Parts/Constructeur-Partie mécanique: SLM.
Builder-Elec. Parts/Constructeur-Partie électrique: BBC.
Traction Motors: 4 single phase commutator type, frame mounted with jackshaft/side rod drive.
Moteurs de traction: 4 moteurs à courant alternatif monophasé à collecteurs, fixés au châssis avec transmission par faux-essieux et bielles.
One Hour Rating/Puissance horaire: 1520 kW.
Maximum Tractive Effort/Effort de traction max.: 177 kN.
Driving Wheel Dia./Diamètre des roues motrices: 1530 mm.
Pony Wheel Dia./Diamètre des roues porteuses: 950 mm.
Weight/Masse: 110 tonnes.
Overall Length/Longeur hors tout: 16.56 m.
Max. Speed/Vitesse maximale: 75 km/h.
New Class No./Nouveau numéro de série: 496.

12320 **B** WT |

CLASS/SERIE Be4/7 1Bo1Bo1

The survivor of a class of 6 locos, a design from the early years of electrification which never went into series production. It is now a museum loco.

La seule survivante d'une série de six locomotives. Il s'agissait de prototypes dans les premières années de l'électrification, prototypes qui ne furent jamais produits en série. Maintenant une locomotive historique.

Built/Date de mise en service: 1922.
Builder-Mech. Parts/Constructeur-Partie mécanique: SLM.
Builder-Elec. Parts/Constructeur-Partie électrique: SAAS.
Traction Motors: 8 single phase commutator type, body mounted with hollow axle drive.
Moteurs de traction: 8 moteurs à courant alternatif monophasé à collecteurs, fixés dans la caisse avec transmission Westinghouse-Sécheron à arbres creux.
One Hour Rating/Puissance horaire: 1790 kW.
Maximum Tractive Effort/Effort de traction max.: 196 kN.
Driving Wheel Dia./Diamètre des roues motrices: 1610 mm.
Pony Wheel Dia./Diamètre des roues porteuses: 950 mm.
Weight/Masse: 111 tonnes.
Overall Length/Longeur hors tout: 16.30 m.
Max. Speed/Vitesse maximale: 80 km/h.
New Class No./Nouveau numéro de série: 497.

12504 **B** BI |

CLASS/SERIE Ce6/8 II — 1CC1

The 'Crocodile' configuration arose from the need to build a locomotive with high power, adequate adhesion weight and the ability to negotiate tight curves. Two motors in each frame are geared to a single shaft connected to the driving wheels by coupling rods. This loco was modernised and uprated in 1947, being reclassified Be6/8 II and renumbered 13253. It reverted to its original classification and number on becoming a museum loco. The specification is from rebuilding.

La silhouette «crocodile» émana du besoin d'une locomotive de haute puissance avec adhérence suffisante mais qui se comportait bien dans des courbes serrées. Dans chaque châssis, il y a deux moteurs qui actionnent un des deux faux-essieux avec transmission aux roues par une bielle-triangle à coulisseau. Cette locomotive a été modernisée en 1947, reclassifiée Be6/8 II et renumérotée 13253. Elle a repris sa classification et son numéro d'origine en devenant une locomotive historique, mais elle reste dans sa version modernisée.

Built/Date de mise en service: 1920.
Builder-Mech. Parts/Constructeur-Partie mécanique: SLM.
Builder-Elec. Parts/Constructeur-Partie électrique: MFO.
Traction Motors: 4 single phase commutator type, bogie mounted with jackshaft/side rod drive.
Moteurs de traction: 4 moteurs à courant alternatif monophasé à collecteurs, montés sur les bogies avec transmission par faux-essieux et bielles.
One Hour Rating/Puissance horaire: 2688 kW.
Maximum Tractive Effort/Effort de traction max.: 294 kN.
Driving Wheel Dia./Diamètre des roues motrices: 1350 mm.
Pony Wheel Dia./Diamètre des roues porteuses: 950 mm.
Weight/Masse: 126 tonnes.
Overall Length/Longeur hors tout: 19.46 m.
Max. Speed/Vitesse maximale: 65 km/h.
New Class No./Nouveau numéro de série: 698.

14253 **B** ER |

CLASS/SERIE Ce6/8 III — 1CC1

This loco represents the 2nd series of 18 'Crocodiles'. Renumbered 13305 in 1956, it also reverted to its original number on becoming a museum loco.

Cette machine représente la 2me série de 18 «crocodiles». Renumérotée 13305 en 1956, elle a repris son numéro d'origine en devenant une locomotive historique.

Built/Date de mise en service: 1926.
Builder-Mech. Parts/Constructeur-Partie mécanique: SLM.
Builder-Elec. Parts/Constructeur-Partie électrique: MFO.
Traction Motors: 4 single phase commutator type, bogie mounted with jackshaft/side rod drive.
Moteurs de traction: 4 moteurs à courant alternatif monophasé à collecteurs, montés sur les bogies avec transmission par faux-essieux et bielles.
One Hour Rating/Puissance horaire: 1820 kW.

Maximum Tractive Effort/Effort de traction max.: 294 kN.
Driving Wheel Dia./Diamètre des roues motrices: 1350 mm.
Pony Wheel Dia./Diamètre des roues porteuses: 950 mm.
Weight/Masse: 131 tonnes.
Overall Length/Longeur hors tout: 20.06 m.
Max. Speed/Vitesse maximale: 65 km/h.
New Class No./Nouveau numéro de série: 698.

14305 **B**	BS	

CLASS/SERIE Ee3/3 C

The first production electric shunters of the SBB, developed from the Ee3/4 of 1923 (now withdrawn). As with the subsequent variations, they have a single motor geared to a layshaft and driving through a jackshaft and coupling rods. However, unlike later Ee3/3, these locomotives have a cab at one end, and a shunter's platform at the other.

La série Ee3/3 qui est un développement des Ee3/4 de 1923 (qui sont maintenant toutes radiées) fut la première classe de locomotives de manoeuvres électriques de série des CFF. Comme les versions suivantes, elles sont monomoteurs avec trois essieux entraînés par bielles à partir d'un faux-essieu. Cependant, cette série se distingue des autres Ee3/3 par sa cabine à une extremité et sa plate-forme à l'autre.

Built/Date de mise en service: 1928.
Builder-Mech. Parts/Constructeur-Partie mécanique: SLM.
Builder-Elec. Parts/Constructeur-Partie électrique: BBC.
Traction Motors: 1 single phase frame mounted with jackshaft/side rod drive.
Moteur de traction: 1 moteur à courant alternatif monophasé à collecteurs, fixé au châssis avec transmission par faux-essieux et bielles.
One Hour Rating/Puissance horaire: 428 kW.
Maximum Tractive Effort/Effort de traction max.: 88 kN.
Driving Wheel Dia./Diamètre des roues motrices: 1040 mm.
Weight/Masse: 45 tonnes.
Overall Length/Longeur hors tout: 9.06 m.
Max. Speed/Vitesse maximale: 40 km/h.
New Class No./Nouveau numéro de série: 930.

16313	GE	16315	BN	16319	LZ	16321	BE	16325	RS
16314	LS	16316	BN	16320	LZ	16324	BE	16326	RS

CLASS/SERIE Ee3/3 C

A development of the previous class, with a centre cab and a shunter's platform at one end.

Version modifiée de la série précédente avec une cabine centrale et une plate-forme à une seule extremité.

Built/Date de mise en service: 1930–1.
Builder-Mech. Parts/Constructeur-Partie mécanique: SLM.
Builder-Elec. Parts/Constructeur-Partie électrique: BBC.
Traction Motors: 1 single phase frame mounted with jackshaft/side rod drive.
Moteur de traction: 1 moteur à courant alternatif monophasé à collecteurs, fixé au châssis avec transmission par faux-essieux et bielles.
One Hour Rating/Puissance horaire: 428 kW.
Maximum Tractive Effort/Effort de traction max.: 88 kN.
Driving Wheel Dia./Diamètre des roues motrices: 1040 mm.
Weight/Masse: 45 tonnes.
Overall Length/Longeur hors tout: 9.15 m (9.894 m *).
Max. Speed/Vitesse maximale: 40 km/h.
New Class No./Nouveau numéro de série: 930.
* Rebuilt with extended buffer beams for fitting of auto couplers.
* Transformée avec traverses renforcées pour accepter attelages automatiques.

16331 **R**	LS	16335 **R**	BI	16339	BI	16343	BE	16347	ER
16332	LS	16336	BI	16340 **R** *	BI	16344	ER	16348 **R**	OL
16333	LS	16337	BI	16341	BI	16345	ER	16349	OL
16334	LS	16338	BI	16342	BE	16346	ER	16350	OL

CLASS/SERIE Ee3/3 C

This development of the standard electric shunter has a centre cab, and shunter's platforms at both ends.

Encore une version différente des Ee3/3 avec cabine centrale et plate-formes aux deux extrémités.

Built/Date de mise en service: 1932–47.
Builder-Mech. Parts/Constructeur-Partie mécanique: SLM.
Builder-Elec. Parts/Constructeur-Partie électrique: BBC (BBC/MFO/SAAS*).
Traction Motors: 1 single phase frame mounted with jackshaft/side rod drive.
Moteur de traction: 1 moteur à courant alternatif monophasé à collecteurs, fixé au châssis avec transmission par faux-essieux et bielles.
One Hour Rating/Puissance horaire: 428 kW (502 kW*).
Maximum Tractive Effort/Effort de traction max.: 88 kN (98 kN*).
Driving Wheel Dia./Diamètre des roues motrices: 1040 mm.
Weight/Masse: 45 tonnes (39 tonnes*).
Overall Length/Longeur hors tout: 9.75 m (9.51 m *).
Max. Speed/Vitesse maximale: 40 km/h (50 km/h*).
New Class No./Nouveau numéro de série: 930.

16351	OL	16363	WT	16375		LS	16391	*	BS	16403	*	LZ
16352	OL	16364	WT	16376		LS	16392	*	BS	16404	*	LZ
16353	BE	16365	WT	16381 R	*	ZU	16393	*	BS	16405	*	LZ
16354	RS	16366	BI	16382	*	RS	16394	*	OL	16406	*	LZ
16355	RS	16367	BR	16383	*	BI	16395	*	OL	16407	*	LZ
16356	RS	16368	BR	16384	*	BI	16396	*	OL	16408	*	LZ
16357	WT	16369	BR	16385	*	BI	16397	*	OL	16409	*	LZ
16358	WT	16370	LS	16386	*	LS	16398	*	OL	16410	*	LZ
16359	RS	16371	LS	16387	*	BN	16399	*	OL	16411	*	LZ
16360 R	RS	16372	LS	16388	*	BN	16400	*	OL	16412	*	LZ
16361	RS	16373	LS	16389	*	BN	16401	*	OL	16413	*	LZ
16362	WT	16374	LS	16390 R	*	BN	16402	*	OL	16414	*	LZ

CLASS/SERIE Ee3/3 C

The final development of the Ee3/3./Version finale des Ee3/3.

Built/Date de mise en service: 1951–66.
Builder-Mech. Parts/Constructeur-Partie mécanique: SLM.
Builder-Elec. Parts/Constructeur-Partie électrique: BBC/MFO/SAAS.
Traction Motors: 1 single phase frame mounted with jackshaft/side rod drive.
Moteur de traction: 1 moteur à courant alternatif monophasé à collecteurs, fixé au châssis avec transmission par faux-essieux et bielles.
One Hour Rating/Puissance horaire: 502 kW.
Maximum Tractive Effort/Effort de traction max.: 118 kN.
Driving Wheel Dia./Diamètre des roues motrices: 1040 mm.
Weight/Masse: 45 tonnes (44 tonnes*).
Overall Length/Longeur hors tout: 9.51 m.
Max. Speed/Vitesse maximale: 45 km/h.
New Class No./Nouveau numéro de série: 930.

16421	LS	16429	RS	16437		ZU	16445	*	OL	16453	*	BI
16422	LS	16430	RS	16438		ZU	16446	*	OL	16454	*	BI
16423 R	LS	16431 R	ZU	16439		ZU	16447	*	OL	16455	*	BI
16424	BN	16432 R	ZU	16440 R		ZU	16448	*	OL	16456	*	BI
16425	BN	16433 R	ZU	16441	*	BE	16449	*	OL	16457	*	BR
16426	RS	16434 R	ZU	16442	*	BE	16450	*	LZ	16458	*	BR
16427 R	RS	16435 R	ZU	16443	*	BE	16451 R	*	BN	16459	*	BR
16428	RS	16436 R	ZU	16444	*	OL	16452	*	BN	16460	*	BR

CLASS/SERIE Ee3/3 II C

The dual-voltage version of the Ee3/3, which can be used under the 25 kV 50 Hz wires of the SNCF. 16501–6 are used around Basel where the SNCF ac electrification extends into the SBB station. 16511–9 were built for the SNCF (C 20151–9) for use around Basel, but were sold to the SBB in 1971. Their dual-voltage capability sees little use at present but the mw facility is put to use for yard shunting. There are detail differences within the class.

Version bi-courant de la Ee3/3 qui peut être utilisée sur les lignes SNCF électrifiées à 25 kV 50 Hz. Les 16501 à 6 sont employées autour de Bâle où les caténaires SNCF arrivent jusque dans la gare CFF. Les 16511 à 19 furent construites pour la SNCF (C 20151 à 9) pour être utilisées autour de Bâle mais toutes furent vendues aux CFF en 1971. Elles sont peu utilisées sous 25 kV en ce moment mais souvent en UM pour les manoeuvres dans les triages. Il existe quelques différences de détails entre membres de la classe.

Built/Date de mise en service: 1957–63
Builder-Mech. Parts/Constructeur-Partie mécanique: SLM.
Builder-Elec. Parts/Constructeur-Partie électrique: BBC*, MFO†, SAAS (remainder/autres).
Traction Motors: 1 dc. (single phase a.c.†) frame mounted with jackshaft/side rod drive.
Moteur de traction: 1 moteur à courant continu (courant alternatif monophasé†) à collecteurs, entièrement suspendu avec transmission par faux-essieux et bielles.
One Hour Rating/Puissance horaire: 506 kW (525 kW†).
Maximum Tractive Effort/Effort de traction max.: 132 kN (128 kN†).
Driving Wheel Dia./Diamètre des roues motrices: 1040 mm.
Weight/Masse: 46 tonnes (52 tonnes m).
Overall Length/Longeur hors tout: 9.510 m (9.42 m).
Max. Speed/Vitesse maximale: 45 km/h.
System/Courant: 15 kV, 16⅔ Hz/25kV 50Hz.
New Class No./Nouveau numéro de série: 932.

m mw fitted./couplables en UM.
§ fitted with thyristorsdotées de thyristors.

16501 * BS	16504 † BS	16511 mBN	16514 mBI	16517 R mBR
16502 § BS	16505 BS	16512 mBI	16515 mBN	16518 R mBR
16503 † BS	16506 BS	16513 mBI	16516 R mBR	16519 R mBR

CLASS/SERIE Ee3/3 IV — C

The four-voltage version of the Ee3/3, for use at border stations. It differs from the others in having two dc motors, one geared directly to the centre and one to the end axle, there being no intermediate jackshaft. They are to be found at Genève where the SNCF 1500 V dc system extends into the station, and at Chiasso for use under the FS 3000 V dc wires. The 25 kV facility is not used at present.

La version quadri-courant de la Ee 3/3 pour les gares frontalières. La série se distingue des autres Ee3/3 par ses deux moteurs à courant continu, qui actionnent directement, sans l'intermédiaire d'un faux-essieu, l'un l'essieu central, l'autre l'essieu d'extrémité. Elles sont utilisées à Genève sous le 1500V de la SNCF et à Chiasso sous le 3000 V des FS. Pour l'instant, elles ne fonctionnent pas sous 25 kV.

Built/Date de mise en service: 1962–3.
Builder-Mech. Parts/Constructeur-Partie mécanique: SLM.
Builder-Elec. Parts/Constructeur-Partie électrique: SAAS.
Traction Motors: 2 d.c. series wound, axle suspended with side rod drive.
Moteurs de traction: 2 moteurs série à courant continu, suspendus par l'essieu avec transmission par bielles.
One Hour Rating/Puissance horaire: 390 kW.
Maximum Tractive Effort/Effort de traction max.: 118 kN.
Driving Wheel Dia./Diamètre des roues motrices: 1040 mm.
Weight/Masse: 48 tonnes.
Overall Length/Longeur hors tout: 10.02 m.
Max. Speed/Vitesse maximale: 60 km/h.
System/Courant: 1500 V dc/continu /3000 V dc/continu /15 kV 16⅔ Hz/ 25 kV 50 Hz.
New Class No./Nouveau numéro de série: 934.

16551 GE	16553 GE	16555 GE	16557 BE	16559 BE
16552 GE	16554 GE	16556 GE	16558 BE	16560 BE

CLASS/SERIE Ee6/6 — CC

A design for heavy yard shunting, effectively a pair of Ee3/3 combined as one loco. Both locos are used in Muttenz Yard near Basel.

▼Class Ae3/6 I No. 10643 is uncoupled from a 'Regionalzug' (local train) on arrival at Chur on 21/09/87. *C.P. Boocock*

▼▼Class Ee6/6 II No. 16820 stands on Lausanne depot on 18/08/ 85. *E. Dunkling*

▲▲La Ae3/6 I 10643 est détellée d'un train régional à Coire. 21/09/87. *C.P. Boocock*

▲La Be6/6 II 16820 au dépôt de Lausanne. 18/08/85. *E. Dunkling*

En fait deux Ee3/3 en une locomotive. Les deux locomotives sont utilisées pour le débranchement de rames lourdes au triage de Bâle Muttenz.
Built/Date de mise en service: 1952.
Builder-Mech. Parts/Constructeur-Partie mécanique: SLM.
Builder-Elec. Parts/Constructeur-Partie électrique: BBC/SAAS.
Traction Motors: 2 single phase bogie mounted with jackshaft/side rod drive.
Moteurs de traction: 2 moteurs à courant alternatif monophasé à collecteurs, montés sur les bogies avec transmission par faux-essieux et bielles.
One Hour Rating/Puissance horaire: 1008 kW.
Maximum Tractive Effort/Effort de traction max.: 235 kN.
Driving Wheel Dia./Diamètre des roues motrices: 1040 mm.
Weight/Masse: 90 tonnes.
Overall Length/Longeur hors tout: 14.84 m.
Max. Speed/Vitesse maximale: 45 km/h.
New Class No./Nouveau numéro de série: 961.

16801 R	BS	16802	BS

CLASS/SERIE Ee6/6 II CoCo

A modern design of heavy yard loco which replaced some converted 'Crocodiles' previously used for such work; fitted with 3-phase traction motors supplied through an inverter. They can be radio controlled and are to be found in the yards at Limmattal (Zürich), Buchs, Winterthur, Schaffhausen, Muttenz (Basel), Denges (Lausanne) and Bern.

Des locomotives modernes conçues pour des manoeuvres lourdes et dotées de moteurs triphasés alimentés par un onduleur. Elles ont remplacé quelques «Crocodiles» modernisés dans les grands triages. Elles peuvent être télécommandées et sont utilisées dans les triages de Zurich Limmattal, Buchs, Winterthour, Schaffhouse, Bâle Muttenz, Lausanne Denges et Berne.

Built/Date de mise en service: 1980.
Builder-Mech. Parts/Constructeur-Partie mécanique: SLM.
Builder-Elec. Parts/Constructeur-Partie électrique: BBC.
Traction Motors: 6 3-phase axle hung, nose suspended.
Moteurs de traction: 6 moteurs triphasés suspendus par le nez.
One Hour Rating/Puissance horaire: 730 kW.
Maximum Tractive Effort/Effort de traction max.: 360 kN.
Driving Wheel Dia./Diamètre des roues motrices: 1260 mm.
Weight/Masse: 111 tonnes.
Overall Length/Longeur hors tout: 17.40 m.
Max. Speed/Vitesse maximale: 85 km/h.
New Class No./Nouveau numéro de série: 962.

16811	ZU	16813	ZU	16815	WT	16817	LS	16819	LS
16812	RS	16814	WT	16816	BS	16818	LS	16820	BN

CLASS/SERIE Eem6/6 (Em6/6*) C+C

An unusual design of electro-diesel shunter, comprising two close coupled Ee3/3 IV chassis, with the cab and electrical gear mounted on one and a diesel engine on the other. However, starting with 17006 in 1984, the class is being converted to diesel electric. They are used for yard shunting in Basel and Chiasso.

Une locomotive de manoeuvre «amphibie» de conception originale – deux châssis Ee3/3 IV couplés en permanence, avec cabine et équipement électrique sur l'un, et un moteur diesel sur l'autre. Cependant, on a commencé, avec la 17006 en 1984, à transformer la série en diesel-électrique uniquement. Elles sont utilisées pour les manoeuvres dans les triages de Bâle et Chiasso.

Built/Date de mise en service: 1970–1.
Builder-Mech. Parts/Constructeur-Partie mécanique: SLM.
Builder-Elec. Parts/Constructeur-Partie électrique: SAAS.
Traction Motors: 4 d.c. series wound, axle suspended with side rod drive.
Moteurs de traction: 4 moteurs série à courant continu avec transmission par bielles.
One Hour Rating/Puissance horaire: 393 kW (diesel) 780 kW (electric/électrique).
Maximum Tractive Effort/Effort de traction max.: 235 kN.
Driving Wheel Dia./Diamètre des roues motrices: 1040 mm.
Weight/Masse: 104 tonnes.

Overall Length/Longeur hors tout: 17.875 m.
Max. Speed/Vitesse maximale: 65 km/h.
Engine/Moteur: SLM 12YD20 TrTH 895 kW.
New Class No./Nouveau numéro de série: .

17001	BE	17003	BE	17004	*	BS	17005	*	BS	17006	*	BS
17002	BE											

CLASS/SERIE Re4/4 450 BoBo

These are single-ended locos to work push-pull trains on the Zürich S-Bahn, which commenced operation in May 1990. They have 3-phase traction motors, SLM 'shifting axle drive', which allows radial adjustment of the axles within the bogies, and regenerative braking. The class was to have been numbered in the 10500 series. Although presently allocated to Zürich, the class will be transferred to Oberwinterthur when the new purpose-built depot there is completed. It is planned to order another 50 locomotives.

Ce sont des locomotives à une seule cabine de conduite, construites pour les rames réversibles utilisées sur le RER de Zurich qui fut inauguré en mai 1990. Elles sont dotées de moteurs triphasés, du système SLM d'essieux auto-orientables et du freinage à récupération. Bien qu' affectée au dépôt de Zurich, la série sera transférée à Oberwinterthour dès que le dépot RER sera complété. A l'origine, l'intention était de numéroter la classe dans la série 10500. Une commande supplémantaire de 50 locomotives est envisagée.

Built/Date de mise en service: 1989 onwards.
Builder-Mech. Parts/Constructeur-Partie mécanique: SLM.
Builder-Elec. Parts/Constructeur-Partie électrique: ABB.
Traction Motors: 4 3-phase axle-hung, nose suspended.
Moteurs de traction: 4 moteurs triphasés suspendus par le nez.
One Hour Rating/Puissance horaire: 3200 kW.
Maximum Tractive Effort/Effort de traction max.: 240 kN.
Driving Wheel Dia./Diamètre des roues motrices: 1100 mm.
Weight/Masse: 78 tonnes.
Overall Length/Longeur hors tout: 18.40 m.
Max. Speed/Vitesse maximale: 130 km/h.

450 000-5	**S**	ZU	
450 001-3	**S**	ZU	
450 002-1	**S**	ZU	Oberwinterthur
450 003-9	**S**	ZU	Zollikon
450 004-7	**S**	ZU	Stettbach
450 005-4	**S**	ZU	Kilchberg
450 006-2	**S**	ZU	Rafz
450 007-0	**S**	ZU	
450 008-8	**S**	ZU	Riesbach
450 009-6	**S**	ZU	Hedingen
450 010-4	**S**	ZU	
450 011-2	**S**	ZU	Oberrieden
450 012-0	**S**	ZU	Schwamendingen
450 013-8	**S**	ZU	
450 014-6	**S**	ZU	Seuzach
450 015-3	**S**	ZU	Erlenbach
450 016-1	**S**	ZU	Altstetten
450 017-9	**S**	ZU	Bubikon
450 018-7	**S**	ZU	Hirslanden–Hottingen
450 019-5	**S**	ZU	Stäfa
450 020-3	**S**	ZU	Pfäffikon
450 021-1	**S**	ZU	
450 022-9	**S**	ZU	
450 023-7	**S**	ZU	
450 024-5	**S**		
450 025-2	**S**		
450 026-0	**S**		
450 027-8	**S**		
450 028-6	**S**		
450 029-4	**S**		
450 030-2	**S**		
450 031-0	**S**		
450 032-8	**S**		
450 033-6	**S**		
450 034-4	**S**		
450 035-1	**S**		
450 036-9	**S**		
450 037-7	**S**		
450 038-5	**S**		
450 039-3	**S**		
450 040-1	**S**		
450 041-9	**S**		
450 042-7	**S**		
450 043-5	**S**		
450 044-3	**S**		
450 045-0	**S**		
450 046-8	**S**		
450 047-6	**S**		
450 048-4	**S**		
450 049-2	**S**		
450 050-0	**S**		
450 051-8	**S**		
450 052-6	**S**		
450 053-4	**S**		
450 054-2	**S**		
450 055-9	**S**		
450 056-7	**S**		
450 057-5	**S**		
450 058-3	**S**		
450 059-1	**S**		

450 060-9 **S**
450 061-7 **S**
450 062-5 **S**
450 063-3 **S**
450 064-1 **S**
450 065-8 **S**
450 066-6 **S**
450 067-4 **S**
450 068-2 **S**
450 069-0 **S**
450 070-8 **S**
450 071-6 **S**
450 072-4 **S**
450 073-2 **S**
450 074-0 **S**
450 075-7 **S**
450 076-5 **S**
450 077-3 **S**
450 078-1 **S**
450 079-9 **S**
450 080-7 **S**
450 081-5 **S**
450 082-3 **S**
450 083-1 **S**
450 084-9 **S**
450 085-6 **S**
450 086-4 **S**
450 087-2 **S**
450 088-0 **S**
450 089-8 **S**
450 090-6 **S**
450 091-4 **S**
450 092-2 **S**
450 093-0 **S**
450 094-8 **S**

CLASS/SERIE Re4/4 460 BoBo

A new class of high speed locos for the 'Bahn 2000' project. They will operate with new express push-pull stock, initially between Zürich and Lausanne. They were originally to have been numbered in the 10700 series.

Une nouvelle série de locomotives à grande vitesse pour le projet «Bahn 2000». Elles seront utilisées avec de nouvelles rames réversibles express, d'abord entre Zurich et Lausanne. A l'origine, l'intention était de numéroter la classe dans la série 10700.

Built/Date de mise en service: 1991 onwards.
Builder-Mech. Parts/Constructeur-Partie mécanique: SLM.
Builder-Elec. Parts/Constructeur-Partie électrique: ABB.
Traction Motors: 4 3-phase fully suspended.
Moteurs de traction: 4 moteurs triphasés entièrement suspendus.
One Hour Rating/Puissance horaire: 6100 kW.
Maximum Tractive Effort/Effort de traction max.: .
Driving Wheel Dia./Diamètre des roues motrices: .
Weight/Masse: 80 tonnes.
Overall Length/Longeur hors tout: .
Max. Speed/Vitesse maximale: 230 km/h.

460 000-3
460 001-1
460 002-9
460 003-7
460 004-5
460 005-2
460 006-0
460 007-8
460 008-6
460 009-4
460 010-2
460 011-0
460 012-8
460 013-6
460 014-4
460 015-1
460 016-9
460 017-7
460 018-5
460 019-3
460 020-1
460 021-9
460 022-7
460 023-5
460 024-3
460 025-0
460 026-8
460 027-6
460 028-4
460 029-2
460 030-0
460 031-8
460 032-6
460 033-4
460 034-2
460 035-9
460 036-7
460 037-5
460 038-3
460 039-1
460 040-9
460 041-7
460 042-5
460 043-3
460 044-1
460 045-8
460 046-6
460 047-4
460 048-2
460 049-0

460 050-8
460 051-6
460 052-4
460 053-2
460 054-0
460 055-7
460 056-5
460 057-3
460 058-1
460 059-9
460 060-7
460 061-5
460 062-3
460 063-1
460 064-9
460 065-6
460 066-4
460 067-2
460 068-0
460 069-8
460 070-6
460 071-4
460 072-2
460 073-0
460 074-8
460 075-5
460 076-3
460 077-1
460 078-9
460 079-7
460 080-5
460 081-3
460 082-1
460 083-9
460 084-7
460 085-4
460 086-2
460 087-0
460 088-8
460 089-6
460 090-4
460 091-2
460 092-0
460 093-8
460 094-6
460 095-3
460 096-1
460 097-9
460 098-7

PROJECTED CLASSES/SERIES EN PROJET

453. Triple voltage (25 kV 50 Hz, 15 kV 16⅔ Hz, 1500 V dc) version of 450 for suburban work in the Basel and Genève areas./ Une version tri-courant (25 kV 50 Hz, 15 kV 16⅔ Hz, 1500 V continu) de la 450 pour les banlieues de Bâle et Genève.

463. Triple voltage (25 kV 50 Hz, 15 kV 16⅔ Hz, 1500 V dc) version of 460 to allow through workings into other countries on international services./
Une version tri-courant (25 kV 50 Hz, 15 kV 16⅔ Hz, 1500 V continu) de la 460 pour les services internationaux en pays étrangers.

The first Class RE 4/4 460 rolled off the SLM production lines at Winterthur on November 12th 1990. 460 000-3 was due to be fitted out with electrical equipment at ABB, Zürich before being delivered to the SBB in May 1991 *ABB*

La première unité de la série RE 4/4 460 est sortie des ateliers de SLM, Winterthour le 12. Novembre 1990. La 460 000-3 recevra son équipement électrique à l'usine ABB de Zurich avant d'être livrée aux CFF courant Mai 1991 *ABB*

DIESEL LOCOMOTIVES/ LOCOMOTIVES DIESEL

Bm4/4 CLASS BoBo

Locos for shunting and trip working on non-electrified tracks.
Des machines pour manoeuvres et trains de marchandises légers sur lignes non-électrifiées.

Built/Date de mise en service: 1960–70.
Builder-Mech. Parts/Constructeur-Partie mécanique: SLM.
Builder-Elec. Parts/Constructeur-Partie électrique: SAAS.
Engine/Moteur: SLM 12YD20TrTH of/de 895 kW.
Transmission: Electric/Electrique.
Maximum Tractive Effort/Effort de traction max.: 216 kN.
Driving Wheel Dia./Diamètre des roues motrices: 1040 mm.
Weight/Masse: 72 tonnes.
Overall Length/Longeur hors tout: 12.65 m. (13.21 m*, 13.15 m†).
New Class No./Nouveau numéro de série: 840.

* Rebuilt with extended buffer beams for additional shunter protection.
* Modifiée avec des traverses renforcées pour une meilleure protection du personnel de manoeuvres.

18401	*	BE	18411		BI	18420		RS	18429	†	ZU	18438	†	BS
18402		BE	18412		GE	18421		ZU	18430	†	BE	18439	†	BS
18403		BE	18413		BI	18422	R	ZU	18431	†	BE	18440	R †	BS
18404		BE	18414		BN	18423		ZU	18432	†	BS	18441	†	BS
18405		BE	18415		BN	18424	R	ZU	18433	†	BS	18442	†	BS
18406		BE	18416		BI	18425		WT	18434	R †	BS	18443	†	BS
18407		GE	18417		GE	18426		ZU	18435	†	BS	18444	†	BS
18408		GE	18418		RS	18427	†	ZU	18436	†	BS	18445	†	BS
18409		LS	18419		WT	18428	†	ZU	18437	†	BS	18446	†	BS
18410		LS												

Bm4/4 II CLASS BoBo

The survivor of pair of elderly diesels which have had a varied life, being moved around as electrification progressed. Nowadays it sees little use, being retained as the breakdown train engine at Olten.

Un ancien diesel qui a vu son utilisation changer avec le progrès de l'électrification. Aujourd'hui elle n'est utilisée que pour tracter le train de secours à Olten.

Built/Date de mise en service: 1939.
Builder-Mech. Parts/Constructeur-Partie mécanique: SLM.
Builder-Elec. Parts/Constructeur-Partie électrique: BBC.
Engine/Moteur: Sulzer of/de 820 kW.
Transmission: Electric/Electrique.
Maximum Tractive Effort/Effort de traction max.: 112 kN.
Driving Wheel Dia./Diamètre des roues motrices: 1040 mm.
Weight/Masse: 66 tonnes.
Overall Length/Longeur hors tout: 14.90 m.
Max. Speed/Vitesse maximale: 75 km/h.
New Class No./Nouveau numéro de série: 841.

18451 OL

Am4/4 CLASS BB

An interesting second hand purchase in 1987, these were formerly part of the well-known DB V 200 Class (later Class 220). They have been acquired for use on works trains in connection with track improvements and new lines as part of the 'Bahn 2000' project.

Ces locomotives sont les célèbres V 200 (plus tard série 220) des DB et furent rachetées par les CFF en 1987 pour remorquer des trains de travaux relatifs à la construction de nouvelles lignes et la modification de tracé pour le projet "Rail 2000".

Built/Date de mise en service: 1957–9.
Builder/Constructeur: Mak (KM*).
Engines/Moteurs: 2 Maybach MD12V538TA of 809 kW each./de 809 kW chacun.
Transmission: Hydraulic/Hydraulique.
Maximum Tractive Effort/Effort de traction max.: 189 kN.
Driving Wheel Dia./Diamètre des roues motrices: 950 mm.
Weight/Masse: 80 tonnes.
Overall Length/Longeur hors tout: 18.47 m.
Max. Speed/Vitesse maximale: 100 km/h.
New Class No./Nouveau numéro de série: 843.

Former DB Nos. in brackets./Anciens numéros DB entre parenthèses.

18461 (220 013-7) **R** BN
18462 (220 014-5) **R** BN
18463 (220 015-2) **R** BN
18464 (220 016-0) **R** BN
18465 (220 017-8) **R** BN
18466 (220 053-3) **R** * BN
18467 (220 077-2) **R** * BN

Bm6/6 CLASS CoCo

Centre cab diesels used for yard shunting and trip working. Each bonnet contains its own engine and generator set.

Locomotives avec cabine de conduite centrale pour des manoeuvres de triage et des trains de marchandises légers. Il y a un moteur et un générateur sous chaque capot.

Built/Date de mise en service: 1954–61.
Builder-Mech. Parts/Constructeur-Partie mécanique: SLM.
Builder-Elec. Parts/Constructeur-Partie électrique: BBC/SAAS.
Engines/Moteurs: 2 Sulzer 6LDA25 of 635 kW each./de 635 kW chacun.
Transmission: Electric/Electrique.
Maximum Tractive Effort/Effort de traction max.: 334 kN.
Driving Wheel Dia./Diamètre des roues motrices: 1040 mm.
Weight/Masse: 106 tonnes.
Overall Length/Longeur hors tout: 17.00 m. (17.56 m*).
Max. Speed/Vitesse maximale: 75 km/h.
New Class No./Nouveau numéro de série: 861.

18501 BS
18502 BS
18503 **R** BS
18504 BS
18505 BE
18506 BE
18507 BE
18508 BE
18509 LS
18510 BR
18511 RS
18512 BN
18513 * WT
18514 WT

Am6/6 CLASS CoCo

Heavy shunting locos, built specifically for use in the new Limmattal Yard near Zürich. They have three phase traction motors supplied from a fixed frequency alternator via frequency conversion equipment.

Machines de manoeuvres lourdes, spécialement conçues pour le nouveau triage de Limmattal près de Zurich. Elles ont des moteurs triphasés alimentés par un alternateur à fréquence fixe et un onduleur.

Built/Date de mise en service: 1976.
Builder-Mech. Parts/Constructeur-Partie mécanique: Thyssen Henschel.
Builder-Elec. Parts/Constructeur-Partie électrique: BBC.
Engine/Moteur: SEMT.
Transmission: Electric/Electrique.
Maximum Tractive Effort/Effort de traction max.: 393 kN.
Driving Wheel Dia./Diamètre des roues motrices: 1260 mm.
Weight/Masse: 111 tonnes.
Overall Length/Longeur hors tout: 17.40 m.
Max. Speed/Vitesse maximale: 85 km/h.
New Class No./Nouveau numéro de série: 863.

18521 ZU
18522 ZU
18523 ZU
18524 ZU
18525 ZU
18526 ZU

Em3/3 CLASS C

General purpose shunting locos found throughout the system.
Des machines de manoeuvres pour tâches moyennes et que l'on trouve partout sur les CFF.

Built/Date de mise en service: 1959* 1962–3.
Builder-Mech. Parts/Constructeur-Partie mécanique: SLM.
Builder-Elec. Parts/Constructeur-Partie électrique: BBC/SAAS.
Engine/Moteur: SLM 6VD20TrTH of 450 kW. (SLM 8YD20TrD of 450 kW*).
Transmission: Electric/Electrique.
Maximum Tractive Effort/Effort de traction max.: 124 kN (118 kN*).
Driving Wheel Dia./Diamètre des roues motrices: 1040 mm.
Weight/Masse: 49 tonnes.
Overall Length/Longeur hors tout: 10.02 m.
Max. Speed/Vitesse maximale: 65 km/h.
New Class No./Nouveau numéro de série: 830.

18801	*	ZU	18810	BS	18818		BE	18826	OL	18834	RS
18802	*	ZU	18811	BS	18819		BE	18827	OL	18835	RS
18803	*	ZU	18812	BS	18820		BE	18828	ZU	18836	RS
18804	*	ZU	18813	BS	18821	R	LZ	18829	WT	18837	BN
18805	*	ZU	18814	BS	18822		LZ	18830	WT	18838	BN
18806	*	ZU	18815	BS	18823		LZ	18831	WT	18839	GE
18807		BS	18816	OL	18824		OL	18832	WT	18840	GE
18808		BS	18817	BE	18825		OL	18833	WT	18841	LS
18809		BS									

831 CLASS Co

An order has been placed for the prototype of a new generation of diesel shunters.
Une commande vient d'être passée pour le prototype d'une nouvelle génération de machines de manoeuvres diesel.

Built/Date de mise en service: 1991.
Builder-Mech. Parts/Constructeur-Partie mécanique: RACO.
Builder-Elec. Parts/Constructeur-Partie électrique: ABB.
Engine/Moteur: 900 kW.
Transmission: Electric/Electrique.
Maximum Tractive Effort/Effort de traction max.:
Driving Wheel Dia./Diamètre des roues motrices:
Weight/Masse: 54 tonnes.
Overall Length/Longeur hors tout: m.
Max. Speed/Vitesse maximale: 80 km/h.

831 000-5	831 001-3	831 002-1

BRÜNIG LINE/LA LIGNE DU BRÜNIG

Although Switzerland possesses a considerable mileage of narrow gauge, only one such line is operated by the SBB. This is the metre gauge Brünig Line running from Interlaken to Luzern. The section between Meiringen and Giswil over the Brünig Pass has stretches of Riggenbach rack. Hence most electric locos, and two of the tractors, are fitted for rack and adhesion operation.

Bien qu'il existe un kilomètrage considérable de lignes à voie étroite en Suisse, il n'y a qu'une seule ligne exploitée par les CFF. Il s'agit de la ligne du Brünig entre Interlaken et Lucerne à voie métrique. La partie entre Meiringen et Giswil qui passe par le col du Brünig a des sections à crémaillère «Riggenbach». La plupart des locomotives électriques et deux des locotracteurs sont donc équipés pour l'exploitation à crémaillère ou en adhérence.

ELECTRIC RAILCARS/AUTOMOTRICES

CLASS/SERIE Deh4/6 (De4/4§) Bo–2–Bo (BoBo§)

These motor luggage vans were built for the electrification of the line and still operate many services, sometimes resorting to double or even triple heading. The outer bogies are used during adhesion working, while on the rack sections the centre rack fitted bogie provides most of the power. Some withdrawal is anticipated as Class 101 enters service and those retained will be refurbished for use on the adhesion sections.

Ces fourgons automoteurs ont été construits lors de l'électrification de la ligne et sont toujours utilisés sur beaucoup de trains, parfois en double ou triple traction. Les deux bogies extérieurs sont utilisés pour la traction en plaine, tandis que le bogie central, qui est doté de roues à pignon, est utilisé pour la traction sur la section à crémaillère. On pense que certains de ces fourgons seront radiés à l'introduction de la série 101 et que ceux qui sont retenus seront modernisés pour utilisation sur les sections sans crémaillère.

Built/Date de mise en service: 1941–2.
Builder-Mech. Parts/Constructeur-Partie mécanique: SLM.
Builder-Elec. Parts/Constructeur-Partie électrique: BBC (MFO†, SAAS*§).
One Hour Rating/Puissance horaire: 930 kW.
Maximum Tractive Effort/Effort de traction max.: 102 kN (adhesion/adhérence), 216 kN (rack/crémaillère).
Driving Wheel Dia./Diamètre des roues motrices: 900 mm.
Pony Wheel Dia./Diamètre des roues porteuses: 710 mm.
Weight/Masse: 54 tonnes.
Overall Length/Longeur hors tout: 1.46 m.
Max. Speed/Vitesse maximale: 75 km/h (adhesion/adhérence), 33km/h (rack/crémaillère).
New Class No./Nouveau numéro de série: 900.

901	R	MR	905	R	MR	908	R †	MR	911	R †	MR	914	R	MR
902		MR	906	*	MR	909	†	MR	912	R †	MR	915		MR
903	R *	MR	907	R	MR	910	R †	MR	913	R §	MR	916	*	MR
904	R	MR												

ELECTRIC LOCOMOTIVES/ LOCOMOTIVES ELECTRIQUES

CLASS/SERIE HGe4/4 BoBo

To overcome the severely limited capacity of the Deh4/6 on the rack sections, these two locos were built with double the rack haulage capacity of a Deh4/6, but with a lower maximum adhesion speed. Their operation is normally restricted to the Meiringen to Giswil section. With the entry into service of the 101 class, they now are reserve power for the rack section.

Ces deux locomotives furent contruites avec une puissance sur crémaillère double par rapport à celle des Deh4/6 (ces dernières étant trop faibles pour certains trains) mais avec une vitesse maximale réduite en adhérence. Leur utilisation est normalement limitée à la section Meiringen–Giswil. Depuis l'introduction de la série 101, elles sont gardées en réserve pour la section à crémaillère.

Built/Date de mise en service: 1954.
Builder-Mech. Parts/Constructeur-Partie mécanique: SLM.
Builder-Elec. Parts/Constructeur-Partie électrique: BBC/MFO.
Traction Motors: .
One Hour Rating/Puissance horaire: 1600 kW.
Maximum Tractive Effort/Effort de traction max.: 137 kN (adhesion/adhérence), 275 kN (rack/crémaillère).
Driving Wheel Dia./Diamètre des roues motrices: 1028 mm.
Weight/Masse: 54 tonnes.
Overall Length/Longeur hors tout: 1.32 m.
Max. Speed/Vitesse maximale: 50 km/h (adhesion), 33 km/h (rack).
New Class No./Nouveau numéro de série:

1991	MR	MEIRINGEN	1992	MR	GISWIL

CLASS/SERIE 101 (HGe4/4 II) BoBo

These eight locos are based on prototypes 1951–2 (now sold to the FO) to enable all through trains to be worked by this type of loco.

Ces huit machines sont basées sur les prototypes 1951/2 qui ont été vendus aux FO. Ce type de locomotive est utilisé sur tous les trains directs Lucerne–Interlaken.

Built/Date de mise en service: 1989–90.
Builder-Mech. Parts/Constructeur-Partie mécanique: SLM.
Builder-Elec. Parts/Constructeur-Partie électrique: ABB.
Traction Motors:.
One Hour Rating/Puissance horaire: kW.
Maximum Tractive Effort/Effort de traction max.: kN.
Driving Wheel Dia./Diamètre des roues motrices: mm.
Weight/Masse: tonnes.
Overall Length/Longeur hors tout: . m.
Max. Speed/Vitesse maximale: km/h.

101 961-1 **R**	MR	HORW	101 965-2 **R**	MR	LUNGERN
101 962-9 **R**	MR	HERGISWIL	101 966-0 **R**	MR	HASLIBERG-BRÜNIG
101 963-7 **R**	MR	ALPNACH	101 967-8 **R**	MR	BRIENZ
101 964-5 **R**	MR	SACHSEN	101 968-6 **R**	MR	RINEGENBERG

Brünig Line Class 101 No. 101 966–0 'HASLIBERG–BRÜNIG' waits to depart from Interlaken Ost during 1990. *E.H. Sawford*

La 101 966–0 «HASLIBERG–BRÜNIG» de la ligne du Brünig attend le départ de Interlaken Ost en 1990. *E.H. Sawford*

SHUNTING TRACTORS/**LOCOTRACTEURS**

CLASS/**SERIE** Te I — B

The narrow gauge equivalent of the 1–60 series.
L'équivalent de la série 1 à 60 mais pour voie métrique.

Built/Date de mise en service: 1941.
Builder-Mech. Parts/Constructeur-Partie mécanique: SLM.
Builder-Elec. Parts/Constructeur-Partie électrique: MFO.
Traction Motors: .
One Hour Rating/Puissance horaire: 95 kW.
Maximum Tractive Effort/Effort de traction max.: kN.
Driving Wheel Dia./Diamètre des roues motrices: mm.
Weight/Masse: 13 tonnes.
Overall Length/Longeur hors tout: 5.8 m.
Max. Speed/Vitesse maximale: 60 km/h.
New Class No./Nouveau numéro de série:

198	LZ	Hergiswil
199	LZ	Sarnen

CLASS/**SERIE** Te III — Bo

The narrow gauge equivalent of the 139–179 series.
L'équivalent de la série 139 à 179 pour voie métrique.
Built/Date de mise en service: 1962.
Builder-Mech. Parts/Constructeur-Partie mécanique: SLM.
Builder-Elec. Parts/Constructeur-Partie électrique: MFO.
Traction Motors:
Moteurs de Traction:
One Hour Rating/Puissance horaire: 260 kW.
Maximum Tractive Effort/Effort de traction max.: kN.
Driving Wheel Dia./Diamètre des roues motrices: mm.
Weight/Masse: 26 tonnes.
Overall Length/Longeur hors tout: 6.05 m.
Max. Speed/Vitesse maximale: 60 km/h.

201	LZ	Luzern
202	LZ	Giswil
203	MR	Meiringen

CLASS/**SERIE** Tm II — B

The narrow gauge equivalent of the 601–853 series; in fact 980/4 are rebuilds from 709 & 828 in 1987 & 1983 respectively.

L'équivalent de la série 601 à 853 pour voie métrique; en effet, les 980/4 4 furent transformés des 709 et 828 en 1987 et 1983 respectivement.

Built/Date de mise en service: 1959–66.
Builder/Constructeur: RACO.
Engine/Moteur: Saurer C615D of 70 kW.
Transmission: Mechanical/Mécanique.
Maximum Tractive Effort/Effort de traction max.: kN.
Driving Wheel Dia./Diamètre des roues motrices: 600 mm.
Weight/Masse: 10 tonnes.
Overall Length/Longeur hors tout: 5.15 m.
Max. Speed/Vitesse maximale: 45 km/h.

* Fitted for snowplough use./Modifié pour l'utilisation comme chasse-neige.

596		LZ	*Reserve*
597		MR	Brienz
598		MR	*Reserve*
980		MR	Meiringen
981	*	MR	Meiringen
982	*	MR	Meiringen
983		MR	Meiringen
984		LZ	Luzern

▼Class Re4/4 I No. 10017 in red livery stands in the siding alongside the station at Bellinzona with the corridor connection coupled to its train on 06/05/90. *T.N. Bowden*

▼▼Class Re4/4 I No. 10042, one of the later series without corridor connections, enters the west end of Lausanne station with a Regionalzug on 28/07/89. *Stuart Falcus*

▲▲La Re4/4 I 10017 en livrée rouge garée à Bellinzona. Une des portes d'intercirculation est connectée à la rame, 06/05/90. *T.N. Bowden*

▲La Re4/4 I 10042, un des exemplaires plus récents sans portes d'intercirculation arrive à Lausanne avec un train régional, 28/07/89. *Stuart Falcus*

▼Class Re4/4 ^{IV} No. 10102 'Ostermundigen' in Bahn 2000 livery at Brig on 28/07/89. The number is carried on small numerals to the left of the cab door. *Stuart Falcus*

▼▼Preserved Class Ae3/6 ^{II} No. 10439 restored to original brown livery at Olten depot on 23/04/88. *P.W. Cooper*

▲▲La Re4/4 ^{IV} 10102 «Ostermundingen» en livrée «Rail 2000» à Brigue. Le numéro de série, en petit chiffres, se trouve juste à gauche de la porte de la cabine de conduite, 28/07/89. *Stuart Falcus*

▲La Ae3/6 ^{II} 10439 préservée et restaurée dans sa livrée marron d'origine au dépôt d'Olten, 23/04/88. *P.W. Cooper*

▼Class Ae4/7 No. 10905 stands in Winterthur station on 03/09/87. This class will not be receiving the new red livery. *Paul Russenberger*

▼▼Class Re4/4 II No. 11108 in 'Swiss Federal' livery at Luzern, with the 11.13 to Genève-Aéroport made up of Mark III push-pull stock, on 10/09/89. *Paul Russenberger*

▲▲La Ae4/7 10905 à la gare de Winterthour. Cette série ne recevra pas la nouvelle livrée rouge, 03/09/87. *Paul Russenberger*

▲La Re4/4 II 11108 en livrée «Swiss Express» à Lucerne avec un train pour Genève-Aéroport composé d'une rame reversible de voitures Mark III, 10/09/89. *Paul Russenberger*

▼Class Ae6/6 No. 11404 'LUZERN', carrying the chrome decorations fitted to the units of the class named after cantons, at Olten on 20/07/ 89. *Stuart Falcus*

▼▼Class Re6/6 No. 11602 'MORGES', with articulated body which can be seen following an undulation in the track, leaves Erstfield yard with a northbound freight train on 20/07/89. *Stuart Falcus*

▲▲La Ae6/6 11404 «LUZERN» à Olten avec anjoliveurs en chrome qu'arborent toutes les locomotives de la classe qui portent des nomes de cantons, 20/07/89. *Stuart Falcus*

▲La Re6/6 11602 «MORGES» quitte le faisceau d'Erstfeld vers le nord avec un train de marchandises. Noter la caisse articulée qui suit les ondulations de la voie, 20/07/89. *Stuart Falcus*

▼Class Re6/6 No. 11620 'WANGEN BEI OLTEN' after arrival at Luzern in September 1976.
Paul Russenberger

▼▼Class Ee3/3 No. 16371, carrying the red-brown shunter livery, during shunting at the west end of Lausanne station on 29/01/89.
Paul Russenberger

▲▲La Re6/6 11620 «WANGEN BEI OLTEN» aprés son arrivée à Lucerne. Septembre 1976.
Paul Russenberger

▲La Ee3/3 16371 en livrée brun-rouge, manoeuvre en gare de Lausanne, 29/01/89.
Paul Russenberger

▼Class 450 No. 450 009-6 'Hedingen' leaves Wetzikon on a Hinwil–Zürich working on 27th August 1990. *Chris Appleby*

▼▼Class Bm4/4 No. 18443 at Basel depot on 17/08/88. *Bevan Price*

▲▲Class 450 No. 450 009-6 «Hedingen» quitte Wetzikon avec un train de Hinwil à Zürich, 27/08/90. *Chris Appleby*

▲La Bm4/4 18443 au dépôt de Bâle, 17/08/88. *Bevan Price*

▼Class Em6/6 No. 17006 with Em3/3 Class No. 18810 and Class Ee6/6 II No. 16816 at Basel SBB on 23/04/88. *P.W. Cooper*

▼▼Class Am4/4 No. 18462 at Biel depot. This class was purchased from the DB where it ran as Class 220. *Stuart Falcus*

▲▲La Em6/6 17006 avec la Em3/3 18810 et la Ee6/6 II 16816 à Bâle CFF, 23/04/88. *P.W. Cooper*

▲La Am4/4 18462 au dépôt de Bienne. Les locomotives de cette série appartenaient auparavant à la classe 220 de la DB. *Stuart Falcus*

▼Class Tem II No. 286 in the new livery with full ownership lettering 'SBB CFF FFS' at Lachen on 03/09/87. *Paul Russenberger*

▼▼Diminutive Class Ta No. 971 shunts a coach on the traverser at Olten carriage works on 31/05/88. *Chris Appleby*

▲▲La Tem II 286 dans la nouvelle livrée rouge à Lachen. Noter le sigle complet SBB CFF FFS, 03/09/87. *Paul Russenberger*

▲La toute petite Ta 971 manoeuvre une voiture sur le pont transbordeur de l'atelier d'Olten, 31/05/88. *Chris Appleby*

▼Class RABDe12/12 No. 1103 at Rapperswil on 03/09/87. *Paul Russenberger*

▼▼Class RBe4/4 No. 1436 outside Zürich Hauptbahnhof in February 1984. *Paul Russenberger*

▲▲La RABDe12/12 1103 à Rapperswil, 03/09/87. *Paul Russenberger*

▲La RBe4/4 1436 à Zurich Hauptbahnhof, Fevrier 1984. *Paul Russenberger*

▼Class BDe4/4 No. 1639 at Schaffhausen on a working to Winterthur on 26/08/74. *Paul Russenberger*

▼▼Class RBDe4/4 No. 2119 'Rivera-Bironico' at Olten on 31/05/89. The non-driving trailer coaches are formed from older, refurbished vehicles. *T.N. Hall*

▲▲La BDe4/4 1639 à Schaffhouse avec un train pour Winterthour, 26/08/84. *Paul Russenberger*

▲La RBDe4/4 2119 «Rivera-Bironico» à Olten. Les remorques intermédiaires sont d'anciennes voitures modernisées, 31/05/89. *T.N. Hall*

Brünig line Class Deh4/6 rack-and-adhesion No. 912 waits to depart from Interlaken Ost on 10/07/89. *Stuart Falcus*

La Deh4/6 912 de la ligne du Brünig, qui peut être exploitée en adhérence ou en crémaillère, attend le départ à Interlaken Ost, 10/07/89. *Stuart Falcus*

▼BLS Class Re4/4 No. 182 'Kandergrund' at Thun about to depart for Brig via the Lötschberg Tunnel on 28/01/89. *Paul Russenberger*

▼▼BLS Class Ae8/8 No. 273 at Brig BLS depot on 28/07/89. Although not named, these twin units carry the emblems of the cantons of Bern and Wallis, one on each unit. *Stuart Falcus*

▲▲La Re4/4 182 «Kandergrund» du BLS est prête à partir de Thoune pour Brigue via le tunnel du Lötschberg, 28/01/89. *Paul Russenberger*

▲La Ae8/8 273 au dépôt BLS de Brigue. Bien que non bapisées, ces locomotives doubles portent les armes des cantons de Berne et Valais, 28/07/89. *Stuart Falcus*

▼GBS Class RBDe4/4 No. 736 at Spiez on a local working to Interlaken Ost during May 1990. *T.N. Bowden*

▼▼BLS Class ABDe4/8 No. 753 enters Thun from Bern via Belp passing EBT Bt Class driving trailer second No. 383 on 28/01/89. *Paul Russenberger*

▲▲La RBDe4/4 736 du GBS à Spiez avec un train régional pour Interlaken Ost, Mai 1990. *T.N. Bowden*

▲La ABDe4/8 753 du BLS arrive à Thoune avec un train de Berne via Belp at croise la remorque pilots Bt 383 du EBT, 28/01/89. *Paul Russenberger*

▼RhB Class Ge2/4 No. 222 shunting at Landquart on 16/05/84. *Nick Bartlett*

▼▼RhB Class Ge6/6 'Baby Crocodile' No. 412 leaving Surava on a Thusis to Samedan mixed train on 26/06/89. *Nick Bartlett*

▲▲La Ge2/4 222 du RhB manoeuvre à Landquart, 16/05/84. *Nick Bartlett*

▲La Ge6/6 «bébé crocodile» 412 du RhB quitte Surava avec un train mixte de Thusis à Samedan, 26/06/89. *Nick Bartlett*

▼RhB Arosa line Class ABe4/4 No. 487 waits in the street opposite the main station at Chur on 03/08/89. This section of line is to be rebuilt in tunnel to avoid street running. *J. Ramsay*

▼▼RhB rebuilt Class Ge4/4 I No. 601 'Albula' enters Filisur on 30/05/89. *T.N. Hall*

▲▲La ABe4/4 487 de la ligne d'Arosa du RhB attend en face de la gare principale de Coire. Cette section de ligne sera bientôt déviée par un tunnel pour éviter l'exploitation sur route en ville, 03/08/89. *J. Ramsay*

▲La Ge4/4 I modernisée 601 «Albula» du RhB, arrive à Filisur, 30/05/89. *T.N. Hall*

▼RhB Ge4/4 Class No. 631 'Untervaz' arrives at Filisur with a freight from Chur on 21/09/87.
Colin Boocock

▼▼Preserved RhB G3/4 Class No. 1 'Rhätia' pilots preserved G4/5 Class No. 108 out of Zernez with a centenary special. *S.A. Sugden*

▲▲La Ge4/4 631 «Untervaz» du RhB arrive à Filisur avec un train de marchandises de Coire, 21/09/87.
Colin Boocock

▲La G3/4 No. 1«Rhätia» et la G4/5 108, toutes les deux préservées par le RhB, quittent Zernez en double traction en tête d'un train spécial pour le centenaire du RhB. *S.A. Sugden*

CLASS/SERIE Tm III B

Purchased second hand from SWEG (Germany) in 1982.
Acheté d'occasion de SWEG (Allemagne) en 1982.

Built/Date de mise en service: 1957.
Builder/Constructeur: Gmeinder.
Engine/Moteur: Saurer of 165 kW.
Transmission: Hydraulic/Hydraulique.
Maximum Tractive Effort/Effort de traction max.: kN.
Driving Wheel Dia./Diamètre des roues motrices: mm.
Weight/Masse: 24 tonnes.
Overall Length/Longeur hors tout: 7.23 m.
Max. Speed/Vitesse maximale: 60 km/h.

599 LZ Alpnach Dorf

CLASS/SERIE Tmh B

The rack and adhesion version of the Tm II class for use on works trains in the Brünig Pass.

Une version à crémaillère de la série Tm II pour utilisation sur des trains de travaux au col du Brünig.

Built/Date de mise en service: 1965.
Builder/Constructeur: RACO/VR.
Engine/Moteur: Saurer.
Transmission: Hydraulic/Hydraulique.
Maximum Tractive Effort/Effort de traction max.: kN.
Driving Wheel Dia./Diamètre des roues motrices: mm.
Weight/Masse: 12 tonnes.
Overall Length/Longeur hors tout: 5.35 m.
Max. Speed/Vitesse maximale: 40 km/h (adhesion), 27 km/h (rack).

985 LZ Luzern | 986 MR Meiringen

Brünig Line Class Te III No. 203 shunting at Meiringen in September 1988. *Paul Russenberger*

Le Te III 203 de la ligne du Brünig manoeuvre à Meiringen en Septembre 1988. *Paul Russenberger*

DEPARTMENTAL LOCOMOTIVES/ LOCOMOTIVES DE SERVICES

Several former electric locos remain in use as heating units for carriage preheating and other purposes.

Plusieurs anciennes locomotives électriques sont utilisées maintenant pour le préchauffage des rames et pour d'autres usages.

HEATING UNITS LOCOMOTIVES DE CHAUFFAGE

Class/Série Ae3/6 II

10420 Chiasso
10424 Aarau
10428 Basel/Bâle Wolf
10429 Chiasso
10448 Basel/Bâle Wolf
10449 Linthal
10459 Stein–Säckingen

Class/Série Ae4/7

10977 Basel/Bâle Wolf
10983 Genève
10989 Basel/Bâle Wolf

OTHER EX-LOCOS AUTRES ANCIENNES LOCOMOTIVES

30 85 94–25054 ex Te II 228

SNOWPLOUGHS/CHASSES-NEIGE

Xrote	50	SLM/MFO	1944	MR	Meiringen
Xrotm	51	Beil	1986	MR	Meiringen
Xrotm	97	SLM/SAAS/Beilhack	1967	ER	Erstfeld
Xrotm	98	SLM/SAAS/Beilhack	1967	ER	Biasca
Xrote	99	SLM/MFO	1946	LS	Lausanne
Xtm	101	RACO/Beilhack/Deutz	1969	MR	Meiringen
Xtm	102	RACO/Beilhack/Deutz	1972	ER	Airolo
Xtm	103	RACO/Beilhack/Deutz	1972	LZ	Konolfingen
Xtm	104	RACO/Beilhack/Deutz	1971	ZU	Ziegelbrücke
Xtm	105	RACO/Beilhack/Deutz	1972	WT	Wetzikon
Xtm	106	RACO/Beilhack/Deutz	1972	BR	Brig/Brigue
Xtm	107	RACO/Beilhack/Deutz	1972	BI	Neuchâtel
Xtm	108	RACO/Beilhack/Deutz	1972	LS	Cossonay
Xtm	109	RACO/Beilhack/Deutz	1972	BI	Neuchâtel
Xtm	116	RACO/Beilhack/Deutz	1979	LS	

All the above are rotaries, the Xtm & Xrotm being self propelled, and the others requiring propulsion by a loco. The MR based snowploughs are metre gauge.

Tous les chasse-neige sont rotatifs. Les Xtm et Xrotm sont autopropulsés mais les autres doivent être poussés par une locomotive. Les chasse-neige basés à MR sont à voie métrique.

SWISS PRIVATE RAILWAYS

Around 40% of the railway mileage in Switzerland does not belong to the SBB, but to one of the numerous so-called Private Railways. In fact, apart from some purely tourist lines, the basic difference is that these Private Railways are financed by local government as opposed to the SBB which is financed by central government. Most of these railways are purely local, often providing a branch line service connecting with the SBB, although some, notably the Bern–Lötschberg–Simplon and the Rhätische Bahn, are main line railways in their own right. The railways provide a considerable contrast, ranging from those with some street or roadside running to those up to full main line standard, and of course mountain rack lines.

Many of the railways are narrow gauge, and partly because of this, their operation is mostly self-contained. However, some joint through operation does exist, including some over SBB tracks.

Format:

Due to the large number of numerically small classes, a format has been adopted for all railways except the BLS and RhB using one line for each item of motive power as follows:

1st Column: Classification: see 'Classification of Swiss Motive Power' for details.
2nd Column: Running number.
3rd Column: Owner: only shown to indicate the actual owner where a group of railways have a common numbering scheme.
4th Column: Name (if any).
5th Column: Builder: see 'List of Builders' for abbreviations.
6th Column: No. of seats (if 1st & 2nd class, seating split shown in that order, e.g. 18/30 = 18 1st, 30 2nd).
7th Column: Max. speed in km/h (if rack & adhesion, adhesion speed shown first).
8th Column: Weight in tonnes.
9th Column: Hourly rating in kW (or engine rating for diesel locos).
10th Column: Date of construction (date in brackets indicates date of major rebuilding).

Some railways are under common management, and where these also share a common numbering scheme, they have been grouped together. To assist in locating the various railways, the numbers in brackets after the headings refer to the relevant table nos. in the Swiss Railway timetable.

All Swiss Railways have an official set of initials, and they have been put into alphabetical order of these, except where grouped together as noted above.

Not included are the urban tramways in Basel, Bern, Genève, Lausanne, Neuchâtel or Zürich, nor the numerous cable and funicular railways.

LES CHEMINS DE FER PRIVES SUISSES

Environ 40% du kilométrage du chemin de fer suisse n'appartient pas aux CFF mais à une des nombreuses compagnies «privées». En réalité, mis à part quelques lignes à vocation purement touristique, la seule différence est que les chemins de fer privés sont financés au niveau local tandis que les CFF sont financés par l'Etat. La plupart de ces chemins de fer sont purement locaux, n'offrant souvent qu'une seule ligne qui assure la correspondance avec les CFF, bien que certains, comme le BLS et le RhB, sont de «vrais» chemins de fer avec un réseau et des trains à longues distances. Les autres sont très contrastés – certains ont des lignes établies sur route ou en accotement de chaussée, d'autres ont de «grandes lignes» et bien sûr dans ce pays montagneux, plusieurs sont entièrement à crémaillère.

Plusieurs compagnies privées ont des lignes à voie étroite et leur exploitation est donc souvent indépendante des autres compagnies. Cependant, certaines exploitent des trains directs entre deux réseaux, y compris sur les voies CFF dans certains cas.

Format:

A cause du nombre important de petites séries, un format a été adopté pour tous les réseaux sauf le BLS et le RhB – une ligne de données est utilisée pour chaque série de matériel comme suit:

1re colonne: Classification – voir «Classification du matériel moteur Suisse».
2me colonne: Numéro de série.
3me colonne: Propriétaire – seulement pour indiquer le propriétaire là où un groupe de réseaux a un système de numérotation commun.
4me colonne: Nom (s'il y en a)
5me colonne: Constructeur – voir «Liste des Constructeurs»
6me colonne: Nombre de places (s'il existe 1re et 2me classe, la partage des places est indiqué dans cet ordre, par exemple 18/30 = 18 1re, 30 2me).
7me colonne: Vitesse max. en km/h (si le matériel marche à crémaillère et en adhérence, la vitesse en adhérence est indiquée d'abord).
8me colonne: Poids en tonnes.
9me colonne: Puissance horaire en kW (ou puissance du moteur pour machines diesel).
10me colonne: Date de construction (une date entre parenthèses indique la date d'une transformation majeure).

Certains réseaux sont gérés en commun. Nous les avons groupés ensemble là où il existe un système de numérotation commun. Pour aider le lecteur à situer chaque réseau, le nom de chaque compagnie est suivi d'un numéro entre parenthèses qui indique le numéro de tableau horaire applicable dans l'indicateur suisse.

Chaque réseau suisse a un sigle officiel, et nous avons classé ceux-ci par ordre alphabétique, sauf lorsque plusieurs réseaux sont groupés (voir plus haut).

Nous n'avons pas inclu ni les réseaux de tramways urbains de Bâle, Berne, Genève, Lausanne, Neuchâtel ou Zurich, ni les nombreux chemins de fer funiculaires.

INDEX TO PRIVATE RAILWAYS/ INDEXE DES CHEMINS DE FER PRIVES SUISSES

AB	Appenzellerbahnen
AL	Aigle Leysin
AOMC	Aigle Ollon Monthey Champéry
ARB	Arth Rigi Bahn
ASD	Aigle Sépey Diablarets
BAM	Bière Apples Morges
BD	Bremgarten Dietikon
BLM	Bergbahn Lauterbrunnen Mürren
BLS	Bern Lötschberg Simplon
BN	Bern Neuenberg (part of BLS Group/ une partie du groupe BLS) (Neuenberg = Neuchâtel)
BOB	Berner Oberland Bahnen
BRB	Brienz Rothorn Bahn
BT	Bodensee Toggenburg
BTI	Biel Täuffelen Ins (part of OSST/intégré dans le OSST)
BVB	Bex Villars Bretaye
BVZ	Brig Visp Zermatt
CEV	Chemins de Fer Electriques Veveysans
CJ	Chemins de Fer du Jura
CMN	Chemins de Fer des Montagnes Neuchâtel
Db	Dolderbahn
EBT	Emmental Burgdorf Thun
FART	Ferrovie Autolinee Regionali Ticinese
FB	Forchbahn
FLP	Ferrovia Lugano Ponte Tresa
FO	Furka Oberalp
FW	Frauenfeld Wil
GBS	Gürbetal Bern Schwarzenburg (part of BLS Group/une partie du groupe BLS)
GFM	Gruyère Fribourg Morat
GGB	Gornergratbahn
JB	Jungfraubahn
KLB	Kriens Luzern Bahn
LEB	Lausanne Eschallens Bercher
LG	Lausanne Gare
LO	Lausanne Ouchy (included with LG/inclu avec le LG)

LSE	Luzern Stans Engelberg
MC	Martigny Châtelard
MG	Monte Generoso
MGN	Montreux Glion Naye
MIB	Meiringen Innertkirchen Bahn
MO	Martigny Orsières
MOB	Montreux Oberland Bernois
MThB	Mittel Thurgau Bahn
NStCM	Nyon St Cergue Morez
OC	Orbe Chavornay
OeBB	Oensingen Balsthal Bahn
OSST	Oberaargau Solothurn Seeland Transport
PB	Pilatus Bahn
PBr	Pont Brassus Bahn
PTT	Post Telephon Telegraph
RBS	Regionalverkehr Bern Solothurn
RhB	Rhätische Bahn
RHB	Rorschach Heiden Bahn
RhW	Rheineck Walzenhausen
RVO	Regionalverkehr Oberaargau (part of OSST/intégré dans le OSST)
RVT	Régional de Val de Travers
SATEB	S.A. des Transports Emosson Barbarine
SEZ	Spiez Erlenbach Zweisimmen (part of BLS Group/une partie du groupe BLS)
SMB	Solothurn Münster Bahn (part of EBT Group/une partie du groupe EBT) (Münster = Mautier)
SNB	Solothurn Neiderbipp Bahn (part of OSST/intégré dans le OSST)
SOB	Schweizerische Sudostbahn
SPB	Schynige Platte Bahn
SSIF	Società Subalpina di Imprese Ferroviarie (included with FART/inclu avec le FART)
ST	Sursee Triengen
STB	Sensetalbahn
SZU	Sihltal Zürich Uetliberg
TB	Trogener Bahn
VHB	Vereinigte Huttwil Bahnen (part of EBT Group/une partie du groupe EBT)
VRB	Vitznau Rigi Bahn
WAB	Wengernalpbahn
WB	Waldenburgerbahn
WM	Wohlen Meisterschwanden (included with BD/inclu avec le BD)
WSB	Wynental und Suhrentalbahn
YSC	Yverdon St Croix

BLS GROUP OF RAILWAYS/LE GROUPE BLS

Bern Lötschberg Simplon (230, 300, 310) **BLS**
Bern Neuenberg (220, 296) **BN**
Gürbetal Bern Schwarzenburg (297, 298) **GBS**
Spiez Erlenbach Zweisimmen (320) **SEZ**

The BLS Group of railways is second only in route mileage to the RhB among the Swiss Private Railways, and the only one with through express and international services. The Lötschberg Pass forms part of the Bern to Milano main line, and extensive joint through working occurs with the SBB. The railway also provides the principal services to Interlaken, operates frequent suburban services from Bern, and the branch to Zweisimmen connects with the MOB.

Le groupe des compagnies de chemins de fer BLS est le deuxième, en termes de kilométrage, des chemins de fer privés suisses, et le seul avec des express directs et des services internationaux. La ligne du col du Lötschberg fait partie de la principale ligne entre Zurich et Milan et les services sont exploités en commun avec les CFF. Le BLS exploite aussi les principaux trains pour Interlaken, des services fréquents dans la banlieue de Berne et la ligne de Zweisimmen qui assure une correspondance avec le MOB.

Electrical system/Système: 15 kV 16⅔ Hz.
Depots/Dépots: Spiez, Bern Holligen, Brig, Schwarzenberg, Erlenbach, Zweisimmen.
Gauge/Voie: 1435 mm.

Note: Unless shown as belonging to one of the three subsidiary companies (BN, GBS, SEZ), all motive power is owned by the BLS proper. In fact, much of the stock is in common usage throughout the system. All motive power is allocated to Spiez, the works and principal depot.

N.B.: Le matériel appartient au BLS lui-même sauf celui indiqué comme appartenant à une des trois filiales (BN, GBS ou SEZ). En réalité, la plupart du matériel est utilisé partout sur le réseau sans tenir compte de son appartenance. Tout le matériel est entretenu à Spiez, atelier et dépôt principal.

Livery: Electric locos: Brown
Tractors: Red, except Ta 1–2 which are yellow
Railcars: Blue & cream, except 761–3, 796 which are green

Livrée: Locomotives électriques: Marron
Locotracteurs: Rouge, sauf les Ta 1 et 2 qui sont en jaune.
Automotrices: Bleu et crème, sauf les 761 à 3 et 796 qui sont vertes.

ELECTRIC LOCOMOTIVES
LOCOMOTIVES ELECTRIQUES

CLASS Re4/4 BoBo

The standard BLS electric loco, found everywhere on all types of work.
La locomotive électrique standard du BLS est utilisée sur tous les types de train partout sur le réseau.

Built/Date de mise en service: 1964–83.
Builder-Mech. Parts/Constructeur-Partie mécanique: SLM.
Builder-Elec. Parts/Constructeur-Partie électrique: BBC.
Traction Motors: 4 d.c. type, fully suspended with BBC spring drive.
Moteurs de traction: 4 moteurs à courant continu, entièrement suspendus avec transmission à ressorts BBC.
One Hour Rating/Puissance horaire: 4990 kW.
Maximum Tractive Effort/Effort de traction max.: 314 kN.
Driving Wheel Dia./Diamètre des roues motrices: 1250 mm.
Weight/Masse: 80 tonnes.
Overall Length/Longeur hors tout: 15.47 (15.10 m *).
Max. Speed/Vitesse maximale: 140 km/h.

All locos mw and push-pull fitted./Toutes sont couplables en UM et dotées de la réversibilité.

161 * DOMODOSSOLA
162 * COURT
163 * GRENCHEN
164 * LENGNAU

165	*	MOUTIER	181	INTERLAKEN
166	*	AESCHI	182	KANDERGRUND
167	*	AUSSERBERG	183	KANDERSTEG
168	*	BALTSCHIEDER	184	KRATTIGEN
169	*	BÖNIGEN	185	LALDEN
170	*	BRIG-GLIS	186	LEISSIGEN
171	*	DÄRLIGEN	187	MUND
172	*	EGGERBERG	188	NATERS
173	*	LÖTSCHENTAL	189	NIEDERGESTELN
174		FRUTIGEN	190	RARON
175		GAMPEL	191	REICHENBACH
176		HOHTENN	192	SPIEZ
177	SEZ	ZWEISIMMEN	193	STEG
178	GBS	SCHWARZENBURG	194	THUN
179	BN	BERN	195	UNTERSEEN
180	BN	VILLE DE NEUCHÂTEL		

CLASS Ae6/8 1CoCo1

These elderly locos, built for main line work on the Lötschberg route are now being withdrawn. The survivors are used on local freights, and as a reserve for use at times of heavy traffic.

Ces vieilles locomotives, qui furent construites pour remorquer les trains principaux sur la ligne du Lötschberg sont en cours d'amortissement. Les survivantes remorquent des trains de marchandises locaux et sont retenues en réserve pour les périodes de trafic important.

Built/Date de mise en service: 1939–43.
Builder-Mech. Parts/Constructeur-Partie mécanique: SLM.
Builder-Elec. Parts/Constructeur-Partie électrique: SAAS.
Traction Motors: 12 single phase, fully suspended with SAAS spring drive.
Moteurs de traction: 12 moteurs à courant alternatif monophasé à collecteurs, entièrement suspendus avec transmission à ressorts Sécheron.
One Hour Rating/Puissance horaire: 4416 kW.
Maximum Tractive Effort/Effort de traction max.: 353 kN.
Driving Wheel Dia./Diamètre des roues motrices: 1350 mm.
Pony Wheel Dia./Diamètre des roues porteuses: 950 mm.
Weight/Masse: 140 tonnes.
Overall Length/Longeur hors tout: 20.26 m.
Max. Speed/Vitesse maximale: 100 km/h.

Rheostatic brake fitted./Dotées du freinage rhéostatique.

205 | 206 | 207 | 208

CLASS Ae4/4 BoBo

A very advanced design at the time of its introduction, this was the first electric type to achieve 1000 hp per axle. Now used on local duties, including the push-pull car carriers through the Lötschberg Tunnel. Nos. 253–6 have been rebuilt to the Ae8/8 class, detailed next.

Locomotives d'une conception très moderne lors de leur introduction. Elles furent les premières machines avec plus de 1000 cv par essieu. Maintenant elles sont utilisées sur des trains locaux, y compris les rames réversibles porte-autos par le tunnel du Lötschberg. Les 253 à 6 furent transformées en Ae8/8 (voir ci-dessous).

Built/Date de mise en service: 1944–55.
Builder-Mech. Parts/Constructeur-Partie mécanique: SLM.
Builder-Elec. Parts/Constructeur-Partie électrique: BBC.
Traction Motors: 4 single phase fully suspended with BBC flexible disc drive.
Moteurs de traction: 4 moteurs à courant alternatif monophasé à collecteurs, entièrement suspendus avec transmission élastique.
One Hour Rating/Puissance horaire: 3238 kW.
Maximum Tractive Effort/Effort de traction max.: 235 kN.
Driving Wheel Dia./Diamètre des roues motrices: 1250 mm.
Weight/Masse: 80 tonnes.
Overall Length/Longeur hors tout: 15.60 m.
Max. Speed/Vitesse maximale: 125 km/h.

All locos mw and push-pull fitted, rheostatic brake fitted.
Couplables en UM et dotées de la réversibilité et du freinage rhéostatique.

251 |252 |257 |258

CLASS Ae8/8 BoBo+BoBo

These are double locos, in effect a pair of Ae4/4 class permanently coupled, with the cabs at the inner ends removed. In fact, 274/5 are rebuilds of 253–6. Used on heavy freights.

Ce sont en fait deux Ae4/4 couplées en permanence avec suppression des deux cabines de conduites du milieu. Les 274 et 275 sont les 253 à 6 transformées. Utilisées sur les trains de marchandises lourds.

Built/Date de mise en service: 1959–63, 1948–52 *.
Builder-Mech. Parts/Constructeur-Partie mécanique: SLM.
Builder-Elec. Parts/Constructeur-Partie électrique: BBC.
Traction Motors: 8 single phase fully suspended with BBC flexible disc drive.
Moteurs de traction: 8 moteurs à courant alternatif monophasé à collecteurs, entièrement suspendus avec transmission élastique.
One Hour Rating/Puissance horaire: 6476 kW.
Maximum Tractive Effort/Effort de traction max.: 471 kN.
Driving Wheel Dia./Diamètre des roues motrices: 1250 mm.
Weight/Masse: 160 tonnes.
Overall Length/Longeur hors tout: 30.23 m.
Max. Speed/Vitesse maximale: 125 km/h.

All locos are mw & rheostatic brake fitted.
Toutes sont couplables en UM et dotées du freinage rhéostatique.
* Rebuilt 1965–6 from Ae4/4 253–256./Transformées en 1965/6 des Ae4/4 253 à 256.

271 |272 |273 |274 * |275*

CLASS Ce4/4 BB

A class built for mixed traffic duties at the time of electrification. The survivors are used on local freight work around Bern & Thun. They were built as 1BB1, rebuilt to BB in the 1950s. An unrebuilt example of the class (307) is an operational preserved loco.

Cette série fut construite pour tout type de trains lors de l'électrification. Les survivantes sont utilisées sur des trains de marchandises locaux autour de Berne et Thoune. A l'origine c'était des 1BB1, mais elles furent transformées en BB pendant les années 50. Une machine non-transformée (307) est utilisée comme locomotive historique.

Built/Date de mise en service: 1920–4, rebuilt 1954–6/transformées 1954 à 6.
Builder-Mech. Parts/Constructeur-Partie mécanique: SLM.
Builder-Elec. Parts/Constructeur-Partie électrique: BBC.
Traction Motors: 4 single phase bogie mounted with jackshaft/side rod drive.
Moteurs de traction: 4 moteurs à courant alternatif monophasé à collecteurs, montés sur les bogies avec transmission par faux-essieux et bielles.
One Hour Rating/Puissance horaire: 736 kW.
Maximum Tractive Effort/Effort de traction max.: 108 kN.
Driving Wheel Dia./Diamètre des roues motrices: 1230 mm.
Weight/Masse: 64 tonnes.
Overall Length/Longeur hors tout: 12.34 m.
Max. Speed/Vitesse maximale: 65 km/h.

311 GBS | 313 GBS | 315 BN | 316

CLASS Ee3/3 C

A classic centre-cab jackshaft drive shunter, similar to the SBB locos. Used as station pilot at Spiez.

Une machine de manoeuvres typiquement suisse, avec cabine centrale et transmission par faux-essieu, similaire aux locomotives CFF. Utilisée pour les manoeuvres en gare de Spiez.

Built/Date de mise en service: 1943.
Builder-Mech. Parts/Constructeur-Partie mécanique: SLM.
Builder-Elec. Parts/Constructeur-Partie électrique: SAAS.
Traction Motors: 1 single phase frame mounted with jackshaft/side rod drive.
Moteurs de traction: 1 moteur à courant alternatif monophasé à collecteurs, monté sur le châssis avec transmission par faux-essieux et bielles.
One Hour Rating/Puissance horaire: 452 kW.
Maximum Tractive Effort/Effort de traction max.: 88 kN.
Driving Wheel Dia./Diamètre des roues motrices: 1040 mm.
Weight/Masse: 38 tonnes.
Overall Length/Longeur hors tout: 9.2 m.
Max. Speed/Vitesse maximale: 40 km/h.

401

CLASS Eea3/3 C

A new design of electric shunter fitted with auxiliary batteries for use on non-electrified sidings, based on the latest Ee3/3 for the PTT. It will operate around Ütendorf.

◀ BLS Class Ae6/8 Class No. 206 pauses at Frutigen on a northbound freight on 21/08/85.
E. Dunkling

◀La Ae6/8 206 du BLS à l'arrêt à Frutigen avec un train de marchandises vers le nord. 21/08/85.
E. Dunkling

Un nouveau type de machine de manoeuvres électrique dotée d'accumulateurs pour des manoeuvres sur faisceaux non-électrifiés et basée sur les dernières Ee3/3 des PTT. Son utilisition est prévue à Ütendorf.

Built/Date de mise en service: Due 1991./Livraison prévue en 1991.
Builder-Mech. Parts/Constructeur-Partie mécanique: SLM.
Builder-Elec. Parts/Constructeur-Partie électrique: ABB.
Overall Length/Longeur hors tout: 11.20 m.
Max. Speed/Vitesse maximale: km/h.

402 GBS

ELECTRIC RAILCARS/AUTOMOTRICES

CLASS RBDe4/4 BoBo

Modern railcars, found on local services throughout the system, particularly in the Bern area. They operate with matching driving and intermediate trailers as 2- and 3-car sets. Fitted with thyristor control.

Des automotrices modernes qui sont utilisées sur tout le BLS, en particulier au départ de Berne. Elles sont formées en élements doubles ou triples (avec remorque intermédiaire). Dotées de thyristors.

Built/Date de mise en service: 1982–90.
Builder-Mech. Parts/Constructeur-Partie mécanique: SIG/SWS.
Builder-Elec. Parts/Constructeur-Partie électrique: BBC.
Traction Motors:
One Hour Rating/Puissance horaire: 1700 kW.
Maximum Tractive Effort/Effort de traction max.: 186 kN.
Driving Wheel Dia./Diamètre des roues motrices: 940 mm.
Weight/Masse: 69.7 tonnes.
Overall Length/Longeur hors tout: 25.0 m.
Max. Speed/Vitesse maximale: 125 km/h.
Accommodation/Aménagement intérieur: –/55 1T.

721		725	GBS	729	GBS	733	SEZ	737	BN	740
722		726	GBS	730	BNS	734	GBS	738	BN	741
723	SEZ	727	GBS	731		735	GBS	739		742
724	SEZ	728	GBS	732	SEZ	736	GBS			

CLASS ABDe4/8 2Bo+Bo2

Twin units for local services. The power equipment is carried at the inner ends of the vehicles. 744 & 745 recently renumbered from 742 & 741 to accommodate the new RBDe4/4 739–42.

Des éléments à deux caisses pour des services régionaux. L'équipement de puissance se trouve à l'extremité opposée de la cabine de conduite. Les 744 et 745 furent auparavant les 742 et 741, mais furent renumérotées à cause de l'introduction des RBDe4/4 739 à 742.

Built/Date de mise en service: 1945–6.
Builder-Mech. Parts/Constructeur-Partie mécanique: SIG.
Builder-Elec. Parts/Constructeur-Partie électrique: SAAS.
Traction Motors:
One Hour Rating/Puissance horaire: 708 kW.
Maximum Tractive Effort/Effort de traction max.: 59 kN.
Driving Wheel Dia./Diamètre des roues motrices: 920 mm.
Weight/Masse: 85 tonnes.
Overall Length/Longeur hors tout: 46.80 m.
Max. Speed/Vitesse maximale: 110 km/h.
Accommodation/Aménagement intérieur: 18/56 1T + –/64 1T.

743	BN	744	GBS	745	SEZ

CLASS ABDe4/8 2Bo+Bo2

Twin units for local services. They normally work with driving trailers as 3-car sets (746–50 have only one driving cab, and thus cannot work as 2-car sets).

Des éléments à deux caisses pour des services régionaux. En général, elles sont formées en éléments de trois caisses avec une voiture pilote (les 746 à 750 n'ont qu'une cabine de conduite et donc ne peuvent pas être utilisés en éléments de deux caisses).

Built/Date de mise en service: 1954, 1957 †, 1964 *.
Builder-Mech. Parts/Constructeur-Partie mécanique: SIG/BBC/BLS.
Builder-Elec. Parts/Constructeur-Partie électrique: SAAS.
Traction Motors:
One Hour Rating/Puissance horaire: 1176 kW.
Maximum Tractive Effort/Effort de traction max.: 98 kN.
Weight/Masse: 85, 90†, 96* tonnes.
Overall Length/Longeur hors tout: 47.465 m, 47.30 m†, 47.80 m*.
Max. Speed/Vitesse maximale: 125 km/h.
Accommodation/Aménagement intérieur: 24/40 1T+–/64 1T (24/32 1T+–/56 1T*).

746
747
748
749 †
750 †
751 *
752 * BN
753 * GBS
754 * BN
755 * BN

CLASS Be4/4 BoBo

Motor coaches, made up into sets as required with driving and intermediate trailers.
Motrices avec deux cabines de conduite qui sont couplées avec des remorques si nécessaire.

Built/Date de mise en service: 1953–6.
Builder-Mech. Parts/Constructeur-Partie mécanique: SIG.
Builder-Elec. Parts/Constructeur-Partie électrique: SAAS.
Traction Motors
One Hour Rating/Puissance horaire: 1472 kW.
Maximum Tractive Effort/Effort de traction max.: 128 kN.
Driving Wheel Dia./Diamètre des roues motrices: 1040 mm.
Weight/Masse: 68 tonnes.
Overall Length/Longeur hors tout: 23.70 m.
Max. Speed/Vitesse maximale: 120 km/h.
Accommodation/Aménagement intérieur: –/60 1T.

761 BN
762 BN
763 GBS

De4/5 CLASS A1ABo

The last survivor of 6 motor luggage vans, currently temporarily used as a heating unit at Spiez. It was built with passenger accommodation, rebuilt to a baggage van in the 1940s.

Le dernier survivant de six fourgons automoteurs, il est utilisé temporairement pour le préchauffage de rames à Spiez. Il fut construit pour transporter des voyageurs mais fut transformé en fourgon pendant les années 40.

Built/Date de mise en service: 1929.
Builder-Mech. Parts/Constructeur-Partie mécanique: SLM/SIG.
Builder-Elec. Parts/Constructeur-Partie électrique: SAAS.
Traction Motors:
One Hour Rating/Puissance horaire: 1176 kW.
Maximum Tractive Effort/Effort de traction max.: 108 kN.
Driving Wheel Dia./Diamètre des roues motrices: 1040 mm.
Weight/Masse: 70 tonnes.
Overall Length/Longeur hors tout: 20.90 m.
Max. Speed/Vitesse maximale: 90 km/h.

796

TRACTORS/LOCOTRACTEURS

A varied selection of tractors are in use for light shunting and departmental operation.

Une sélection variée de locotracteurs qui sont utilisés pour des manoeuvres et des trains de service.

Class *Série*	*No.* *No.*	*Rly.* *C.F.*	*Builder* *Constructeur*	*km/h* *km/h*	*Tonnes* *Tonnes*	*kW* *kW*	*Date* *Date*
Ta	1		BLS	15	4.5	6	1941
Ta	2		BLS	6.5	8.6	5.5	1975
Te^{I}	11		SLM/MFO	45	15	96	1950
Te^{I}	12		SLM/MFO	45	15	96	1950
Te^{I}	13		SLM/MFO	45	15	96	1950
Te^{I}	14		SLM/MFO	45	15	96	1950
Te^{I}	15	BN	SLM/MFO	45	15	96	1954
Te^{I}	16	BN	SLM/MFO	45	15	96	1954
Te^{I}	17	BN	SLM/MFO	45	15	96	1954
Tm	26		BLS/VW/VR	22	3.9	33	1963
Te2/3	31		SLM/MFO/BLS	45	36	360	1925
Te2/3	32		SLM/MFO/BLS	45	36	360	1925
Te	33		BLS/SAAS	45	21	294	1960
Tem	41		SLM/MFO/BBC/SAAS	65	30	258/146	1960
Tem	42		SLM/MFO/BBC/SAAS	65	30	258/146	1960
Tem	43		BLS/MFO/BBC/SAAS	65	30	258/146	1965
Tem	45		BLS/SLM/MFO/SAAS/DZ	65	30	258/180	1960
Tem	46		BLS/SLM/MFO/SAAS/DZ	65	30	258/180	1960
Tem	55		BLS/MFO/BBC/SAAS	65	30	258/146	1967
Tem	56		BLS/MFO/BBC/SAAS	65	30	258/146	1967
Tem	57		BLS/MFO/BBC/SAAS	65	30	258/146	1967
Tem	58		BLS/MFO/BBC/SAAS	65	30	258/146	1967
Tm	61		BLS/SLM/DZ	45	9	74	1974
Tm	62		BLS/SLM/DZ	45	9	74	1968
Tm	63		BLS	45	8.4	74	1960
Tm	64		BLS/SLM/DZ	45	9	74	1962
Tm	65		BLS/SLM/DZ	45	9	74	1963
Tm	66		BLS/SLM/DZ	45	9	74	1965
Tm	67	BN	BLS/SLM/DZ	45	9	74	1965
Tm	68	BN	BLS/SLM/DZ	45	9	74	1965
Tm	69	SEZ	BLS/SLM/DZ	45	9	74	1968
Tm	70		BLS/SLM/DZ	45	9	74	1972
Tm	71		BLS/SLM/DZ	45	9	74	1975
Tm	72		BLS/SLM/DZ	45	9	74	1974
Tm	75	SEZ	STAD/MERC	30	15	57	1952
Tm	81		ROBEL/DZ	63	18	67	1971
Tm	82		RACO/DZ	75	19	176	1977
Tm	83	SEZ	RACO/DZ	75	19	176	1980
Tm	84	GBS	RACO/DZ	75	19	176	1980
Tm	85	BN	RACO/DZ	75	19	176	1980
Tm	86		RACO/DZ	75	19	176	1983
Tm	87		RACO/DZ	75	19	176	1983
Tm	88		RACO/DZ	75	19	176	1983
Tm	91		STAD/VM/BBC	80	38	618	1980
Tm	92		STAD/VM/BBC	80	38	618	1980
Tm	93		STAD/VM/BBC	80	38	618	1980
Tm	94		STAD/VM/BBC	80	38	618	1981
Tm	95	GBS	STAD/MB/BBC	80	29	350	1984
Tm	96	GBS	STAD/MB/BBC	80	29	350	1984
Tm	97	BN	STAD/MB/BBC	80	29	350	1984
Tm	98	BN	STAD/MB/BBC	80	29	350	1985
Xrote	101		RACO/DZ/BEIL	60	25	166/191	1971

RHÄTISCHE BAHN/ **LES CHEMINS DE FER RHETIQUES**

In terms of route mileage the RhB is the largest of the Swiss Private Railways. It operates all the lines in south east Switzerland, connecting with the SBB at Chur and Landquart, and serving the major tourist centre of St. Moritz. Branches also serve Disentis, Arosa, Scuol–Tarasp and Tirano (the latter being in Italy). Although the main system is electrified at 11 kV 16⅔ Hz ac, several of the branches, all at one time being separate companies, are electrified on dc. These are:

Berninabahn (BB) (St. Moritz–Tirano). (1000 V dc).
Chur Arosa (ChA). (2000 V dc, now under conversion to 11 kV ac).
Bellinzona–Mesocco (BM) (an isolated 1500 V dc line, now freight only with just the section Castione Arbedo–Cama still in use).

All the lines of the RhB are very scenic, particularly the Berninabahn.
Gauge: 1000 mm.
Depots: Lanquart, Chur, Davos Platz, Samedan (main system), Chur Sand (ChA), Pontresina (BB), Poschiavo (BB), Grono (BM).

En termes de kilomètres de voie, le RhB est le plus grand des chemins de fer privés en Suisse. Il exploite toutes les lignes dans le sud-est de la Suisse, dessert l'importante ville touristique de St Moritz et assure des correspondances avec les CFF à Coire et Landquart. Les lignes affluentes desservent Disentis, Arosa, Scuol–Tarasp et Tirano (cette dernière se trouve en Italie). Bien que le réseau principal soit électrifié à 11kV 16⅔ Hz monophasé, plusieurs autres lignes, qui appartenaient auparavant à d'autres sociétés, sont électrifiées en continu. Il s'agit du:

Berninabahn (BB) (St. Moritz–Tirano). (1000 V continu).
Chur Arosa (ChA). (2000 V continu, en train d'être convertie à 11 kV monophasé).
Bellinzona–Mesocco (BM). (une ligne à 1500 V continu purement marchandises, isolée du reste du RhB; seule la section Castione–Arbedo à Cama est toujours exploitée).
Toutes les lignes du RhB sont très pittoresques, en particulier le BB.

Ecartement: 1000 mm.
Dépôts: réseau principal – Landquart, Coire, Davos Platz, Samedan; ChA –Coire Sand; BB – Pontresina, Poschiavo; BM – Grono.

LOCOS (MAIN SYSTEM) **LOCOMOTIVES (RESEAU PRINCIPAL)**

CLASS/**SERIE** Ge2/4 (Gem2/4*) 1B1

Built as mixed traffic locos at the time of electrification, these three locos were rebuilt in 1943 as shunters, with new off-centre-cab superstructure. They are used around Chur, Landquart and Samedan. One loco (211) was rebuilt with auxiliary batteries; it was further rebuilt with an auxiliary diesel engine in 1967.

Conçues pour des services de ligne lors de l'électrification, ces trois machines furent transformées en locomotives de manoeuvre en 1943 avec cabine de conduite décentrée. Elles sont utilisées autour de Coire, Landquart et Samedan. 211 a d'abord reçu des accumulateurs et en 1967 fut transformée une deuxième fois; elle est maintenant dotée d'un moteur diesel.

Built: 1913, rebuilt 1943 ex 202/6/1 (* further rebuilt 1967).
Construction: 1913; transformées en 1943 des 202/6/1 (* transformée à nouveau en 1967).
Builder-Mech. Parts/Constructeur-Partie mécanique: SLM.
Builder-Elec. Parts/Constructeur-Partie électrique: BBC/SAAS.
Engine/Moteur: Deutz F12L714 172 kW *.
Traction Motor: 1 single phase frame mounted with side rod drive.
Moteur de traction: 1 moteur à courant alternatif monophasé à collecteurs, monté sur le châssis avec transmission par bielles.
One Hour Rating/Puissance horaire: 228 kW (170 kW on diesel power/en mode diesel*).
Maximum Tractive Effort/Effort de traction max.: 60 kN.
Driving Wheel Dia./Diamètre des roues motrices: 1070 mm.
Pony Wheel Dia./Diamètre des roues porteuses: 710 mm.

▼RhB Class Ge2/4 No. 212 inside Samedan Depot on 19/08/85. *E. Dunkling*

▼▼RhB Class Gm2/2 No. 232 at the rear of a 'Rhätische Bahn 100' special near Wiesen on 25/06/89. *Mrs M. Boocock*

▲▲La Ge2/4 212 du RhB dans le dépôt de Samedan. 19/08/85. *E. Dunkling*

▲La Gm2/2 232 à l'arrière du train spécial pour le centenaire du RhB près de Wienen. 25/06/89. *Mrs M. Boocock*

Weight/Masse: 33 tonnes.
Overall Length/Longeur hors tout: 8.7 m.
Max. Speed/Vitesse maximale: 55 km/h.

211 * |212 |213

CLASS/SERIE Ge3/3 C

Modern shunting locos, a single motor drives all wheels through cardan shafts. Used at Landquart & Chur.

Des machines de manoeuvre modernes avec un seul moteur et transmission par cardans. Utilisées à Landquart et Coire.

Built/Date de mise en service: 1984.
Builder-Mech. Parts/Constructeur-Partie mécanique: RACO.
Builder-Elec. Parts/Constructeur-Partie électrique: BBC.
Traction Motor: 1 single phase frame mounted with cardan shift drive.
Moteur de traction: 1 moteur à courant alternatif monophasé à collecteurs, monté sur le châssis avec transmission par cardans.
One Hour Rating/Puissance horaire: 425 kW.
Maximum Tractive Effort/Effort de traction max.: 102 kN.
Driving Wheel Dia./Diamètre des roues motrices: 920 mm.
Weight/Masse: 33 tonnes.
Overall Length/Longeur hors tout: 8.64 m.
Max. Speed/Vitesse maximale: 40 km/h.

214 |215

CLASS/SERIE Ge2/4 1B1

Originally part of the same class as 211–3, but when rebuilt for shunting in 1945/6 retained the original box cab. Since the delivery of 214/5, they are mainly held in reserve for use at Samedan and Landquart.

A l'origine dans la même série que les 211 à 3, ces deux machines ont retenu leurs cabines d'origine malgré leur transformation pour des manoeuvres en 1945/6. Depuis l'introduction des 214–5, elles sont maintenues en réserve à Samedan et Landquart.

Built: 1913, rebuilt 1945–6 ex 203–4.
Date de mise en service: 1913,transformées en 1945–6 des 203–4.
Builder-Mech. Parts/Constructeur-Partie mécanique: SLM.
Builder-Elec. Parts/Constructeur-Partie électrique: BBC.
Traction Motor: 1 single phase frame mounted with side rod drive.
Moteur de traction: 1 moteur à courant alternatif monophasé à collecteurs, monté sur le châssis avec transmission par bielles.
One Hour Rating/Puissance horaire: 428 kW.
Maximum Tractive Effort/Effort de traction max.: 59 kN.
Driving Wheel Dia./Diamètre des roues motrices: 1070 mm.
Pony Wheel Dia./Diamètre des roues porteuses: 710 mm.
Weight/Masse: 31.8 tonnes.
Overall Length/Longeur hors tout: 8.7 m.
Max. Speed/Vitesse maximale: 55 km/h.

221 |222

CLASS/SERIE Gm3/3 C

Diesel shunters used at Landquart and Chur, they have a 2-speed transmission giving different characteristics for shunting & line operation.

Des locotracteurs diesel avec transmission à double réduction – pour les services de ligne ou manoeuvres. Elles sont utilisées à Landquart et Coire.

Built/Date de mise en service: 1975–6.
Builder/Constructeur: Moyse.
Engine/Moteur: MTU of 396 kW.
Transmission: Hydraulic/hydraulique.
Maximum Tractive Effort/Effort de traction max.: 153 kN.
Driving Wheel Dia./Diamètre des roues motrices: 920 mm.

Weight/Masse: 34 tonnes.
Overall Length/Longeur hors tout: 7.96 m.
Max. Speed/Vitesse maximale: 55 km/h.

231 |232 |233

CLASS/SERIE Gm4/4 BB

A diesel purchased in 1988 from the Brohltalbahn in Germany for use on construction work on the new Vereina Tunnel.

Une locomotive diesel rachetée du Brohltalbahn en Allemagne en 1988 pour des trains de travaux lors de la construction du tunnel de Vereina.

Built/Date de mise en service: 1988.
Builder/Constructeur: Mak.
Engines/Moteurs: 2 x 150 kW.
Transmission: Hydraulic/hydraulique.
Maximum Tractive Effort/Effort de traction max.: kN.
Driving Wheel Dia./Diamètre des roues motrices: mm.
Weight/Masse: tonnes.
Overall Length/Longeur hors tout: m.
Max. Speed/Vitesse maximale: km/h.

241

CLASS/SERIE Gm4/4 BB

Two diesel locos on order, also for use on construction work on the Vereina Tunnel.

Deux locomotives diesel en commande pour des trains de travaux lors de la construction du tunnel de Vereina.

Built/Date de mise en service: On order/En commande.
Builder/Constructeur: Gmeinder/Kaelble/RhB.
Engine/Moteur: Caterpillar 560 kW.
Transmission: Hydraulic/hydraulique.
Maximum Tractive Effort/Effort de traction max.: 165 kN.
Driving Wheel Dia./Diamètre des roues motrices: mm.
Weight/Masse: tonnes.
Overall Length/Longeur hors tout: 11.70 m.
Max. Speed/Vitesse maximale: 60 km/h.

242 243

CLASS/SERIE Ge4/6 1D1

The last survivor of an assortment of locos of this wheel arrangement dating from the time of electrification. Now in reserve at Samedan. The body contains two traction motors geared to a single layshaft driving through an additional layshaft and coupling rods.

La dernière machine d'un groupe de locomotives avec la même disposition d'essieux, toutes construites lors de l'électrification. La caisse contient deux moteurs engrenés sur un seul axe transmettant le mouvement par un réducteur et une transmission à bielles. Maintenant en réserve à Samedan.

Built/Date de mise en service: 1914.
Builder-Mech. Parts/Constructeur-Partie mécanique: SLM.
Builder-Elec. Parts/Constructeur-Partie électrique: MFO.
Traction Motors: 2 single phase frame mounted with side rod drive.
Moteurs de traction: 2 moteurs à courant alternatif monophasé à collecteurs, montés sur le châssis avec transmission par bielles.
One Hour Rating/Puissance horaire: 588 kW.
Maximum Tractive Effort/Effort de traction max.: 106 kN.
Driving Wheel Dia./Diamètre des roues motrices: 1070 mm.
Pony Wheel Dia./Diamètre des roues porteuses: 710 mm.
Weight/Masse: 56.3 tonnes.
Overall Length/Longeur hors tout: 11.10 m.
Max. Speed/Vitesse maximale: 55 km/h.

353

CLASS/*SERIE* Ge6/6 CC

The survivors of 15 'Baby Crocodiles' built in the 1920s to the same configuration as their SBB counterparts. They are used on local freight and mixed trains over most of the system.

Les derniers de 15 "bébé crocodiles" construits pendant les années 20 avec les mêmes dispositions de leurs grandes soeurs aux CFF. Elles sont utilisées partout sur le réseau sur des trains de marchandises locaux et des trains mixtes.

Built/Date de mise en service: 1925–9.
Builder-Mech. Parts/Constructeur-Partie mécanique: SLM.
Builder-Elec. Parts/Constructeur-Partie électrique: BBC/MFO.
Traction Motors: 2 single phase frame mounted with jackshaft/side rod drive.
Moteurs de traction: 2 moteurs à courant alternatif monophasé à collecteurs, montés sur le châssis avec transmission par faux-essieux et bielles.
One Hour Rating/Puissance horaire: 794 kW.
Maximum Tractive Effort/Effort de traction max.: 172 kN.
Driving Wheel Dia./Diamètre des roues motrices: 1070 mm.
Weight/Masse: 66 tonnes.
Overall Length/Longeur hors tout: 13.30 m.
Max. Speed/Vitesse maximale: 55 km/h.

411 | 412 | 413 | 414 | 415

CLASS/*SERIE* Ge4/4 I BoBo

Mixed traffic locos, now undergoing extensive refurbishment. They will see use on push-pull trains on the Arosa line when this is converted to ac.

Des locomotives pour trafic mixte qui sont en cours de modernisation profonde. Elles seront utilisées sur des rames réversibles sur la ligne d'Arosa après sa conversion à 11kV.

Built/Date de mise en service: 1947 (601–604), 1953 (605–610)).
Builder-Mech. Parts/Constructeur-Partie mécanique: SLM.
Builder-Elec. Parts/Constructeur-Partie électrique: BBC/MFO.
Traction Motors: 4 single phase fully suspended with BBC spring drive.
Moteurs de traction: 4 moteurs à courant alternatif monophasé à collecteurs, entièrement suspendus avec transmission à ressorts BBC.
One Hour Rating/Puissance horaire: 1176 kW.
Maximum Tractive Effort/Effort de traction max.: 142 kN.
Driving Wheel Dia./Diamètre des roues motrices: 1070 mm.
Weight/Masse: 47 tonnes.
Overall Length/Longeur hors tout: 12.10 m.
Max. Speed/Vitesse maximale: 80 km/h.

All fitted with regenerative brakes./ Toutes sont dotées du freinage à récupération
† Rebuilt with new cabs and fitted for push-pull & mw operation.
† Transformées avec nouvelles cabines et couplables en UM et dotées de la reversabilité.

601 † ALBULA
602 † BERNINA
603 † BADUS
604 CALANDA
605 † SILVRETTA
606 KESCH
607 † SURSELVA
608 † MADRISA
609 † LINARD
610 VIAMALA

CLASS/*SERIE* Ge4/4 II BoBo

The standard RhB electric, used throughout the ac system, fitted with thyristor control & dc motors.

La locomotive électrique standard du RhB, qui est utilisée partout sur le réseau principal. Dotées de thyristors et des moteurs à courant continu.

Built/Date de mise en service: 1973 (* 1984–5).
Builder-Mech. Parts/Constructeur-Partie mécanique: SLM.
Builder-Elec. Parts/Constructeur-Partie électrique: BBC.
Traction Motors: 4 pulsating current fully suspended with BBC spring drive.
Moteurs de traction: 4 moteurs à courant continu, entièrement suspendus avec transmission à ressorts BBC.

▼The last surviving RhB Class Ge4/6 No. 353 at Davos Platz on 25/06/89. *C.P. Boocock*

▼▼RhB Class Ge6/6 II No. 706 'Disentis/Muster' stands at Chur with a train for St. Moritz. Note that the body is in two halves articulated about a horizontal hinge at the bottom and the name is given first in German and then in Romansch. *C.P. Boocock*

▲▲La dernière survivante de la série Ge4/6 du RhB, la 353 est vue à Davos Platz. 25/06/89. *C.P. Boocock*

▲La Ge6/6 II 706 «Disentis/Muster» du RhB à Coire avec un train pour St. Moritz. Notez la caisse articulée et le nom en allemand et romanch. *C.P. Boocock*

One Hour Rating/Puissance horaire: 1648 kW.
Maximum Tractive Effort/Effort de traction max.: 179 kN.
Driving Wheel Dia./Diamètre des roues motrices: 1070 mm.
Weight/Masse: 50 tonnes.
Overall Length/Longeur hors tout: 12.96 m.
Max. Speed/Vitesse maximale: 90 km/h.

All fitted with regenerative brakes./Dotées du freinage à récupération.

611		LANDQUART	623	*	BONADUZ
612		THUSIS	624	*	CELERINA/SCHLARIGNA
613		DOMAT/EMS	625	*	KÜBLIS
614		SCHIERS	626	*	MALANS
615		KLOSTERS	627	*	REICHENAU–TAMINS
616		FILISUR	628	*	S-CHANF
617		ILANZ	629	*	TIEFENCASTEL
618		BERGÜN/BRAVUOGN	630	*	TRUN
619		SAMEDAN	631	*	UNTERVAZ
620		ZERNEZ	632	*	ZIZERS
621	*	FELSBERG	633	*	ZUOZ
622	*	AROSA			

CLASS/SERIE Ge4/4 III — BoBo

A new design of general purpose locomotive on order.
Un nouveau type de locomotive en commande.

Built/Date de mise en service: On order/En commande.
Builder-Mech. Parts/Constructeur-Partie mécanique: SLM.
Builder-Elec. Parts/Constructeur-Partie électrique: ABB.
Traction Motors:
Moteurs de traction:
One Hour Rating/Puissance horaire: 2500 kW.
Maximum Tractive Effort/Effort de traction max.: 200 kN.
Driving Wheel Dia./Diamètre des roues motrices: 1070 mm.
Weight/Masse: approx. 60 tonnes.
Overall Length/Longeur hors tout: 15.50 m.
Max. Speed/Vitesse maximale: 100 km/h.

641	642	643	644	645	646

CLASS/SERIE Ge6/6 — BoBoBo

Articulated locos, mainly used on heavy trains between Chur and St. Moritz. The two halves of the body are joined by a hinge with its axis horizontal; the centre bogie has some sideplay.

Des locomotives articulées qui sont utilisées pour remorquer des trains lourds entre Coire et St Moritz. Le bogie du centre dispose d'un certain débattement.

Built/Date de mise en service: 1958 *, 1965 †.
Builder-Mech. Parts/Constructeur-Partie mécanique: SLM.
Builder-Elec. Parts/Constructeur-Partie électrique: MFO/BBC.
Traction Motors: 6 single phase fully suspended with BBC spring drive.
Moteurs de traction: 6 moteurs à courant alternatif monophasé à collecteurs, entièrement suspendus avec transmission à ressorts BBC.
One Hour Rating/Puissance horaire: 1764 kW.
Maximum Tractive Effort/Effort de traction max.: 214 kN.
Driving Wheel Dia./Diamètre des roues motrices: 1070 mm.
Weight/Masse: 65 tonnes.
Overall Length/Longeur hors tout: 14.50 m.
Max. Speed/Vitesse maximale: 80 km/h.

701	*	RAETIA	705	†	PONTRESINA/PUNTRASCHIGNA
702	*	CURIA	706	†	DISENTIS/MUSTER
703	†	ST. MORITZ	707	†	SCUOL
704	†	DAVOS			

CLASS/SERIE Gem4/4 BoBo

These electro-diesels are the only main-line locos that can be used throughout the system. They operate as electrics on the Berninabahn and as diesel elsewhere. Used on the Bernina Express between Samedan and Tirano, on snowplough duties, and on works trains.

Ce sont des machines "amphibies" qui sont les seules à pouvoir parcourir tout le réseau RhB. Elles sont utlisées en mode électrique sur le BB et en diesel ailleurs. Elles remorquent le Bernina Express entre Samedan et Tirano, et en plus peuvent pousser des chasse-neige et remorquer des trains de travaux.

Built/Date de mise en service: 1968.
Builder-Mech. Parts/Constructeur-Partie mécanique: SLM.
Builder-Elec. Parts/Constructeur-Partie électrique: BBC/MFO/SAAS/Cummins.
Diesel Engines/Moteurs Diesel: 2 Cummins VT12-825B1 463 kW.
Moteurs de traction: 4 moteurs à courant alternatif monophasé à collecteurs, suspendus par le nez.
Traction Motors: 4 single phase axle hung nose suspended.
One Hour Rating/Puissance horaire: 680 kW (electric), 926 kW (diesel).
Maximum Tractive Effort/Effort de traction max.: 192 kN.
Driving Wheel Dia./Diamètre des roues motrices: 920 mm.
Weight/Masse: 50 tonnes.
Overall Length/Longeur hors tout: 13.54 m.
Max. Speed/Vitesse maximale: 65 km/h.

Fitted for mw operation; can also mw with ABe4/4 41–9 under electric traction only.
Couplables en UM entre eux et avec les Abe4/4 41 à 49 en mode électrique seulement.

801	STEINBOCK	802	MURMELTIER

ELECTRIC RAILCARS (MAIN SYSTEM)
AUTOMOTRICES ELECTRIQUES (RESEAU PRINCIPAL)
CLASS/SERIE ABe4/4

Used on local services in the Samedan area, operating with driving trailers BDt 1721–3.
Utilisées avec les voitures pilotes BDt 1721 à 3 pour des services locaux autour de Samedan.

Built/Date de mise en service: 1939–40.
Builder-Mech. Parts/Constructeur-Partie mécanique: SWS.
Builder-Elec. Parts/Constructeur-Partie électrique: BBC/MFO.
Traction Motors:
One Hour Rating/Puissance horaire: 440 kW.
Maximum Tractive Effort/Effort de traction max.: 78 kN.
Driving Wheel Dia./Diamètre des roues motrices: 850 mm.
Weight/Masse: 39 tonnes.
Overall Length/Longeur hors tout: 18.00 m.
Max. Speed/Vitesse maximale: 70 km/h.
Wheel Arrangement/Disposition des essieux: BoBo.
Accommodation/Aménagement intérieur: 12/28 1T.

501	502	503	504

CLASS/SERIE Be4/4

Single ended motor coaches (gangwayed at the non-driving end), used on local services around Chur, operating as 3-car sets with driving trailers ABD 1711–6 and intermediate trailers B2411–6. They are fitted with thyristor control, dc motors & electropneumatic brakes.

Motrices avec cabine de conduite à une extremité et porte d'intercirculation à l'autre. Formées en éléments de 3 caisses avec voitures pilotes ABD 1711 à 6 et remorques B 2411 à 6, elles sont utilisées pour des services locaux autour de Coire. Dotées de thyristors, moteurs à courant continu et du freinage électropneumatique.

Built/Date de mise en service: 1971 (* 1979).
Builder-Mech. Parts/Constructeur-Partie mécanique: FFA/SIG.
Builder-Elec. Parts/Constructeur-Partie électrique: SAAS.

Traction Motors:
One Hour Rating/Puissance horaire: 776 kW.
Maximum Tractive Effort/Effort de traction max.: 112 kN.
Driving Wheel Dia./Diamètre des roues motrices: 750 mm.
Weight/Masse: 44.6 tonnes.
Overall Length/Longeur hors tout: 18.70 m.
Max. Speed/Vitesse maximale: 90 km/h.
Wheel Arrangement/Disposition des essieux: BoBo.
Accommodation/Aménagement intérieur: –/40 1T.

511	512	513	514	515	*	516	*

STOCK OF DC BRANCHES
MATERIEL DES AUTRES LIGNES

CLASS/***SERIE*** ABe4/4 (BDe4/4*)

The survivors, all much rebuilt, of the original Berninabahn stock. Used on works duties and as reserve power, on the BB and ChA. Fitted with track brakes for street running in Chur and Tirano.

Les dernières survivantes, transformées en profondeur, des automotrices du Berninabahn. A part quelques trains de travaux, elles sont gardées en réserve pour les BB et ChA. Dotées de freins à patin pour les sections de voie dans les rues de Coire et Tirano.

Built/Date de mise en service: 1908–11.
Builder-Mech. Parts/Constructeur-Partie mécanique: SIG.
Builder-Elec. Parts/Constructeur-Partie électrique: SAAS (SAAS/MFO *§).
Traction Motors:
One Hour Rating/Puissance horaire: 382 kW (426 kW *§).
Maximum Tractive Effort/Effort de traction max.: 55 kN (57 kN *§).
Driving Wheel Dia./Diamètre des roues motrices: 850 mm.
Weight/Masse: 30 tonnes (31 tonnes †).
Overall Length/Longeur hors tout: 13.93 m (14.66 m *†).
Max. Speed/Vitesse maximale: 55 km/h.
Wheel Arrangement/Disposition des essieux: BoBo.
Accommodation/Aménagement intérieur: 12/27 (12/29 †, 12/31 §, –/36S*).

30	†	32	35	§	36	§	37	§	38 *
31		34							

CLASS/***SERIE*** ABe4/4

These railcars operate most trains on the Berninabahn.
Ces automotrices sont utilisées pour la plupart des trains sur le BB.

Built/Date de mise en service: 1964–5 (* 1972).
Builder-Mech. Parts/Constructeur-Partie mécanique: SWS.
Builder-Elec. Parts/Constructeur-Partie électrique: BBC/MFO/SAAS (*BBC/SAAS).
Traction Motors:
One Hour Rating/Puissance horaire: 680 kW.
Maximum Tractive Effort/Effort de traction max.: 156 kN.
Driving Wheel Dia./Diamètre des roues motrices: 920 mm.
Weight/Masse: 41 tonnes (43 tonnes *).
Overall Length/Longeur hors tout: 16.54 m (16.89 m *).
Max. Speed/Vitesse maximale: 65 km/h.
Wheel Arrangement/Disposition des essieux: BoBo.
Accommodation/Aménagement intérieur: 12/24.

mw & track brake fitted./Couplables en UM et dotées de freins à patin.

41	43	45	47	*	48	*	49 *
42	44	46					

▼RhB Class Be4/4 No. 514 (right) waits to leave Thusis with a stopping service to Chur as 'Baby Crocodile' Class Ge6/6 I (left) arrives with a freight from St. Moritz on 26/06/89. *C.P. Boocock*

▼RhB Bernina Line Class ABe4/4 No. 43 heading a train for Tirano during July 1988. *E.H. Sawford*

▲▲La Be4/4 514 du RhB (à droite) attend le départ de Thusis avec un service omnibus pour Coire alors qu'un «Bébé Crocodile» (à gauche) arrive avec un train de marchandises de St. Moritz. 26/06/89. *C.P. Boocock*

▲La ABe4/4 43 de la ligne de Bernina du RhB remorque un train à destination de Tirano en Juillet 1988. *E.H. Sawford*

CLASS/SERIE ABe4/4

New railcars built to supplement 41–9.
Six nouvelles automotrices pour utiliser avec les 41 à 49.

Built: 1987 (51–3), 1990 (54–6).
Construction: 1987 (51 à 53) ou en commande (54 à 56)
Builder-Mech. Parts/Constructeur-Partie mécanique: SWA.
Builder-Elec. Parts/Constructeur-Partie électrique: ABB.
Traction Motors:
One Hour Rating/Puissance horaire: 1016 kW.
Maximum Tractive Effort/Effort de traction max.: 178 kN.
Driving Wheel Dia./Diamètre des roues motrices: mm.
Weight/Masse: 47 tonnes.
Overall Length/Longeur hors tout: 16.90 m.
Max. Speed/Vitesse maximale: 65 km/h.
Wheel Arrangement/Disposition des essieux: BoBo.
Accommodation/Aménagement intérieur: 12/16.

mw & track brake fitted./Couplables en UM et dotées de freins à patin.

51	POSCHIAVO	53	TIRANO	55
52	BRUSIO	54		56

CLASS/SERIE De2/2

An ex-BB motor luggage van, much rebuilt and now used for shunting at Campocologno.

Un fourgon automoteur ex BB qui fut transformé en profondeur. Utilisé maintenant pour des manoeuvres à Campocologno.

Built/Date de mise en service: 1909, rebuilt/transformé 1980.
Builder-Mech. Parts/Constructeur-Partie mécanique: SIG.
Builder-Elec. Parts/Constructeur-Partie électrique: Alioth.
Traction Motors:
One Hour Rating/Puissance horaire: 147 kW.
Maximum Tractive Effort/Effort de traction max.: kN.
Driving Wheel Dia./Diamètre des roues motrices: 850 mm.
Weight/Masse: 14 tonnes.
Overall Length/Longeur hors tout: 7.15 m.
Max. Speed/Vitesse maximale: 45 km/h.
Wheel Arrangement/Disposition des essieux: Bo.

151

CLASS/SERIE Ge2/2

A pair of ex-BB electric locos, normally used for shunting around Poschiavo.
Deux locomotives électriques ex BB. Utilisées normalement pour des manoeuvres autour de Poschiavo.

Built/Date de mise en service: 1911.
Builder-Mech. Parts/Constructeur-Partie mécanique: SIG.
Builder-Elec. Parts/Constructeur-Partie électrique: Alioth.
Traction Motors:
One Hour Rating/Puissance horaire: 242 kW.
Maximum Tractive Effort/Effort de traction max.: kN.
Driving Wheel Dia./Diamètre des roues motrices: 975 mm.
Weight/Masse: 16 tonnes (18 tonnes*).
Overall Length/Longeur hors tout: 7.72 m.
Max. Speed/Vitesse maximale: 45 km/h.
Wheel Arrangement/Disposition des essieux: Bo.

161	162 *

CLASS/SERIE ABDe4/4 (ABe4/4*, BDe4/4†)

481–8 are the normal motive power on the Chur–Arosa line, while 491 is the last remaining RhB car on the Bellinzona–Mesocco line (the reserve car here is a hired AB car). When the

Chur–Arosa line is converted to ac, 481–6 will be withdrawn, and 487–8 rebuilt to driving trailers.

La série 481–488 assure l'essentiel de la traction sur la ligne Coire–Arosa. La 491 est la seule automotrice RhB qui subsiste sur la ligne Bellinzone–Mesocco (l'automotrice de réserve est louée au AB). Dès que la ligne Coire–Arosa sera convertie à 11kV monophasé, les 481–486 seront radiées et les 487–488 seront transformées en voitures pilotes.

Built/Date de mise en service: 1957–8 (* 1973).
Builder-Mech. Parts/Constructeur-Partie mécanique: SWS.
Builder-Elec. Parts/Constructeur-Partie électrique: BBC (BBC/SAAS *).
Traction Motors:
One Hour Rating/Puissance horaire: 500 kW (676 kW †).
Maximum Tractive Effort/Effort de traction max.: 113 kN.
Driving Wheel Dia./Diamètre des roues motrices: 920 mm.
Weight/Masse: 43 tonnes (45 tonnes*, 41 tonnes†).
Overall Length/Longeur hors tout: 17.70 m. (16.70 m *).
Max. Speed/Vitesse maximale: 65 km/h.
Fitted with track brakes./Dotées de freins à patin.

481	483	485	487 *	488 *	491 †
482	484	486			

◀RhB Class Te2/2 No. 73 shunts at Thusis on 26/06/89. *C.P. Boocock*

◀Le Te2/2 73 du RhB à Thusis. 26/06/89. *C.P. Boocock*

◀RhB Class Xm2/2 inspection vehicle No. 9917 standing at Filisur on 26/06/89. *C.P. Boocock*

◀Voiture d'inspection du RhB, la Xm2/2 9917 est vue à Filisur. 26/06/89. *C.P. Boocock*

TRACTORS/SNOWPLOUGHS, ETC
LOCOTRACTEURS, CHASSES-NEIGE, ETC.

As with other Swiss railways, the RhB owns a selection of tractors and snowploughs, plus an assortment of other departmental motive power. 9213–4 are self-propelled steam rotary snowploughs, still occasionally used at times of severe weather.

Comme les autres chemins de fer suisses, le RhB a une sélection de locotracteurs et de chasse-neige, plus un assortiment d'autre matériel de service. 9213–4 sont des chasses-neige à vapeur autopropulsés qui sont utilisés ponctuellement par très mauvais temps.

Tm2/2	56	RACO/SLM	30	9	41	1969
Tm2/2	57	RACO/SLM	30	9	41	1965
Tm2/2	58	RACO/SLM	30	9	41	1965
Tm2/2	59	RACO/SLM	30	9	41	1965
Tm2/2	60	RACO/SLM	30	9	41	1965
Tm2/2	61	RACO/SLM	30	9	41	1965
Tm2/2	62	RACO/SLM	30	9	41	1962
Tm2/2	63	RACO/SLM	30	9	41	1962
Tm2/2	64	RACO/SLM	30	9	37	1957
Tm2/2	65	RACO/SLM	30	9	37	1957
Tm2/2	66	RACO/SLM	30	9	37	1957
Tm2/2	67	RACO/SLM	30	9	37	1957
Tm2/2	68	RACO/SAU/SCIN	20	3.5	19	1948
Te2/2	71	SLM/SAAS	30	13	97	1946
Te2/2	72	SLM/SAAS	30	13	97	1946
Te2/2	73	SLM/SAAS	30	13	97	1946
Te2/2	74	SE/GSEG	50	24	216	1969
Te2/2	75	SE/GSEG	50	24	216	1969
Ta1/2	80	WIND	3.9	9.2	6	1980
Tm2/2	81	RACO/RhB	50	24	336	1987
Tm2/2	82	RACO/RhB	50	24	336	1987
Tm2/2	83	RACO/RhB	50	24	336	1987
Tm2/2	84	RACO/RhB	50	24	336	1987
Tm2/2	85	RACO/RhB	50	24	336	1990
Tm2/2	86	RACO/RhB	50	24	336	1990
Tm2/2	87	RACO/RhB	50	24	336	1990
Tm2/2	88	RACO/RhB	50	24	336	1990
Tm2/2	89	RACO/RhB	50	24	336	1990
Tm2/2	91	RACO/SAU	40	10.5	48	1959
Tm2/2	92	RACO/SAU	40	10.5	48	1959
Tm2/2	93	SCH/DZ	35	21	172	1971
Xrotd6/6	9213	SLM	36	63.5	-	1910
Xrotd6/6	9214	SLM	36	64	-	1912
Xrote	9215	SIG/DMG/PUCH/RhB	36	21.5	74	1908
Xrotm	9216	RACO/BEIL	55	15	164	1958
Xrotmt	9217	BEIL/JMR/DZ	55	38	670	1981
Xrotet	9218	RACO/BEIL	55	24	522	1967
Xrotet	9219	RACO/BEIL	55	24	522	1967
Xm2/2	9912	RACO/SAU	30	10	41	1962
Xm2/2	9913	DMG/PUCH/SAU	35	10.4	48	1934
Xm2/2	9914	RhB/SAU/MFO	55	19	112	1950
Xm2/2	9915	PFING/SAU/MFO	55	20	112	1958
Xm2/2	9916	RACO/NEN/DZ	40	13	100	1963
Xm2/2	9917	STAD/RhB/DZ	55	27	224	1974
Xm2/2	9918					1990
Xe4/4	9920	SIG/Alioth	45	31	298	1908

▼Appenzellerbahnen (ex-AB) Class ABe4/4 No. 41 stands at Herisau on 30/01/89.
Paul Russenberger

▼▼Appenzellerbahnen (ex-SGA) Class ABDeh4/4 No. 5 stands at Heirsau in the older SGA green and cream livery on 07/04/86. *G.B. Wise*

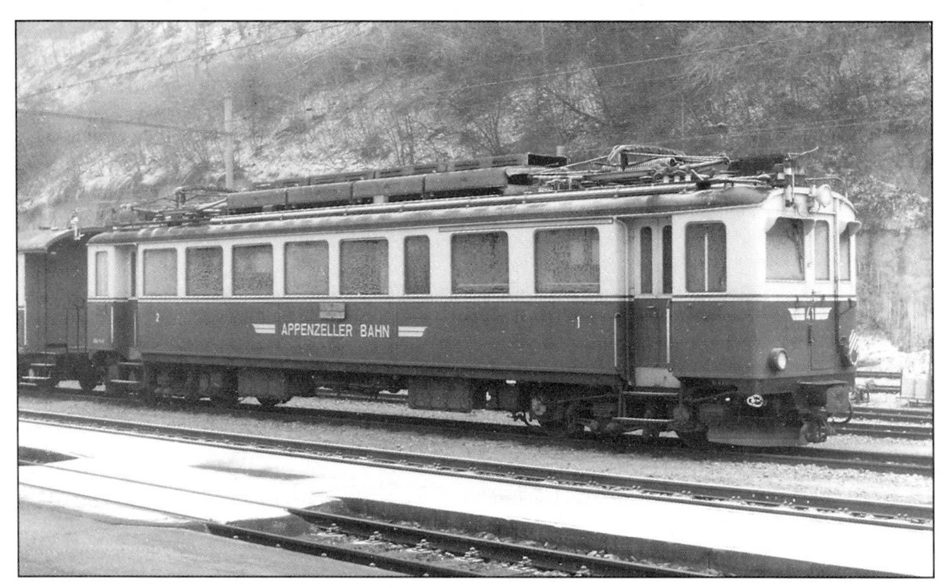

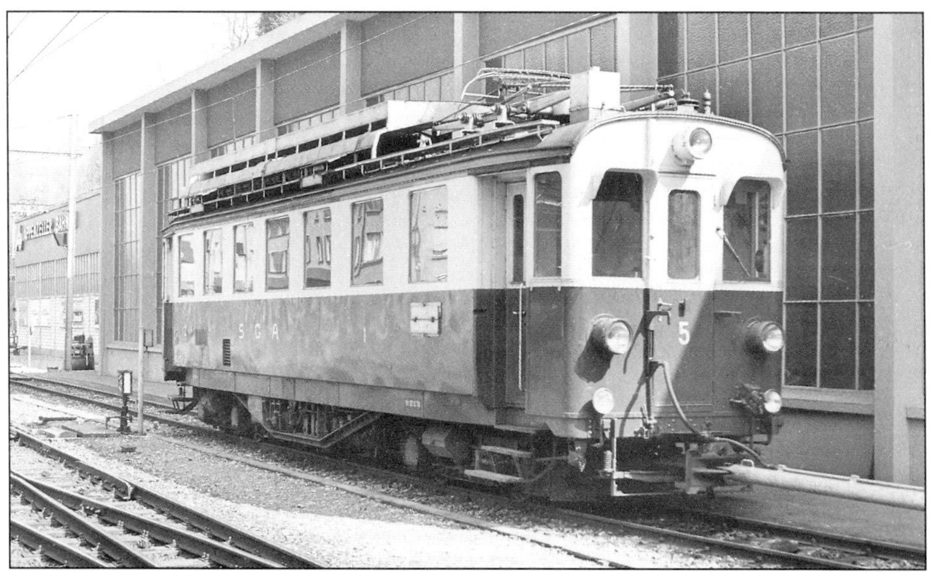

▲▲La ABe4/4 41 du Appenzellerbahnen (anciennement du AB) à Herisau. 30/01/89.
Paul Russenberger

▲La ABDeh4/4 5 du Appenzellerbahnen (anciennement du SGA), dans l'ancienne livrée vert et crème du SGA, à Herisau. 07/04/86. *G.B. Wise*

APPENZELLERBAHNEN (854, 855, 856) AB

After many years of common management, the Appenzellbahn (AB) and St Gallen–Gais–Appenzell (SGA) merged in 1988 to form the Appenzellerbahnen. The former SGA is partly rack and some of the latest stock is intended for operation throughout the system.

Après plusieurs années de gestion commune, le Appenzellbahn (AB) et le St Gallen Gais Appenzell (SGA) ont fusionnés en 1988 pour devenir le Appenzellerbahnen. L'ancien SGA a des sections à crémaillère et le dernier matériel est conçu pour être exploité en adhèrence ou à crémaillère.

Gauge/Ecartement: 1000 mm.
Electrical System/Courant: 1500 V dc/continu.
Depots/Dépôts: Gais, Herisau, Wasserauen, Appenzell.

Class *Série*	*No.* *No*	*Name* *Nom*	*Builder* *Constructeur*	*Seats* *Places*	*km/h* *km/h*	*Tonnes* *Tonnes*	*kW* *kW*	*Built* *Date*
ABDeh4/4	1		SLM/SIG/BBC	6/39	40/24	40	450	1931
ABDeh4/4	2		SLM/SIG/BBC	6/39	40/24	40	450	1931
ABDeh4/4	4		SLM/SIG/BBC	6/39	40/24	40	450	1931
ABDeh4/4	5		SLM/SIG/BBC	6/39	40/24	40	450	1931
ABDeh4/4	6	ALTSTÄTTEN	SLM/BBC	6/32	55/25	35.6	480	1953
ABDeh4/4	7		SLM/BBC	6/32	55/25	35.6	480	1953
ABDeh4/4	8		SLM/BBC	6/32	55/25	35.6	480	1953
BDeh4/4	11	ST GALLEN	FFA/SLM/BBC	40	65/40	44.5	830	1981
BDeh4/4	12	TEUFEN	FFA/SLM/BBC	40	65/40	44.5	830	1981
BDeh4/4	13	BÜHLER	FFA/SLM/BBC	40	65/40	44.5	830	1981
BDeh4/4	14	GAIS	FFA/SLM/BBC	40	65/40	44.5	830	1981
BDeh4/4	15	APPENZELL	FFA/SLM/BBC	40	65/40	44.5	830	1981
Xe2/3	17		SLM/SIG/Alioth	16	35	20.4	90	1911
BDe4/4	31	GOSSAU	FFA/SIG/BBC	39		36		1985
BDe4/4	32	HERISAU	FFA/SIG/BBC	39		36		1985
BDe4/4	33	GONTEN	FFA/SIG/BBC	39		36		1985
ABe4/4	41		SIG/MFO	12/40	65	34.2	455	1933
ABe4/4	42		SIG/MFO	12/40	65	34.2	455	1933
ABe4/4	43		SIG/MFO	12/40	65	34.2	455	1933
ABe4/4	44		SIG/MFO	14/34	65	35	515	1949
ABe4/4	45		SIG/MFO	14/34	65	35	515	1949
BDe4/4	46	WALDSTATT	FFA/SIG/BBC	32	65	37.8	565	1968
BDe4/4	47	URNÄSCH	FFA/SIG/BBC	32	65	37.8	565	1968
Te2/2	49		SWS/MFO/AB	-	45	12	95	1955
De4/4	50		FFA/MFO/AB	-	65	32.5	455	1966
Xm1/2	51		SWS/SIG/SAU/AB	-	45	15	75	1962
ABDm2/4	56		SIG/SZ/MFO	6/24	50	32	185	1929
Xrotm2/2	99		RACO/BEIL/DZ	-	30	18	150	1974
Tm2/2	501		OK/LMG	-	18	18.5	105	1957

On order/En commande 2 BDe4/4, 2 BDeh4/4, 1 De4/4

AIGLE–LEYSIN (125) AL

This railway is under common management with the AOMC, ASD and BVB as the Transports Publics du Chablais (TPC). The differing electrical and rack systems prevent full integration. The AL has street running in Aigle and then climbs steeply with rack assistance.

Cette compagnie est gérée par les Transports Publics du Chablais (TPC) qui gère aussi les AOMC, ASD et BVB. Les quatre réseaux ne peuvent pas être intégrés à cause de leurs différents systèmes d'électrification et de crémaillères. Le AL traverse la ville d'Aigle avec la voie établie sur route et puis grimpe abruptement à l'aide d'une crémaillère.

Gauge/Ecartement: 1000 mm.
Electrical System/Courant: 1300 V dc/continu.
Depots/Dépôts: Aigle, Leysin Feydey.

He2/2	12		SLM/MFO/SIG	-	7.5	20.3	264	1915
Te2/2	101		ACMV/AL/BBC	-	20	11.6	82	1949
BDeh2/4	201		SLM/BBC	48	25/15	24.5	250	1946

Appenzellerbahnen (ex-SGA) Class ABDeh4/4 No. 8 arrives ar Appenzell with the 10.56 from St. Gallen in the St. Gallen–Gais–Appenzell red and white livery on 07/04/86. *G.B. Wise*

La ABDeh4/4 8 du Appenzellerbahnen (anciennement du SGA) arrive à Appenzell avec un train de St. Gall. Elle porte la livrée rouge et blanc de l'ancien SGA. 07/04/86. *G.B. Wise*

BDeh2/4	202		SLM/BBC	48	25/15	24.5	250	1946
BDeh2/4	203		SLM/BBC	48	25/15	24.5	250	1946
BDeh4/4	301		SIG/SAAS	48	40/24	33	596	1966
BDeh4/4	302		SIG/SAAS	48	40/24	33	596	1966
BDeh4/4	303	YVORNE	ACMV/SLM/BBC	32	40/25	36	752	1987
BDeh4/4	304	OLLON	ACMV/SLM/BBC	32	40/25	36	752	1987

AIGLE–OLLON–MONTHEY–CHAMPERY (126) AOMC

Really two separate lines radiating from Monthey, only the line to Champéry has rack sections. Hence the adhesion only cars are restricted to the Aigle line.

En réalité deux lignes distinctes qui commencent à Monthey. Seule la ligne de Champéry a des sections à crémaillère. Les automotrices sans crémaillère sont alors limitées à la ligne d'Aigle.

Gauge/Ecartement: 1000 mm.
Electrical System/Courant: 850 V dc/continu.
Depot/Dépôt: Monthey.

BDeh4/4	1	VAUD	ACMV/SLM/BBC	32	65/30	40	600	1987
BDeh4/4	2	VALAIS	ACMV/SLM/BBC	32	65/30	40	600	1987
BDeh4/4	11	LA HAUTE CIME	SWP/BBC	40	50/18	30.4	368	1954
BDeh4/4	12	LA CIME DE L'EST	SWP/BBC	40	50/18	30.4	368	1954
BDeh4/4	13	LES DENTS BLANCHES	SWP/BBC	40	50/18	30.4	368	1954
BDeh4/4	14	LES DENTS DE MORCLES	SWP/BBC	40	50/18	30.4	368	1954
Be4/4	101		SWP/BBC	44	65	27	382	1966
Be4/4	102		SWP/BBC	44	65	27	382	1966
Be4/4	103		SWP/BBC	44	65	27	382	1966
Be4/4	104		SWP/BBC	44	65	27	382	1966
Be4/4	105		SWP/BBC	44	65	27	382	1966

ARTH RIGI BAHN (602) ARB

A pure rack line starting from above Arth Goldau SBB station and running side by side with the VRB at the summit of the Rigi mountain.

Une ligne purement à crémaillère qui commence au-dessus de la gare CFF d'Arth Goldau et qui longe le VRB au sommet du Mont Rigi.

Gauge/Ecartement: 1435 mm.
Electrical System/Courant: 1500 V dc/continu.
Depots/Dépôts: Arth Goldau, Rigi Kulm.

BDhe2/3	6	SWS/MFO	60	15	23.5	395	1911
BDhe2/4	7	SIG/MFO	60	15	25.5	455	1925
He2/3	8	SLM/MFO	-	15	30.4	455	1930
BDhe2/4	11	SLM/SAAS	60	21	26.5	485	1949
BDhe2/4	12	SLM/SAAS	60	21	26.5	485	1949
BDhe2/4	13	SLM/SAAS	60	21	26.5	485	1954
BDhe2/4	14	SLM/SAAS	60	21	26.5	485	1967
Bhe4/4	15	SLM/BBC	60	18.6	30.3	835	1982

AIGLE–SEPEY–DIABLERETS (124) ASD

Recently under threat of closure, this line has now been modernised. The original 1913 stock operated all services until delivery of the new ACMV cars.

Après des menaces de fermeture jusqu'à récemment, cette ligne est en cours de modernisation. Les automotrices de 1913 eurent le monopole des services jusqu'à la livraison des nouvelles voitures ACMV.

Gauge/Ecartement: 1000 mm.
Electrical System/Courant: 1350 V dc/continu.
Depots/Dépôts: Aigle, Les Diablerets.

ABDe4/4	1		SWS/BBC	8/32	50	25	240	1913
ABDe4/4	2		SWS/BBC	8/32	50	25	240	1913
ABDe4/4	11		SWS/BBC	8/32	50	25	240	1913
BDe4/4	401	ORMONT DESSOUS	ACMV/SIG/SLM/BBC	32	65	32.5	724	1987

BDe4/4	402	ORMONT DESSUS	ACMV/SIG/SLM/BBC	32	65	32.5	724	1987
BDe4/4	403	OLLON	ACMV/SIG/SLM/BBC	32	65	32.5	724	1987
BDe4/4	404	AIGLE	ACMV/SIG/SLM/BBC	32	65	32.5	724	1987

BIÈRE–APPLES–MORGES (156) BAM

Unusually for Switzerland, this light railway is electrified on high voltage ac. Once threatened with closure, new cars were delivered a few years ago. Car 14 was originally 13, renumbered for superstitious reasons!

Cette ligne à intérêt local est électrifiée en monophasé, ce qui est insolite en Suisse. Menacée de fermeture il y a quelques années, la ligne s'est dotée récemment de voitures modernes. L'automotrice 14 fut numérotée 13 à l'origine. On a changé le numéro pour des raisons de supersticion.

Gauge/Ecartement: 1000 mm.
Electrical System/Courant: 15 kV 16⅔ Hz ac/monophasé.
Depots/Dépôts: Bière, L'Isle.

BDe4/4	1		SWS/SAAS	40	65	36	500	1943
BDe4/4	2		SWS/SAAS	40	65	36	500	1943
BDe4/4	3		SWS/SAAS	40	65	36	500	1943
BDe4/4	4		SWS/SAAS	40	65	36	500	1943
BDe4/4	5		SWS/SAAS	40	65	37	500	1949
Be4/4	11		ACMV/HESS/BBC	40		44.5	780	1981
Be4/4	12		ACMV/HESS/BBC	40		44.5	780	1981
Be4/4	14		ACMV/HESS/BBC	40		44.5	780	1981
Tm2/2	–		RACO		–		310	

BREMGARTEN–DIETIKON (654) BD
WOHLEN–MEISTERSCHWANDEN (654) WM

Two railways under common management but with totally different characteristics. The BD is a metre gauge light railway with mostly roadside running. The line continues from Bremgarten to Wohlen as mixed gauge, BD standard gauge diesels hauling freight on this section. The WM is a short standard gauge branch, under threat of closure to passengers recently, although this threat now seems to have receded.

Ces deux compagnies sont gérées en commun mais ont des charactéristiques complètement différentes. Le BD est un chemin de fer d'interet local à écartement métrique, construit en accotement de chaussée. Cette ligne continue de Bremgarten à Wohlen avec une voie à écartement mixte. Les diesels BD à écartement normal remorquent des marchandises sur cette section. Le WM est une courte ligne à écartement normal, qui fut récemment menacée de fermeture au trafic voyageurs, bien que cette menace semble s'éloigner maintenant.

Gauge/Ecartement: 1000 mm (Bremgarten West–Dietikon), mixed/mixte 1000/1435 mm (Wohlen–Bremgarten West), 1435 mm (WM, Wohlen–Fahrwangen–Meisterschwanden).
Electrical System/Courant: 1200 V dc/continu (BD), 15 kV, 16⅔ Hz ac/monophasé (WM).
Depots/Dépôts: Bremgarten (BD, 1000 mm), Bremgarten West (BD, 1435 mm), Fahrwangen, Meisterschwanden (WM).

Metre Gauge Stock/Matériel Metrique: (all BD/tout BD).

BDe8/8	1	KANTON AARGAU	SWS/MFO	93	70	50.5	580	1969
BDe8/8	2	KANTON ZÜRICH	SWS/MFO	93	70	50.5	580	1969
BDe8/8	3	WOHLEN	SWS/MFO	93	70	50.5	580	1969
BDe8/8	4	BREMGARTEN	SWS/MFO	93	70	50.5	580	1969
BDe8/8	5	ZUFIKON	SWS/MFO	93	70	50.5	580	1969
BDe8/8	6	BERIKON	SWS/MFO	93	70	50.5	580	1969
BDe8/8	7	WIDEN	SWS/MFO	93	70	50.5	580	1969
BDe8/8	8	RUDOLFSTETTEN	SWS/MFO	93	70	50.5	580	1969
BDe8/8	9	DIETIKON	SWS/MFO	93	70	50.5	580	1969
BDre4/4	10		SWS/MFO		45	32	172	1928
BDe4/4	11		SWS/MFO	24	45	32	172	1932
Tm2/2	51		STAD/BBC/SAU	–	50	13	88	1967
Tm2/2	52		STAD/BBC/SAU	–	50	13	88	1968

On order: 5 Be4/8 from SIG/ABB, due 1992 (90 km/h, 600 kW).
En commande: 5 Be4/8 de SIG/ABB, pour livraison en 1992 (90 km/h, 600 kW).

Standard Gauge Stock/Matériel Normal:

WM:

BDe4/4	1		SIG/SWS/SAAS/BBC/MFO	48	100	63	1076	1966
BDe4/4	2		SIG/SWS/SAAS/BBC/MFO	48	100	63	1076	1966
BDe2/4	3		SWS/SAAS	60	75	39.5	330	1938
Em2/2	101		SIG/BBC/SAU	–	55	38	243	1961
Em4/4	151	HANS REY	CEM/POY	–	55	72	442	1968
Ta2/2	-		BBC	–	15	9.9	9	1915

BD

Em2/2	102		SIG/BBC/SAU	–	55	38	243	1966
Em2/2	103		STAD/HESS/MB/GM/BBC	–	80	39.5	700	1984

BERGBAHN LAUTERBRUNNEN MÜRREN (313) BLM

Under common management with the BOB, JB, SPB & WAB, the BLM runs from Grütschalp (where there is a funicular connection from Lauterbrunnen) to Mürren. The line runs along a mountain ledge, serving an area with no road access.

Le BLM est une ligne de Grütschalp (où il existe une correspondance pour Lauterbrunnen en funiculaire) à Mürren qui est gérée en commun avec les BOB, JB, SPB et WAB. La ligne longe une crête montagneuse et dessert une région inaccessible par route.

Gauge/Ecartement: 1000 mm.
Electrical System/Courant: 550 V dc/continu.
Depot/Dépôt: Grütschalp.

BDe2/4	11	SIG/MFO	40	25	17.5	100	1913
Be4/4	21	SIG/BBC/SAAS	48	30	25	200	1967
Be4/4	22	SIG/BBC/SAAS	48	30	25	200	1967
Be4/4	23	SIG/BBC/SAAS	48	30	25	200	1967
Xrotm	25	PETER/FORD	–	25	5	125	1956

BERNER OBERLAND BAHNEN (311,312) BOB

This line runs from Interlaken to Lauterbrunnen and Grindelwald, at both of which connections are made with the WAB. There are rack sections beyond Zweilütschinen on both routes.

Cette ligne va de Interlaken Ost à Lauterbrunnen et à Grindelwald où il existe des correspondances avec le WAB. Il y a des sections à crémaillère au-delà de Zweilütschinen sur les deux routes.

Gauge/Ecartement: 1000 mm.
Electrical System/Courant: 1500 V dc/continu.
Depot/Dépôt: Zweilütschinen.

Tm2/2	1	CHRIGEL	STAD/SAU/BBC/MFO	–	30	15	110	1946
HGe3/3	24		SLM/BBC/MFO	–	45/15	35.6	294	1914
HGe3/3	29		SLM/MFO	–	45/15	36.5	300	1926
HGm2/2	31		STECK/SLM/DZ	–	30	20	283	1985
ABDeh4/4	301		SLM/BBC	10/32	70/30	40	632	1949
ABDeh4/4	302		SLM/BBC	10/32	70/30	40	632	1949
ABDeh4/4	303		SLM/BBC	10/32	70/30	40	632	1949
ABeh4/4	304		SLM/SIG/BBC	12/32	60/30	44	1000	1965
ABeh4/4	305		SLM/SIG/BBC	12/32	60/30	44	1000	1965
ABeh4/4	306		SLM/SIG/BBC	12/32	60/30	44	1000	1965
ABeh4/4	307		SLM/SIG/BBC	12/32	60/30	44	1000	1965
ABeh4/4	308		SLM/SIG/BBC	12/32	60/30	44	1000	1965
ABeh4/4	309		SLM/SIG/BBC	12/32	60/30	44	1000	1979
ABeh4/4	310		SLM/SIG/BBC	12/32	60/30	44	1000	1979
ABeh4/4 II	311	GRINDELWALD	SLM/BBC	12/24	70/30	45	1256	1986
ABeh4/4 II	312	INTERLAKEN	SLM/BBC	12/24	70/30	45	1256	1986
ABeh4/4 II	313	LAUTERBRUNNEN	SLM/BBC	12/24	70/30	45	1256	1986

BT Class RBDe4/4 No. 76 'LICHTENSTEIG' at the station of the same name on a Rapperswil–St. Gallen–Romanshorn working on 07/10/87. *Graham Scott-Lowe*

La RBDe4/4 76 du BT «LICHTENSTEIG» à le gare du même nom avec un train Rapperswil–St. Gall–Romanshorn. 07/10/87. *Graham Scott-Lowe*

BRIENZER–ROTHORN BAHN (475) BRB

One of the few non-electrified lines in Switzerland, the BRB was entirely steam operated until diesel locos were introduced to augment the fleet in the 1970s. However, most trains remain steam, and the railway has now ordered two new steam locos from SLM! The line is pure rack, and boasts the greatest height difference between lowest and highest stations of any Swiss railway.

Le BRB est une des rares lignes non-électrifiées en Suisse, et fut entièrement exploité en traction à vapeur jusqu'à l'introduction de locomotives diesel dans les années 70. Cependant, la plupart des trains sont toujours à vapeur et la compagnie vient de passer une commande pour deux machines à vapeur au SLM ! La ligne est totalement à crémaillère et se distingue par la plus grande différence d'altitude entre les deux terminus en Suisse.

Gauge/Ecartement: 800 mm.
Depot/Dépôt: Brienz.

HII/3	1		SLM	–	9.5	17		1892
HII/3	2		SLM	–	9.5	17		1891
HII/3	3		SLM	–	9.5	17		1892
HII/3	4		SLM	–	9.5	17		1892
HII/3	5		SLM	–	9.5	17		1891
HII/3	6		SLM	–	9.5	20		1933
HII/3	7		SLM	–	9.5	20		1936
Hm2/2	8		RC/BÜH/CAT/PLEI/MG	–	14	12.3	415	1973
Hm2/2	9		STECK/MTU/BIBUS	–	14	13.5	485	1975
Hm2/2	10		STECK/MTU/BIBUS	–	14	13.5	485	1975
Hm2/2	11	OIGAWA	STECK/BOWIL	–				1987
HII/3	12		SLM	–				1992
HII/3	13		SLM	–				1993

100 years old – and still running! BRB Class H2/3 No. 5 rests at Rothorn Kulm on 06/10/85. *E.H. Sawford*

100 ans et toujours en service! La H2/3 5 du BRB à Rothorn Kulm. 06/10/85. *E.H. Sawford*

BODENSEE TOGGENBURG (853, 870) BT

This railway forms the eastern section of the Luzern to Romanshorn route, some services hence being jointly operated with the SBB and the SOB. A joint BT/SBB Wil to Nesslau service also operates.

Ce chemin de fer constitue la partie orientale de la route Lucerne-Romanshorn et certains trains sont alors exploités en commun avec les CFF et le SOB. Le service Wil-Nesslau est aussi exploité en commun par le BT et les CFF.

Gauge/Ecartement: 1435 mm.
Electrical System/Courant: 15 kV 16⅔ Hz ac/monophasé.
Depots/Dépôts: Herisau, Nesslau-Neu St Johann.

Tm2/2	1		RACO/SAU	-	45	10	70	1962
Tm2/2	2		RACO/SAU	-	45	10	70	1964
Tm2/2	4	HERCULES	RACO/DZ	-	80	18	200	1977
Tm2/2	5		SLM/SAU	-	45	10	70	1925
TmIV	6	MAX	SLM/MAN	-	60	30	280	1971
TmIV	7	MORITZ	SLM/MAN	-	60	30	280	1973
Tm2/2	8*		RACO/HÜR	-	45	7	22	1937
Tm2/2	10	ANTONIO	SIG/BBC/SAU	-	55	38	243	1960
Be4/4	11		SLM/SAAS	-	80	66	1180	1931
Be4/4	12		SLM/SAAS	-	80	66	1180	1931
Te III	35		SLM/MFO	–	65	28	239	1966
BDe2/4	41		SLM/SIG/SAAS	48	90	59	590	1932
BDe2/4	42		SLM/SIG/SAAS	48	90	58	590	1932
Be3/4	43	TINO	SIG/SAAS	46	80	68	885	1938
BDe4/4	50	EGNACH	SIG/BBC	32	110	70	2100	1960
BDe4/4	51	EBNAT–KAPPEL	SIG/BBC	32	110	73	2100	1966
BDe4/4	52	KRUMENTAL	SIG/BBC	32	110	73	2100	1966
BDe4/4	53	NESSLAU	SIG/BBC	32	110	73	2100	1967
RBDe4/4	71	MUOLEN	FFA/SIG/BBC	48	125	71	1700	1982
RBDe4/4	72	HÄGGENSCHWIL	FFA/SIG/BBC	48	125	71	1700	1982
RBDe4/4	73	ROGGWIL–BERG	FFA/SIG/BBC	48	125	71	1700	1982
RBDe4/4	74	MOGELSBERG	FFA/SIG/BBC	48	125	71	1700	1982
RBDe4/4	75	BRUNNADERN	FFA/SIG/BBC	48	125	71	1700	1982
RBDe4/4	76	LICHTENSTEIG	FFA/SIG/BBC	48	125	71	1700	1982
Re4/4	91	ROMANSHORN	SLM/BBC	-	130	68	3200	1987
Re4/4	92	WITTENBACH	SLM/BBC	-	130	68	3200	1987
Re4/4	93	ST GALLEN	SLM/BBC	-	130	68	3200	1987
Re4/4	94	HERISAU	SLM/BBC	-	130	68	3200	1987
Re4/4	95	DEGERSHEIM	SLM/BBC	-	130	68	3200	1988
Re4/4	96	WATTWIL	SLM/BBC	-	130	68	3200	1988

* ex SBB/CFF 533

BEX–VILLARS–BRETAYE (127, 128, 129) BVB

This rack and adhesion line is normally run in two sections, Bex–Villars and Villars–Bretaye. In addition, there is a local tram service from Bex to Bévieux which meets most SBB trains at Bex.

Cette ligne avec sections à crémaillère est normalement exploitée en deux parties, Bex–Villars et Villars–Col de Bretaye. En plus, il existe un service de tramway local de Bex à Bévieux qui offre une correspondance avec la plupart des trains CFF à Bex.

Gauge/Ecartement: 1000 mm.
Electrical System/Courant: 700 V dc/continu.
Depots/Dépôts: Bévieux, Villars.

He2/2	2	SLM/IEG	-	10	14.8	162	1900
Be2/2	8	SWS/MFO	18	35	12.7	108	1907
Be2/2	9	SWS/MFO	20	37	15	108	1915
Be2/3	15	SWS/SLM/MFO	28	40	15	96	1948
Be2/3	16	SWS/SLM/MFO	28	40	15	96	1948
BDeh2/4	21	SLM/MFO	53	35/18	19	96	1940
BDeh2/4	22	SLM/MFO	53	35/18	19	96	1940

BDeh2/4	23	SLM/MFO	53	35/18	19	96	1941
BDeh2/4	24	SLM/MFO	53	35/18	19	96	1941
BDeh2/4	25	SLM/MFO	53	35/18	19	96	1944
BDeh2/4	26	SLM/MFO	53	35/18	19	96	1945
HGe4/4	31	SIG/MFO	-	35	24.4	368	1953
HGe4/4	32	SIG/MFO	-	35	24.4	368	1964
Te2/2	42	SIG/BVB/ACEC/MFO	-	35	8.5	108	1898
BDeh4/4	81	SLM/SWP/SAAS	24	40/16	36.5	720	1977
BDeh4/4	82	SLM/SWP/SAAS	24	40/16	36.5	720	1977
BDeh4/4	83	ACMV/SLM/BBC	24	40/25	37	652	1987
Xrote	313						
Xe4/4	1501	SWS/BBC	-	35	15	148	1941

BRIG–VISP–ZERMATT (140, 141) BVZ

This line provides the transport link to Zermatt to which road traffic is not permitted. Hence, in addition to the main service from Brig, there is a frequent shuttle service from Täsch (the end of the valley road) to Zermatt. Through coaches also operate to Chur & St Moritz via the FO & RhB.

Cette ligne assure le lien avec Zermatt où la circulation routière est interdite. Il existe alors, mis à part le service principal Brigue–Zermatt, une navette fréquente entre Täsch (ville où la route se termine) et Zermatt. Des voitures directes sont acheminées de Zermatt à Coire et St Moritz en passant par le FO et RhB.

Gauge/Ecartement: 1000 mm.
Electrical System/Courant: 11 kV 16⅔ Hz ac/monophasé.
Depots/Dépôts: Visp, Brig Glisergrund, Zermatt.

HGe4/4 II	1		SLM/ABB	–	90/35	64	1932	1990
HGe4/4 II	2		SLM/ABB	–	90/35	64	1932	1990
HGe4/4 II	3		SLM/ABB	–	90/35	64	1932	1990
HGe4/4 II	4		SLM/ABB	–	90/35	64	1932	1990
HGe4/4 II	5		SLM/ABB	–	90/35	64	1932	1990
HGe4/4	11		SLM/SWS/MFO	–	45/25	46.8	736	1929
HGe4/4	12		SLM/SWS/MFO	–	45/25	46.8	736	1929
HGe4/4	13		SLM/SWS/MFO	–	45/25	46.8	736	1929
HGe4/4	14		SLM/SWS/MFO	–	45/25	46.8	736	1929
HGe4/4	15		SLM/SWS/MFO	–	45/25	46.8	736	1930
HGe4/4	16		SLM/MFO	–	45/25	45	736	1939
Deh4/4	21	STALDEN	SIG/SLM/SAAS	–	65/35	49	1094	1975
Deh4/4	22	ST NIKLAUS	SIG/SLM/SAAS	–	65/35	49	1094	1975
Deh4/4	23	RANDA	SIG/SLM/SAAS	–	65/35	49	1094	1976
Deh4/4	24	TÄSCH	SIG/SLM/SAAS	–	65/35	49	1094	1976
Gm3/3	71		MOY/DZ	–	49	26	191	1975
Gm3/3	72		MOY/DZ	–	49	26	191	1975
Tm2/2	73		SCH/DZ	–	40	21	158	1972
ABDeh6/6	2031		SIG/SLM/SAAS	92	55/30	71	882	1960
ABDeh6/6	2032		SIG/SLM/SAAS	92	55/30	71	882	1960
ABDeh8/8	2041	BRIG	SIG/SLM/SAAS	108	55/30	88	1176	1964
ABDeh8/8	2042	VISP	SIG/SLM/SAAS	108	55/30	88	1176	1965
ABDeh8/8	2043	ZERMATT	SIG/SLM/SAAS	108	55/30	88	1176	1965
Tm2/2	2921		RACO/SLM	–	30	9.8	40	1957
Tm2/2	2922		RACO/DZ	–	30	10.2	40	1959
Xrotm	2931		BEIL	–			222	1987
Xm1/2	2962		STECK/DZ	–	50/21	4.2	66	1982

CHEMINS DE FER ELECTRIQUES VEVEYSANS (112) CEV

Once a much larger system, two sections remain in operation, the adhesion line from Vevey to Blonay and the rack continuation from Blonay to Les Pléiades. Only the modern railcars 71–5 can operate throughout. The Blonay–Chamby museum line was once part of the CEV. The CEV has been part of the MOB from 01/01/90.

Seulement deux sections de ligne – de Vevey à Blonay et sa continuation à crémaillère de Blonay aux Pléiades, subsistent d'un réseau qui était auparavant beaucoup plus grand. Seules les automotrices modernes 71 à 75 sont utilisées sur les deux sections. La ligne «musée» de de Blonay à Chamby (BC) était autrefois une partie du CEV. Le CEV fut absorbé par le MOB le 01/01/90.

Gauge/Ecartement: 1000 mm.
Electrical System/Courant: 900 V dc/continu.
Depots/Dépôts: Vevey, Blonay.

He2/2	1		SLM/MFO/SIG	-	20	17.4	390	1911
He2/2	2		SLM/MFO/SIG	-	20	17.4	390	1911
Xe2/3	12		SWS/SLM/CEV/ACEC	-	45	15.5	114	1902
BDeh2/4	71		SWP/SAAS/BBC	60	50/16	33.8	428	1969
BDeh2/4	72		SWP/SAAS/BBC	60	50/16	33.8	428	1970
BDeh2/4	73		SWP/SAAS/BBC	60	50/16	33.8	428	1970
BDeh2/4	74		SWP/SAAS/BBC	60	50/16	33.8	428	1970
BDeh2/4	75		SWP/SAAS/BBC	60	50/16	33.8	428	1983
Te2/2	81		SWS/MFO/CEV	–	30	12	62	1921
Te2/2	82		CEV/MFO	–	25	9.9	60	1938
BDe4/4	103		SWS/MFO	38	45	22.3	208	1903
BDe4/4	105	ST LEGIER	SWS/MFO	40	45	23.5	208	1913
Xrote	–							

CHEMINS DE FER DU JURA (236, 237, 238) CJ

The CJ comprises two separate systems, a short standard gauge branch linking Porrentruy and Bonfol, and a lengthy metre gauge system meeting the SBB at Chaux de Fonds, Tavannes and Glovelier. Proposals exist to extend the metre gauge from Glovelier to Delémont.

Le CJ consiste en deux systèmes distincts – une courte ligne à écartement normal entre Porrentruy et Bonfol et un réseau assez considérable à voie métrique qui assure des correspondances aves les CFF à La Chaux de Fonds, Tavannes et Glovelier. Il existe un projet pour le prolongement de la ligne de Glovelier jusqu'à Delémont.

Gauge/Ecartement: 1435/1000 mm.
Electrical System/Courant: 15 kV $16\frac{2}{3}$ Hz ac/monophasé (1435 mm), 1500 V dc/continu (1000 mm).
Depots/Dépôts: Bonfol (1435 mm), Tramelan, Saignelégier, Noirmont (1000 mm).

Standard Gauge Stock/Matériel Normal:

BDe4/4	101	BONFOL	SWS/MFO/BBC	60	70	51	640	1968
BDe4/4	102	ALLE	SWS/MFO/BBC	48	70	51	640	1980
De4/4	111	VENDLINCOURT	SWS/BBC	–		40	620	1980
TmIV	181		SLM/MAN	–	60	30	280	1971
Xm1/2	182		ROBEL/DZ	–	50	7.3	62	1961

Metre Gauge Stock/Matériel Metrique:

De4/4	401		SIG/SAAS	–	60	36	544	1952
De4/4	402		SIG/SAAS	–	60	36	544	1953
De4/4	411		SIG/SAAS	–	90	36	544	1953
Xe2/4	503	*	SWS/BBC	32	45	22	126	1913
Te	504		BBC	–	45	15	126	1913
Tm	506		ASPER/SAU	–	40	7.9	88	1953
Gm4/4	508		BL/REN	–	60	49	440	1950
Xm	509		BEIL	–				1985
BDe4/4	601		SIG/SAAS	34	70	26.5	332	1953
BDe4/4	602		SIG/SAAS	34	70	26.5	332	1953
ABDe4/4	603		SIG/SAAS	9/17	70	26.5	332	1953
BDe4/4	604		SIG/SAAS	34	70	26.5	332	1953
BDe4/4	605		SIG/SAAS	34	70	26.5	332	1953
BDe4/4	606		SIG/SAAS	34	70	26.5	332	1953
BDe4/4	607		SIG/SAAS	34	70	26.5	332	1953
BDe4/4	608		SIG/SAAS	34	70	26.5	332	1953
BDe4/4 II	611		FFA/BBC	32				1985
BDe4/4 II	612		FFA/BBC	32				1985
BDe4/4 II	613		FFA/BBC	32				1985
BDe4/4 II	614		FFA/BBC	32				1985

* Restored as museum car BCe2/4 70./Rénové comme voiture musée BCe2/4 70.

CHEMINS DE FER DES MONTAGNES NEUCHÂTELOIS (214, 222) CMN

This railway comprises two separate lines, Chaux de Fonds to Les Ponts de Martel and Le Locle to Les Brenets. The future of both lines has been uncertain for some time, but new stock is now on order. The existing Italian built cars are unusual for Switzerland.

Deux lignes distinctes – La Chaux de Fonds–Les Ponts de Martel et Le Locle–Les Brenets. Après des incertitudes sur l'avenir des deux lignes, une commande pour de nouveau matériel a été passée récemment. Les voitures italiennes sont insolites en Suisse.

Gauge/Ecartement: 1000 mm.
Electrical System/Courant: 1500 V dc/continu.
Depots/Dépôts: Les Brenets, Les Ponts de Martel.

Class	No.	Co.	Name	Builder	Seats	km/h	Tonnes	kW	Built
BDe4/4	1			REG/BBC/SAAS	48	60	23.5	320	1950
BDe4/4	2			REG/BBC/SAAS	48	60	23.5	320	1950
BDe4/4	3			REG/BBC/SAAS	48	60	23.5	320	1950
BDe4/4	4			REG/BBC/SAAS	48	60	23.5	320	1950
BDe4/4	5			REG/BBC/SAAS	48	60	23.5	320	1950
BDe4/4	6			ACMV/ABB		80	34	800	1991
BDe4/4	7			ACMV/ABB		80	34	800	1991
Tm2/2	11			RACO/DZ	–	75	19	177	1983

DOLDERBAHN (732) Db

Converted from a funicular in 1973, this rack railway connects with the Zürich trams at its lower terminus of Romerhof.

Cette ligne à crémaillère fut transformée d'un funiculaire en 1973 et assure la correspondance avec le tramway de Zurich à son terminus inférieur de Romerhof.

Gauge/Ecartement: 1000 mm.
Electrical System/Courant: 600 V dc/continu.
Depot: Dolder. (the upper station is convertible to a depot!).
Dépôt: Dolder. (le terminus supérieur se convertit en dépôt!).

Class	No.	Co.	Name	Builder	Seats	km/h	Tonnes	kW	Built
Bhe1/2	1			SLM/GANG/BBC	26	25	14.4	150	1973
Bhe1/2	2			SLM/GANG/BBC	26	25	14.4	150	1973

EMMENTHAL–BURGDORF–THUN (440) EBT
SOLOTHURN–MÜNSTER BAHN (411) SMB
VEREINIGTE HUTTWIL BAHNEN (441, 442) VHB

These three railways under common management operate an extensive standard gauge network to the east of Bern. Although one branch has closed, much of the fleet has been modernised during recent years.

Ces trois compagnies qui sont gérées en commun exploitent un réseau considérable à voie normale à l'est de Berne. Bien qu'une ligne ait été fermée, une grande partie du parc a été modernisée récemment.

Gauge/Ecartement: 1435 mm.
Electrical System/Courant: 15 kV 16⅔ Hz ac/monophasé.
Depots/Dépôts: Burgdorf, Huttwil, Oberburg.

Class *Série*	*No.* *No*	*Co.* *Cie.*	*Name* *Nom*	*Builder* *Constructeur*	*Seats* *Places*	*km/h* *km/h*	*Tonnes* *Tonnes*	*kW* *kW*	*Built* *Date*
Tm	10	EBT	MAX	DIEMA/DZ	–	40	24	140	1978
Tm	11	EBT		RACO/FORD	–	45	6.5	64	1937
Tm	12	EBT		RACO/SAU	–	45	10	74	1962
Tm	13	EBT		RACO/SAU	–	45	10	74	1972
Tm	14	EBT		RACO/SAU	–	45	10	74	1975
Tm	15	EBT		HEN	–	60	10	54	
Te [1]	21	EBT		SLM/MFO	–	45	12.4	90	1944
Te [1]	22	EBT		SLM/MFO	–	45	12.4	90	1944
Te [1]	23	EBT		SLM/MFO	–	45	12.4	90	1944

▼EBT SMB VHB Class Tm No. 15 in orange livery at Hasle–Rüegsau on 28/01/89. *Paul Russenberger*

▼▼EBT Class Te^{I} No. 26 in brown livery at Hasle–Rüegsau on 28/01/ 89. *Paul Russenberger*

▲▲Le Tm 15 du EBT–SMB– VHB dans la livrée orange à Hasle–Rüegsau. 28/01/89. *Paul Russenberger*

▲Le Te^{I} 26 du EBT dans la livrée marron à Hasle–Rüegsau. 28/ 01/89. *Paul Russenberger*

Te^{I}	24	EBT		SLM/MFO	–	45	12.4	90	1946
Te^{I}	25	EBT		SLM/MFO	–	45	12.4	90	1946
Te^{I}	26	EBT		SLM/MFO	–	45	12.4	90	1946
Te^{I}	27	EBT		SLM/MFO	–	45	12.4	90	1946
Te^{I}	28	EBT		SLM/MFO	–	45	13	90	1955
Te^{I}	29	EBT		SLM/MFO	–	45	13	90	1955
Tm	51	VHB		RACO/MB	–	45	10.5	33	1949
Tm	52	VHB		RACO/SAU	–	45	10	74	1971
Tm	53	VHB		RACO/SAU	–	45	10	74	1971
Tm	54	VHB		RACO/SAU	–	45	10	74	1972
Tm	55	VHB		RACO/SAU	–	45	10	74	1972
Tm	56	VHB		RACO/DZ	–	75	19	177	1980
Tm	57	VHB		HEN	–				
Te^{I}	61	VHB		SLM/MFO	–	45	13	90	1963
Tm	71	SMB		RACO/SAU	–	45	10	74	1964
Tm	72	SMB		RACO/DZ	–	75	19	177	1983
Be4/4	101	EBT		SLM/SAAS	–	80	64.7	1177	1932
Be4/4	102	EBT		SLM/SAAS	–	80	64.7	1177	1932
Be4/4	103	EBT		SLM/SAAS	–	80	64.7	1177	1933
Be4/4	104	EBT		SLM/SAAS	–	80	64.7	1177	1933
Be4/4	105	EBT		SLM/SAAS	–	80	64.7	1177	1933
Be4/4	106	EBT		SLM/SAAS	–	80	64.7	1177	1933
Be4/4	107	EBT		SLM/SAAS	–	80	64.7	1177	1944
Be4/4	108	EBT		SLM/SAAS	–	80	64.7	1177	1953
Re4/4	111	EBT		SLM/BBC/MFO/SAAS	–	120	80	4653	1969
Re4/4	112	EBT		SLM/BBC/MFO/SAAS	–	120	80	4653	1969
Re4/4	113	EBT		SLM/BBC/MFO/SAAS	–	120	80	4653	1983
Te^{III}	121	EBT		SLM/SAAS	–	60	29	257	1945
Te^{III}	122	EBT	(ex SBB 137)	SLM/SAAS	–	60	29	257	1945
Te^{III}	123	EBT		SLM/SAAS	–	60	29	257	1952
Te^{III}	124	EBT		SLM/SAAS	–	60	29	257	1952
Ee3/3	131	EBT		SLM/BBC/MFO/SAAS	–	45	44	508	1967
Ee3/3	132	EBT	(ex SBB 16312)	SLM/BBC	–	40	45	428	1928
Ee3/3	133	EBT	(ex SBB 16322)	SLM/BBC	–	40	45	428	1928
Re4/4	141	VHB		SLM/BBC/MFO/SAAS	–	120	80	4653	1983
Ee3/3	151	VHB	(ex SBB 16323)	SLM/BBC	–	40	45	428	1928
Te^{III}	161	VHB		SLM/SAAS	–	60	29	257	1945
Be4/4	171	SMB		SLM/SAAS	–	80	64.7	1177	1932
Be4/4	172	SMB		SLM/SAAS	–	80	64.7	1177	1932
Re4/4	181	SMB		SLM/BBC/MFO/SAAS	–	120	80	4653	1983
BDe4/4^{II}	201	EBT	BURGDORF	SIG/BBC	32	110	73	2060	1966
RBDe4/4	221	EBT		SWS/SAAS	56	125	71	1340	1973
RBDe4/4	222	EBT		SWS/SAAS	56	125	71	1340	1974
RBDe4/4	223	EBT		SWS/SAAS	56	125	71	1340	1974
RBDe4/4	224	EBT		SWS/SAAS	56	125	71	1340	1974
RBDe4/4	225	EBT		SWS/SAAS	56	125	71	1340	1974
RBDe4/4	226	EBT		SWS/SAAS	56	125	71	1340	1974
RBDe4/4	227	EBT	EMMENTAL	SWS/BBC	56	125	71	1340	1984
RBDe4/4	228	EBT	GERLAFINGEN	SWS/BBC	56	125	71	1340	1985
RBDe4/4	229	EBT	HASLE–RÜEGSAU	SWS/BBC	56	125	71	1340	1985
RBDe4/4	230	EBT	OBERDIESSBACH	SWS/BBC	56	125	71	1340	1985
RBDe4/4	231	EBT	KIRCHBERG–ALCHENFLÜH	SWS/BBC	56	125	71	1340	1985
RBDe4/4	232	EBT	GROSSHÖCHSTETTEN	SWS/BBC	56	125	71	1340	1985
RBDe4/4	233	EBT	LÜTZELFLÜH	SWS/BBC	56	125	71	1340	1985
De4/4	235	EBT		SWS/SIG/BBC/MFO	–	80	67	1177	1981
De4/4	236	EBT		SWS/SIG/BBC/MFO	–	80	67	1177	1981
BDe2/4	240	EBT		SWS/SIG/BBC/MFO	30	80		588	1932
BDe4/4^{II}	251	VHB	HUTTWIL	SIG/BBC	32	110	73	2060	1966
BDe4/4^{II}	252	VHB	WILLISAU	SIG/BBC	32	110	73	2060	1966
RBDe4/4	261	VHB		SWS/SAAS	56	125	71	1340	1973
RBDe4/4	262	VHB	SUMISWALD	SWS/BBC	56	125	71	1340	1985
RBDe4/4	263	VHB	ROHRBACH	SWS/BBC	56	125	71	1340	1985
RBDe4/4	264	VHB	ZELL	SWS/BBC	56	125	71	1340	1985
RBDe4/4	265	VHB	MADISWIL	SWS/BBC	56	125	71	1340	1985

EBT Class Be4/4 No. 107 at Burgdorf on 23/08/85. This type is identical to the Be4/4 Class on the BT. *E. Dunkling*

La Be4/4 107 du EBT à Burgdorf. Cette série est identique au type Be4/4 du BT. 23/08/85. *E. Dunkling*

De4/4	266	VHB		SWS/SIG/BBC/MFO	–	80	67	1177	1981
De4/4	267	VHB		SWS/SIG/BBC/MFO	–	80	67	1177	1981
RBDe4/4	281	SMB		SWS/SAAS	56	125	71	1340	1973
RBDe4/4	282	SMB	LANGENDORF	SWS/BBC	56	125	71	1340	1985
RBDe4/4	283	SMB	CREMINES	SWS/BBC	56	125	71	1340	1985

On order/En commande: 4 Ee3/3 from/de SLM/ABB.

FERROVIE AUTOLINEE REGIONALI TICINESE (620) FART

SOCIETÀ SUBALPINA DI IMPRESE FERROVIARIE (620) SSIF

This international light railway links Locarno in Switzerland with Domodossola in Italy, traversing very spectacular scenery. The SSIF is an Italian company operating the western half of the line, although the through services are jointly operated and the stock is numbered in a common series. The route through Lugano is currently being reconstructed on a new underground alignment.

Ce petit réseau à vocation internationale relie Locarno en Suisse à Domodossola en Italie, en traversant une région hautement pittoresque. Le SSIF est une compagnie italienne qui exploite la partie occidentale de la ligne, bien que les services soient exploités en commun et le matériel est numéroté dans une série commune. Une nouvelle ligne en souterrain est en train d'être construit à Locarno.

Gauge/Ecartement: 1000 mm.
Electrical System/Courant: 1200 V dc/continu.
Depots/Dépôts: Locarno S. Antonio, Ponte Brolla, Camedo (FART), Domodossola, Re (SSIF).

Class *Série*	*No.* *No*	*Co.* *Cie.*	*Name* *Nom*	*Builder* *Constructeur*	*Seats* *Places*	*km/h* *km/h*	*Tonnes* *Tonnes*	*kW* *kW*	*Built* *Date*
ABDe4/4	1	FART		MAN/BBC	12/32	45	28	180	1907 (64)
Xe2/4	4	SSIF		MAN/MFO	–	60	15.2	100	1911
Xe2/4	5	SSIF		MAN/MFO	–	60	15.2	100	1911
Xe2/2	6	FART		MAN/BBC/FART	–	40	11	60	1908 (75)
Xe2/2	7	FART		MAN/BBC	–	40	11	60	1908
ABDe4/4	12	SSIF		CET/BBC	6/30	45	30	310	1923
ABDe4/4	13	SSIF		CET/BBC	6/30	45	30	310	1923
ABDe4/4	16	SSIF		CET/BBC/SSIF	6/30	45	30	310	1923 (75)
ABDe4/4	17	SSIF		CET/BBC	6/30	45	30	310	1923
ABDe4/4	18	SSIF		CET/BBC	6/30	45	30	310	1923
ABe8/8	21	SSIF	ROMA	SWP/TIBB	28/85	60	59	725	1959
ABe8/8	22	FART	TICINO	SWP/TIBB	28/85	60	59	725	1959
ABe8/8	23	SSIF	OSSOLA	SWP/TIBB	28/85	60	59	725	1959
ABe8/8	24	SSIF	VIGEZZO	SWP/TIBB	28/85	60	59	725	1959
ABDe6/6	31	FART	BERNA	SWP/TIBB	18/45	60	45	365	1963
ABDe6/6	32	FART	VALLESE	SWP/TIBB	18/45	60	45	365	1963
ABe6/6	33	SSIF	SEMPIONE	SWP/TIBB	10/72	60	45.5	545	1968
ABe6/6	34	SSIF	PIEMONTE	SWP/TIBB	10/72	60	45.5	545	1968
ABe6/6	35	SSIF	VERBANO	SWP/TIBB	10/72	60	45.5	545	1968
Be4/8	41	FART	PEDEMONTE	SIG/BBC	112	60	46	335	1979
Be4/8	42	FART	MELEZZA	SIG/BBC	112	60	46	335	1979

On Order: 10 ABe4/6 (8 for FART, 2 for SSIF) due 1992./En commande: 10 ABe4/6 (8 pour le FART, 2 pour le SSIF) en 1992. Seats/places 18/64, 80 km/h, 42.5 tonnes, 1080 kW.

FORCHBAHN (731) FB

Once a tramway basically operated as a rural extension of the Zürich system, this light railway has been upgraded mostly to roadside running, but with some sections of private right-of-way. The cars still run over the Zürich tram tracks from the terminus at Stadelhofen (adjacent to the SBB station) to Rehalp.

Autrefois tramway exploité comme une extension rurale du réseau zurichois, cette ligne a été améliorée et est maintenant établie en accotement de chaussée avec quelques sections de plate-forme en site propre. Les voitures utilisent toujours les voies du tramway de Zurich entre le terminus à Stadelhofen (près de la gare CFF) jusqu'à Rehalp.

Gauge/Ecartement: 1000 mm.
Electrical System/Courant: 1200 V dc/continu (600 V over tram tracks/sur le tramway).
Depot/Dépôt: Forch.

Class	No.	Builder	Seats	km/h	Tonnes	kW	Built
CFe2/2	4	SWS/MFO	24	36	20.2	150	1912
Xe4/4	9	SWS/MFO/VBZ	–	70	26	300	1948 (82)
BDe4/4	10	SWS/MFO	40	70	26.5	300	1948
BDe4/4	11	SWS/MFO	40	65	29.4	375	1959
BDe4/4	12	SWS/MFO	40	65	29.4	375	1959
BDe4/4	13	SWS/MFO	40	65	29.4	375	1959
BDe4/4	14	SWS/MFO	40	65	29.4	375	1959
BDe4/4	15	SWS/MFO	40	65	29.4	375	1966
BDe4/4	16	SWS/MFO	40	65	29.4	375	1966
Be8/8	21+22	SWS/SWP/BBC	86	65	42	610	1976
Be8/8	23+24	SWS/SWP/BBC	86	65	42	610	1976
Be8/8	25+26	SWS/SWP/BBC	86	65	42	610	1976
Be8/8	27+28	SWS/SWP/BBC	86	65	42	610	1981
Be8/8	29+30	SWS/SWP/BBC	86	65	42	610	1981
Be8/8	31+32	SWS/SWP/BBC	86	65	42	610	1986

On order/En commande: 4 Be8/8.

FERROVIA LUGANO–PONTE TRESA (635) FLP

The only survivor of several light railways in the Lugano area, the FLP has been modernised and new cars purchased.
La dernière survivante de plusieurs lignes à intérêt local dans la région de Lugano, le FLP a été modernisé et a reçu des voitures nouvelles.

Gauge/Ecartement: 1000 mm.
Electrical System/Courant: 1000 V dc/continu.
Depots/Dépôts: Agno, Ponte Tresa.

ABe4/4	3		SWS/SLM/BBC	16/40	55	29	215	1912 (54)
Ze4/4	4	TRESA	SWS/SLM/SAAS/BBC	16/40	55	30	245	1952 (81)
Be4/4	21	LEMA	SIG/BBC	128	60	48.7	330	1978
Be4/4	22	MALCANTONE	SIG/BBC	128	60	48.7	330	1979
Be4/4	23	VEDEGGIO	SIG/BBC	128	60	48.7	330	1979
Be4/4	24	MAGLIASENA	SIG/BBC	128	60	48.7	330	1979
Be4/4	25	CERESIO	SIG/BBC	128	60	48.7	330	1979

FURKA OBERALP (610) FO

Forming the only east–west rail link across the south of the country, for many years the section of the FO over the Furka pass was only open during the summer. However, in 1982 the new Furka tunnel was opened, facilitating all-year-round operation, but eliminating the spectacular section over the pass itself. Several stretches of rack remain on this scenic line. Through coaches operate from Zermatt (BVZ) to Chur & St Moritz (RhB).

Le seul lien ferroviaire d'ouest en est dans le sud de la Suisse. Pendant très longtemps, la section du FO qui traverse le col de la Furka n'était ouvert qu'en été. Cependant, le tunnel de base de la Furka a été ouvert en 1982, ce qui permet l'exploitation pendant toute l'année mais qui élimine la section spectaculaire par le col lui-même. Il subsiste plusieurs sections de voie à crémaillère sur cette ligne pittoresque. Des voitures directes sont acheminées de Zermatt (BVZ) à Coire et St Moritz (RhB).

Gauge/Ecartement: 1000 mm.
Electrical System/Courant: 11 kV 16⅔ Hz ac/monophasé.
Depots/Dépôts: Brig, Andermatt.

HGe4/4	31		SLM/MFO	–	55/30	46.6	912	1941
HGe4/4	32		SLM/MFO		55/30	46.6	912	1941
HGe4/4	33		SLM/MFO		55/30	46.6	912	1941
HGe4/4	34		SLM/MFO		55/30	46.6	912	1941
HGe4/4	36		SLM/MFO		55/30	46.6	912	1949
HGe4/4	37		SLM/MFO		55/30	46.6	912	1956
BDeh2/4	41		SLM/BBC	48	55/30	37	427	1941
BDeh2/4	42		SLM/BBC	48	55/30	37	427	1941
BDeh2/4	43		SLM/BBC	48	55/30	37	427	1941
BDeh2/4	44		SLM/BBC	48	55/30	37	427	1942
BDeh2/4	45		SLM/BBC	48	55/30	37	427	1942
Deh4/4	51	DISENTIS/MUSTER	SIG/SLM/BBC	–	60/30	48	1032	1972
Deh4/4	52	TAVETSCH/TUJETSCH	SIG/SLM/BBC	–	60/30	48	1032	1972
Deh4/4	53	URSERN	SIG/SLM/BBC	–	60/30	48	1032	1972
Deh4/4	54	GOMS	SIG/SLM/BBC	–	60/30	48	1032	1972
Deh4/4	55	BRIG	SIG/SLM/BBC	–	60/30	48	1032	1972
HGm4/4	61		SLM/BBC/MFO/CUM	–	50/30	54	1134	1968
HGm4/4	62		SLM/BBC/MFO/CUM	–	50/30	54	1134	1968
Gm4/4	71	ELCH	JUNG/MWM	–	40	37.6	652	1966
Ge4/4 III	81	WALLIS	SLM/BBC	–	90	50	1700	1980
Ge4/4 III	82	URI	SLM/BBC	–	90	50	1700	1980
Deh4/4 II	91	GÖSCHENEN	SLM/BBC	–	60/30	51	1032	1979
Deh4/4 II	92	REALP	SLM/BBC	–	60/30	51	1032	1980
Deh4/4 II	93	OBERWALD	SLM/BBC	–	60/30	51	1032	1980
Deh4/4 II	94	FIESCH	SLM/BBC	–	60/30	51	1032	1980
Deh4/4 II	95	ANDERMATT	SLM/BBC	–	60/30	51	1032	1984
Deh4/4 II	96	MÜNSTER	SLM/BBC	–	60/30	51	1032	1984
HGe4/4 II	101	SITTEN/VILLE DE SION	SLM/BBC	–	90/30	64	1932	1986
HGe4/4 II	102	ALTDORF	SLM/BBC	–	90/30	64	1932	1986
HGe4/4 II	103	CHUR/MARCAU DE CUERA	SLM/BBC	–	90/30	64	1932	1986
HGe4/4 II	104	FURKA*	SLM/BBC	–	90/30	64	1932	1986
HGe4/4 II	105	OBERALP†	SLM/BBC	–	90/30	64	1932	1986
HGe4/4 II	106		SLM/ABB	–	90/30	64	1932	1989
HGe4/4 II	107		SLM/ABB	–	90/30	64	1932	1989
HGe4/4 II	108		SLM/ABB	–	90/30	64	1932	1989

Te2/2	4926		SLM/SAAS	–	30	12.7	96	1946
Xrote	4931		SLM/SIG/MFO	–		16	405	1941
Xrote	4932		SLM/SIG/MFO	–		16	405	1943
Xrote	4933		SLM/SIG/MFO	–		16	405	1945
Xrotm	4934		BEIL/DZ/JMR	–	60	32	670	1980
Xrotm	4935		BEIL	–				1986
Tm2/2	4971		SCH/DZ	–	33	21.8	170	1960
Tm2/2	4972		SCH/DZ	–	33	21.8	170	1960
Tm2/2	4973	§	RUHR	–				1958
Tm2/2	4981		DZ	–		15		

* ex SBB 1951
† ex SBB 1952
§ ex DB 333.902

FRAUENFELD–WIL (841) FW

Once threatened with closure, this light railway has now been modernised with new stock and a new depot. The line is mostly roadside running, with street running in Frauenfeld.

Autrefois menacé de fermeture, ce chemin de fer à intérêt local a maintenant été modernisé avec un nouveau matériel et un nouveau dépôt. La ligne est en accotement de chaussée avec la route mais la voie est établie sur route dans la ville de Frauenfeld.

Gauge/Ecartement: 1000 mm.
Electrical System/Courant: 1200 V dc/continu.
Depots/Dépôts: Wil.

Be4/4	11	FRAUENFELD	FFA/BBC					1985
Be4/4	12	MATZINGEN	FFA/BBC					1985
Be4/4	13	WÄNGI	FFA/BBC					1985
Be4/4	14	MÜNCHWILEN	FFA/BBC					1985
Be4/4	15	WIL	FFA/BBC					1985
Be4/4	201*		SWS/MFO	17	55	28	290	1921
Be4/4	203		SWS/MFO	17	55	28	290	1921
Be4/4	205		SWS/MFO	54	65	29.5	460	1947
Be4/4	206		SWS/MFO	54	65	29.5	460	1947

* Restored as museum car/Transformé en automotrice historique BCe4/4 I.
Two cars are on order to replace 205/6.
Deux automotrices sont en commande pour remplacer les 205–6.

GRUYÈRE–FRIBOURG–MORAT (CHEMINS DE FER FRIBOURGEOIS) (253, 254, 255, 256) GFM

This system operates both standard and metre gauge lines. There are two separate standard gauge branches, Fribourg–Ins and Bulle–Romont, plus an extensive metre gauge system centred on Bulle. Connection is made with the MOB at Montbovon.

Cette compagnie exploite des lignes à voie normale et métrique. Il existe deux lignes distinctes à voie normale: Fribourg–Ins et Bulle–Romont plus un réseau considérable à voie métrique autour de Bulle. Il y a correspondance avec le MOB à Montbovon.

Gauge/Ecartement: 1435/1000 mm.
Electrical System/Courant: 15 kV 16⅔ Hz ac/monophasé (1435 mm), 800 V dc/continu (1000 mm).
Depots/Dépôts: Bulle, Fribourg Pérolles (1435 mm), Bulle, Châtel St Denis, Montbovon (1000 mm).

Metre Gauge Stock/Matériel Metrique: (all BD/tout BD).

Te2/2	11	MFO	-	30	16.5	88	1913
Te2/2	12	CEG/ALIOTH	-	50	9	774	1913
Te4/4	13	CEG/ALIOTH	-	45	23	148	1901 (27)
Te4/4	14	CEG/ALIOTH	-	50	21.5	264	1901 (33)

Tm2/2	15		SCH/DZ	-	35	24	168	1971
Tm2/2	16		CFD	-	-	-	-	
GDe4/4	101	VILLE DE BULLE	SLM/BBC	-	90	48.2	1053	1983
GDe4/4	102	NEIRIVUE	SLM/BBC	-	90	48.2	1053	1983
Be4/4	107		SWS/ALIOTH	40	60	27	264	1903
Be4/4	111		SWS/ALIOTH	44	60	27	264	1903
BDe4/4	114		SIG/ALIOTH	22	60	24.5	264	1904
Be4/4	115		SWS/ALIOTH	44	60	29.5	296	1905
Be4/4	121		SWS/MFO	58	75	35	486	1922
Be4/4	131		SWS/BBC	48	75	33	408	1943
Be4/4	132		SWS/BBC	48	75	33	408	1943
Be4/4	133		SWS/BBC	48	75	33	408	1943
BDe4/4	141		SWP/SAAS	46	70	38	648	1972
BDe4/4	142		SWP/SAAS	46	70	38	648	1972
Be4/4	151	LA GRUYÈRE	SIG/SAAS	44	80	32	448	1977
Be4/4	152	CHÂTEL ST DENIS	SIG/SAAS	44	80	32	448	1977

On order/En commande: 2 BDe4/4 from/de ACMV/ABB.

Standard Gauge Stock/**Matériel Normal:**

Te2/2	52		SLM/SAAS	-	20	11.5	44	1947
Tm	81		RACO/SAU	-	30	10.3	81	1943
Tm	82		RACO/VR/MB	-	45	33	236	1964
Tm	83		CEM/BBC	-	35	40	220	1960
Tm	84		KRUPP/MAN	-	40	45.5	324	1963
Ee2/2	91		SIG/BBC	-	75	30	242	1960
ABDe2/4	155		SIG/BBC	16/39	90	48.8	442	1931
ABDe4/4	161		SIG/BBC	18/34	100	56	736	1946
ABDe4/4	162		SIG/BBC	18/34	100	56	736	1946
ABDe4/4	163		SIG/BBC	18/34	100	56	736	1947
ABDe4/4	164		SIG/BBC	18/34	100	56	736	1947
ABDe4/4	165		SIG/BBC	18/34	100	56	736	1947
ABe4/4	166		SIG/BBC	18/58	100	57	736	1947
ABe4/4	167		SIG/BBC	18/58	100	57	736	1948
RABDe4/4	171	LA SARINE	SIG/SWS/BBC	12/31	125	70	1700	1983
RABDe4/4	172	VULLY	SIG/SWS/BBC	12/31	125	70	1700	1983

On order/En commande: 2 RABDe4/4.

GORNERGRATBAHN (142) GGB

A pure rack mountain railway starting from Zermatt. This line and the Jungfraubahn are the only Swiss railways electrified on the 3-phase system which requires two overhead wires.

Une ligne à crémaillère qui commence à Zermatt. Cette ligne et le JB sont les seules en Suisse à être électrifiées au système triphasé qui nécessite deux fils de caténaire, la troisième phase étant acheminée par les rails.

Gauge/Ecartement: 1000 mm.
Electrical System/Courant: 725 V 50 Hz 3-phase/triphasé.
Depot/Dépôt: Zermatt.

He2/2	3001	SLM/SIG/BBC	-	9	13.3	184	1898
He2/2	3002	SLM/SIG/BBC	-	9	13.3	184	1898
He2/2	3003	SLM/SIG/BBC	-	9	11.4	184	1898
Bhe2/4	3011	SLM/BBC	56	14.5	18	190	1947
Bhe2/4	3012	SLM/BBC	56	14.5	18	190	1947
Bhe2/4	3013	SLM/BBC	56	14.5	18	190	1952
Bhe2/4	3014	SLM/BBC	56	14.5	18	190	1952
Bhe2/4	3015	SLM/BBC	56	14.5	18	190	1954
Bhe2/4	3016	SLM/BBC	56	14.5	18	190	1954
Bhe2/4	3017	SLM/BBC	56	14.5	18	190	1958
Bhe2/4	3018	SLM/BBC	56	14.5	18	190	1958
Bhe2/4	3019	SLM/BBC	56	14.5	18	190	1961
Bhe2/4	3020	SLM/BBC	56	14.5	18	190	1961
Bhe2/4	3021	SLM/BBC	56	14.5	18	190	1961

Bhe2/4	3022	SLM/BBC	56	14.5	18	190	1961
Bhe4/8	3041	SLM/BBC	120	14.5	35.7	380	1965
Bhe4/8	3042	SLM/BBC	120	14.5	35.7	380	1965
Bhe4/8	3043	SLM/BBC	120	14.5	35.7	380	1967
Bhe4/8	3044	SLM/BBC	120	14.5	35.7	380	1967
Bhe4/4	3061	SLM/BBC	28	15.3	27.2	380	1981
Bhe4/4	3062	SLM/BBC	28	15.3	27.2	380	1981
Xrote	3931	SLM/MFO	–	–	–	–	1944
Xrote	3932	SLM/BBC	–	–	–	–	1970

JUNGFRAUBAHN (311, 312) JB

This rack line starting at Kleine Scheidegg, where it connects with the WAB, climbs mostly in tunnel through the Eiger and Mönch to its upper terminus at Jungfraujoch below the summit of the Jungfrau. There are superb views here, the highest railway station in Europe. The line is electrified on the 3-phase system.

Cette ligne à crémaillère commence à Kleine Scheidegg, où il existe une correspondance avec le WAB. Sa progression ascendante se fait principalement en tunnel sous les montagnes Eiger et Mönch jusqu'au terminus supérieur de Jungfraujoch en-dessous du sommet de la Jungfrau. Il existe des panoramas superbes, par exemple à Jungfraujoch, la station la plus haute d'Europe. La ligne est électrifiée au système triphasé.

Gauge/Ecartement: 1000 mm.
Electrical System/Courant: 1125 V 50 Hz 3-phase/triphasé.
Depots/Dépôts: Eigergletscher, Kleine Scheidegg.

He2/2	6		SLM/BBC	-	11.5	15	324	1904
He2/2	8		SLM/BBC	–	18.5	15	280	1912
He2/2	9		SLM/BBC	–	18.5	15	280	1912
He2/2	10		SLM/BBC	–	18.5	15	280	1912
He2/2	11		SLM/BBC	–	18.5	15	280	1924
Xrote	51		SLM/MFO	–	12	14	376	1937
BDhe2/4	201		SLM/BBC	41	24	25	440	1955
BDhe2/4	202		SLM/BBC	41	24	25	440	1955
BDhe2/4	203		SLM/BBC	41	24	25	440	1960
BDhe2/4	204		SLM/BBC	41	24	25	440	1960
BDhe2/4	205		SLM/BBC	41	24	25	440	1961
BDhe2/4	206		SLM/BBC	41	24	25	440	1961
BDhe2/4	207	LAKE BIWA/OTSU	SLM/BBC	41	24	25	440	1964
BDhe2/4	208		SLM/BBC	41	24	25	440	1964
BDhe2/4	209		SLM/BBC	41	24	25	440	1964
BDhe2/4	210		SLM/BBC	41	24	25	440	1964
BDhe4/8	211		SLM/ABB					on order/
BDhe4/8	212		SLM/ABB					en commande
BDhe4/8	213		SLM/ABB					on order/
BDhe4/8	214		SLM/ABB					en commande

KRIENS–LUZERN BAHN KLB

Once a steam tramway, passenger service was withdrawn as long ago as 1900 due to the extension of the town tramway system, now itself long since closed. The railway now provides a freight service to a number of private sidings.

Tramway à vapeur à l'origine, cette ligne fut fermée aux voyageurs en 1900 à cause de l'extension du tramway de Lucerne qui est lui-même fermé maintenant. La compagnie offre maintenant une desserte marchandises d'une série d'embranchements industriels.

Gauge/Ecartement: 1435 mm.
Electrical System/Courant: Not electrified/Non-électrifié.
Depot/Dépôt: Kriens.

Em4/4	35	U23A	-	60	50	375	1979

▼LO Class He2/2 No. 123 propels its train out of Ouchy and starts the climb to Lausanne on 03/08/88. *G.B. Wise*

▼La He2/2 123 du LO quitte Ouchy en poussant son train et commence à grimper la rampe vers Lausanne. 03/08/88. *G.B. Wise*

◀LSE Class Tm^{II} No. 102 near the depot at Stansstad in September 1989. *Paul Russenberger*

◀Le Tm^{II} 102 du LSE près du dépôt de Stansstad en Septembre 1989. *Paul Russenberger*

LAUSANNE–ECHALLENS–BERCHER (102) LEB

A light railway serving the area to the north of Lausanne, recently modernised with new stock. The railway is to be extended from the present inconveniently located terminus at Lausanne Chauderon to a new terminus at Flon, nearer the town centre and with an interchange with the LG/LO.

Une ligne à intérêt local qui dessert la région au nord de Lausanne et qui a été modernisée récemment avec du nouveau matériel. La ligne va être prolongée de son terminus actuel de Lausanne Chauderon qui est mal situé, à Flon qui est plus près du centre ville et qui permettra la correspondance avec les LG et LO.

Gauge/Ecartement: 1000 mm.
Electrical System/Courant: 1500 V dc/continu.
Depots/Dépôts: Eschallens, Lausanne Chauderon.

Tm2/2	1		DIEMA					
BDe4/4	21		SWS/SAAS	40	60	30	324	1935
BDe4/4	22		SWS/SAAS	40	60	30	324	1935
BDe4/4	23		SWS/SAAS	40	60	30	324	1936
BDe4/4	25		SWS/SAAS	40	60	30	324	1947
Be4/4	26		SWS/SAAS	40	80	35	588	1966
Be4/4	27		SWS/SAAS	40	80	35	588	1966
Be4/8	30	LAUSANNE	ACMV/SIG/BBC	58+66	80	54.5	752	1985
Be4/8	32	ESCHALLENS	ACMV/SIG/BBC	58+66	80	54.5	752	1985
Be4/8	33	BERCHER	ACMV/SIG/BBC	58+66	80	54.5	752	1985

On order/En commande: 3 Be4/8.

LAUSANNE–GARE (104) LG
LAUSANNE–OUCHY (103) LO

Two short rack lines, originally funiculars, now owned by the municipality. The LO provides a link between the town centre (Flon), the SBB station and Ouchy on Lake Geneva. The LG provides a supplementary service between the town and the station.

Deux courtes lignes à crémaillère, transformées de funiculaires, et qui appartiennent maintenant à la municipalité. Le LO relie le centre ville (Flon) à la gare CFF et à Ouchy sur la rive du Lac Léman. Le LG, qui est parallèle au LO dans le même tunnel, donne un service supplémentaire entre la ville et la gare.

Gauge/Ecartement: 1435 mm.
Electrical System/Courant: 650 V dc/continu.
Depot/Dépôt: Ouchy.

Bhe2/2	111	LG	SLM/SIG/MFO	*	32	18.5	464	1964
Bhe2/2	112	LG	SLM/SIG/MFO	*	32	18.5	464	1964
He2/2	121	LO	SLM/MFO	-	32	18.1	464	1958
He2/2	122	LO	SLM/MFO	-	32	18.1	464	1958
He2/2	123	LO	SLM/MFO	-	32	18.1	464	1958

* Accommodates 154 standing passengers (no seats).
Accomodation pour 154 passagers (pas de sièges).

LUZERN–STANS–ENGELBERG (480) LSE

Once an isolated 3-phase line connecting the lake steamers at Stansstad with the towns of Stans and Engelberg, this railway was modernised and upgraded in the 1960s. A link was built from Stansstad to join the SBB Brunig line at Hergiswil, and most trains now run through to Luzern. At the same time, the electrical system was changed to the SBB standard. There is rack operation near the Engelberg end of the line.

Autrefois le LSE était une ligne isolée à courant triphasé qui reliait le débarcadère des bateaux à Stansstad aux villes de Stans et Engelberg. La ligne a été modernisée pendant les années 60 et prolongée de Stansstad à Hergiswil pour rejoindre la ligne du Brünig des CFF. La ligne fut ré-électrifiée au système CFF et maintenant la plupart des trains ont Lucerne pour terminus. Il existe une section à crémaillère près de Engelberg.

Gauge/Ecartement: 1000 mm.
Electrical System/Courant: 15 kV 16⅔ Hz ac/monophasé.
Depots/Dépôts: Stansstad, Engelberg.

BDeh4/4	1		SWP/SLM/BBC	40	75/20	48	745	1964
BDeh4/4	2		SWP/SLM/BBC	40	75/20	48	745	1964
BDeh4/4	3		SWP/SLM/BBC	40	75/20	48	745	1964
BDeh4/4	4		SWP/SLM/BBC	40	75/20	48	745	1964
BDeh4/4	5		SWP/SLM/BBC	40	75/20	48	745	1964
BDeh4/4	6		SWP/SLM/BBC	40	75/20	48	745	1970
BDeh4/4	7		SWP/SLM/BBC	40	75/20	48	745	1970
BDeh4/4	8		SWP/SLM/BBC	40	75/20	48	745	1980
Tm I	101		RACO/DZ	-	30	6.3	30	1931
Tm II	102		RACO/DZ/VR	-	45	10.4	80	1961
Tm II	103		RACO/DZ/VOITH	-	50	15.2	115	1967
Gm4/4	111	JUMBO	JUNG/MAN	-	40	36	375	1950

MARTIGNY–CHÂTELARD (132) MC

This rack and adhesion line possesses a number of unusual features. From Martigny SBB to Vernayez overhead current collection is used, but the remainder of the line to Châtelard, which includes the rack sections, has 3rd rail. At Châtelard, the MC links with the metre gauge SNCF line from St Gervais, which uses a similar 3rd rail system. Most MC trains continue to Vallorcine, but apart from a limited amount of through operation either side of the border, physical incompatibility between the lines prevent the operation of through services. However, the MC and the SNCF are about to order six new railcar sets to enable a joint through service to be operated.

Cette ligne avec sections à crémaillère a plusieurs particularités intéressantes. Entre Martigny CFF et Vernayez le courant est capté par pantographes mais sur le reste de la ligne jusqu'au Châtelard, où il existe des sections à crémaillère, le captage se fait par un troisième rail. Au Châtelard, le MC rejoint la ligne SNCF à voie métrique de St Gervais qui possède un système similaire de troisième rail. La plupart des trains MC continue sur Vallorcine, mais mis à part quelques incursions de chaque côté de la frontière, l'incompatabilité des deux systèmes empèche un vrai service de trains directs. Cependant, le MC et la SNCF envisagent de commander six nouvelles automotrices afin de pouvoir exploiter un tel service.

Gauge/Ecartement: 1000 mm.
Electrical System/Courant: 800 V dc/continu.
Depot/Dépôt: Vernayez, Finhaut, Le Châtelard.

BDeh4/4	4		SWP/SAAS	52	50/25	37.9	560	1957
BDeh4/4	5		SWP/SAAS	52	50/25	37.9	560	1957
BDeh4/4	6		SWP/SAAS	52	50/25	37.9	560	1957
BDeh4/4	7		SWP/SAAS	52	50/25	37.9	560	1964
BDeh4/4	8		SWP/SAAS	52	50/25	37.9	560	1964
BDeh4/4	14		SLM/SWS/MFO	48	35/9	36.3	176	1908
BDeh4/4	15		SLM/SWS/MFO	48	35/9	37	176	1909
BDe4/4	22		SWS/SAAS	40	45	22.6	110	1908
BDeh4/4	31		SLM/SWS/MFO	32	28/9	40.5	298	1921
BDeh4/4	32		SLM/SWS/MFO	32	28/9	40.5	298	1921
Te2/2	91		SWS/MFO/MC	-	40	16.6	108	1962
Te2/2	92		SWS/MFO/MC	-	40	16.6	108	1962
Tm2/2	204	*	BEIL	-	50	16	149	1982
BDeh4/4	501		SWP/SLM/BBC	44	65/24	41.1	716	1979

* Can be fitted with rotary snowplough, when classification becomes Xtm2/2.
* Peut être doté d'un chasse-neige rotatif – classification devient Xtm2/2.

ERRATUM: Sur les deux pages suivantes, les deux légendes françaises sont inversées.

▼Appenzellerbahnen Class BDe4/4 rack-and-adhesion No. 13 'Bühler' leads driving trailer Class Bt No. 113 on the 16.20 St. Gallen to Appenzell on 19/04/86. *G.B. Wise*

▼▼AL Aigle depot with three generations of rolling stock, among which rack-and-adhesion BDeh2/4 Class Nos. 202 and 201 are prominent on 05/04/88. *Chris Appleby*

▲▲Trois générations de matériel au dépôt d'Aigle du AL avec les BDeh2/4 202 et 201 en premier plan, 05/04/88. *Chris Appleby*

▲La BDe4/4 13 «Bühler» du AB avec remorque pilote Bt 113 assure un train St Gall–Appenzell, 19/04/86. *G.B. Wise*

▼ASD Class BDe4/4 No. 404 'Aigle' at Aigle after arrival from Les Diablerets on 05/04/88. *Chris Appleby*

▼▼BAM Class Be4/4 No. 12 at Morges before departure for Bière on 03/04/88. *Chris Appleby*

▲▲La Be4/4 12 du BAM à Morges juste avant son départ pour Bière, 03/04/88. *Chris Appleby*

▲La BDe4/4 404 «Aigle» du ASD à Aigle aprés son arrivée des Diablerets, 05/04/88. *Chris Appleby*

▼BD Class BDe8/8 No. 4 'Bremgarten' at Wohlen working the 10.45 to Dietikon on 21/04/88.
G.B. Wise

▼▼BOB Class ABeh4/4 No. 305 enters Lütschental heading a Grindelwald to Interlaken Ost working in September 1988. *Paul Russenberger*

▲▲La ABeh4/4 305 du BOB arrive à Lütschental avec un train de Grindelwald à Interlaken Ost, Septembre 1988. *Paul Russenberger*

▲La BDe8/8 No. 4 «Bremgarten» du BD à Wohlen avec un train pour Dietikon, 21/04/88. *G.B. Wise*

▼BVB Class BDe4/4 No. 83 approaches Bex from Villars on 05/04/88. *Chris Appleby*

▼▼BVZ Class Deh4/4 No. 23 'RANDA' at Brig before departure for Zermatt on 27/08/88. *J.D. Davis*

▲▲La BDe4/4 83 du BVB arrive à Bex avec un train de Villars, 05/04/88. *Chris Appleby*

▲La Deh4/4 23 «RANDA» du BVZ à Brigue avec un train pour Zermatt, 27/08/88. *J.D. Davis*

▼CEV Class BDeh2/4 No. 72 leaves Blonay for Les Pléiades in September 1982.
Paul Russenberger

▼▼CJ Class BDe4/4 II No. 614 at Saignélegier on a working to La Chaux-de-Fonds on 02/04/88.
Chris Appleby

▲▲La BDeh2/4 72 du CEV quitte Blonay pour Les Pléiades, Septembre 1982. *Paul Russenberger*

▲La BDe4/4 II 614 du CJ à Saignélegier avec un train pour La Chaux-de-Fonds, 02/04/88.
Chris Appleby

▼EBT SMB VHB Class RBDe4/4 II No. 283 'Crémines' leaves Burgdorf for Solothurn on 28/01/89.
Paul Russenberger

▼▼Forchbahn Class Be8/8 No. 24 and 23 at Zürich Stadelhofen where the line is physically connected to the Zürich tram system on 11/03/86.
G.B. Wise

▲▲La RBDe4/4 II 283 «Crémines» du groupe EBT-SMB-VHB quitte Burgdorf pour Soleure, 28/01/89.
Paul Russenberger

▲Les Be8/8 24 et 23 du FB à Zurich Stadelhofen ou le FB est raccordé au réseau de tramways zurichois, 11/03/86.
G.B. Wise

▼FO Class BDeh2/4 No. 41 and HGe4/4 Class Nos. 32 and 37 at Brig FO depot on 31/05/88.
Chris Appleby

▼▼FW Class Be4/4 No. 14 'Munchwilen' at Wil about to depart for Frauenfeld on 29/06/89.
J.D. Davis

▲▲La BDe2/4 41 et les HGe4/4 32 et 37 au dépôt FO de Brigue, 31/05/ 88. *Chris Appleby*

▲La Be4/4 14 «Munchwilen» du FW s'apprète à quitter Wil pour Frauenfeld, 29/06/89. *J.D. Davis*

▼GFM Class Be4/4 No. 151 'La Gruyère' standing at Montbovon on 20/06/83. *T.N. Hall*

▼▼JB Class He2/2 No. 9 at Kleine Scheidegg before departure for Jungfraujoch on 30/08/88. *J.D. Davis*

▲▲La Be4/4 151 «La Gruyère» du GFM à Montbovon, 20/06/83. *T.N. Hall*

▲La He2/2 9 du JB à Kleine Scheidegg avant son départ pour Jungfraujoch, 30/08/88. *J.D. Davis*

Jungfraubahn BDhe 2/4 No. 204 stands at Kleine Scheidegg in February 1987 below the Eiger through which it will pass on its way to Jungfraujoch. *Paul Russenberger*

La BDhe2/4 204 du JB à Kleine Scheidegg au pied de l'Eiger que le train doit traverser en tunnel pour atteindre Jungfraujoch. *Paul Russenberger*

▼LEB Class Be4/8 No. 32 and 33 at Lausanne Chauderon on 03/08/88. This line is to be extended to Lausanne Flon in the city centre. *G.B. Wise*

▼▼LSE Class BDeh4/4 No. 5 arrives from Engelberg at Hergiswil in September 1989. From here it will continue over the SBB Brünig line metre gauge tracks to Luzern. *Paul Russenberger*

▲▲Les Be4/8 32 et 33 du LEB au terminus de Lausanne Chauderon. Cette ligne doit être prolongée à Lausanne Flon dans le centre ville, 03/08/88. *G.B. Wise*

▲La BDeh4/4 5 du LSE arrive à Hergiswil d'Engelberg. Le train continuera vers Lucerne sur les voies CFF de la ligne du Brünig, Septembre 1989. *Paul Russenberger*

▼MG Class Bhe4/8 No. 13 stands in the street outside Capolago SBB station. *S.A. Sugden*

▼▼MGN Class Bhe2/4 No. 204 berthed at Montreux opposite the MOB station tracks on 04/04/88. *Chris Appleby*

▲▲La Bhe4/8 13 du MG devant la gare CFF de Capolgo. *S.A. Sugden*

▲La Bhe2/4 204 du MGN garée à Montreux en face des voies du MOB, 04/ 04/88. *Chris Appleby*

▼MIB Class Bem4/4 No. 7 at Meiringen on arrival from Innertkirchen during August 1988.
Paul Russenberger

▼▼MOB Class BDe4/4 No. 3003 at Montreux on 18/08/88. *Bevan Price*

▲▲La Bem4/4 7 du MIE aprés son arrivée à Meiringen de Innertkirchen, Aout 1988.
Paul Russenberger

▲La BDe4/4 3003 du MOB à Montreux, 18/08/88. *Bevan Price*

▼NStCM Class Be4/4 No. 204 at Nyon, where the line terminates in the street outside the SBB station, on 29/01/89. *Paul Russenberger*

▼▼Pilatusbahn Class Bhe2/4 No. 25 at Alpnachstad during September 1989. Note the unique Locher rack rail with its horizontal opposed teeth required for the world's steepest rack railway. *Paul Russenberger*

▲▲La Be4/4 204 du NStCM au terminus de Nyon devant la gare CFF, 29/01/89. *Paul Russenberger*

▲La Bhe2/4 25 du PB à Alpnachstad. Noter le système insolite de crémaillères latérales du type Locher nécessaire pour la ligne la plus raide de monde, Septembre 1989. *Paul Russenberger*

▼OSB/SNB Class Be4/4 No. 302 at Solothurn before departing for Langenthal on 28/01/89.
Paul Russenberger

▼▼RhW Class BDeh4/4 No. 1 at Rheineck on 29/05/88. This vehicle has no need for couplings as it is the RhW's sole item of rolling stock. *Chris Appleby*

▲▲La Be4/4 302 du groupe OSB-SNB à Soleure avec un train pour Langenthal, 28/01/89.
Paul Russenberger

▲La BDeh4/4 No. 1 du RhW à Rheineck. Cette voiture n'a pas d'attelages puisqu'elle est l'unique matériel du RhW, 29/05/88. *Chris Appleby*

SOB Class BDe4/4 No. 84 'SATTEL SZ' with Te III Class No. 51 at Einsiedeln on 05/09/87. *Paul Russenberger*

La BDe4/4 84 «SATTEL SZ» et la Te III 51 du SOB à Einsiedeln, 05/ 09/87. *Paul Russenberger*

▼WAB Class BDhe4/8 No. 133 at Kleine Schiedegg while working on the Lauterbrunnen–Wengen–Kleine Scheidegg section of the line on 30/08/ 88. *J.D. Davis*

▼▼VRB Class BDhe4/4 No. 5 and Bhe2/4 Class No. 1 at Vitznau station during September 1987. *Paul Russenberger*

▲▲La BDhe4/8 133 du WAB à Kleine Schiedegg assure un service sur la ligne à Lauterbrunnen via Wengen, 30/08/88. *J.D. Davis*

▲La BDhe4/4 No. 5 et la Bhe2/4 No. 1 du VRB à Vitznau, Septembre 1987. *Paul Russenberger*

MONTE GENEROSO (636) MG

The only mountain rack line south of the Gotthard pass, the MG was electrified as late as 1982. For many years prior to this, the line was diesel operated. Some of the old diesel stock still remains on the line, either stored or for works or reserve use.

La seule ligne de montagne à crémaillère au sud du col du Gothard. La ligne fut exploitée en traction diesel pendant longtemps avant d'être électrifiée en 1982. Certains matériels diesel subsistent mais sont soit garés soit gardés en réserve.

Gauge/Ecartement: 800 mm.
Electrical System/Courant: 650 V dc/continu.
Depot/Dépôt: Capolago.

Hm2/3	1	SLM/MG/VM	-	11.5	11.5	280	1953
Hm2/3	2	SLM/MG/VM	-	11.5	11.7	280	1954
Bhm2/4	4	SIG/BÜS/SAU/MAN	60	18	15.6	335	1957
Hm2/2	7	BÜH/PLEI/MG	-	14	9.8	280	1975
Bhe4/8	11	SLM/SE	96	14	34.1	810	1982
Bhe4/8	12	SLM/SE	96	14	34.1	810	1982
Bhe4/8	13	SLM/SE	96	14	34.1	810	1982
Bhe4/8	14	SLM/SE	96	14	34.1	810	1982

MONTREUX–GLION–NAYE (121) MGN

Formed 1987 by the merger of the Montreux–Glion (MGl) & Glion–Naye (GN), which had operated as a single entity for many years under the management of the MOB. A pure rack line giving excellent views over Lake Geneva.

Créé en 1987 par la fusion du Montreux Glion (MGl) et le Glion Rochers de Naye (GN), qui furent gerés en commun par le MOB pendant longtemps. C'est une ligne entièrement à crémaillère qui donne des panoramas superbes sur le Lac Léman.

Gauge/Ecartement: 800 mm.
Electrical System/Courant: 850 V dc/continu.
Depot/Dépôt: Glion.

HGe2/2	2		SLM/MFO	-	13	14.2	162 1909
HGe2/2	101		SLM/MOB/MFO	-	13	14.5	162 1909 (76)
Bhe2/4	201		SLM/BBC	52	17.5	15.5	150 1938
Bhe2/4	202		SLM/BBC	52	17.5	15.5	150 1938
Bhe2/4	203		SLM/BBC	52	17.5	15.5	150 1938
Bhe2/4	204		SLM/BBC	52	17.5	15.5	150 1938
Bhe2/4	205		SLM/BBC	52	17.5	15.5	150 1938
Bhe2/4	206		SLM/BBC	52	17.5	15.5	150 1947
Bhe2/4	207		SLM/BBC	52	17.5	15.5	150 1949
Bhe2/4	208		SLM/BBC	52	17.5	15.5	150 1966
Bhe4/8	301	MONTREUX	SLM/SE	96	22	34	800 1983
Bhe4/8	302	VEYTAUX	SLM/SE	96	22	34	800 1983
Bhe4/8	303	VILLENEUVE	SLM/SE	96	22	34	800 1983

MEIRINGEN–INNERTKIRCHEN BAHN (474) MIB

Originally built as a construction railway for a hydro-electric scheme, this line was later opened to the public. For many years the line was battery operated, and was only electrified in 1977 using second-hand cars from the OEG (Mannheim).

Cette ligne fut construite en 1926 pour faciliter la construction d'un barrage hydro-électrique et ouverte au public en 1946. L'exploitation était par voitures à accumulateurs jusqu'à l'électrification en 1977. Le matériel consiste en tramways d'occasion rachetés de OEG (Mannheim).

Gauge/Ecartement: 1000 mm. **Electrical System/Courant:** 1200 V dc/continu.
Depot/Dépôt: Innertkirchen.

Bem4/4	6	FUCHS/BBC(M)/VW/SBB(MR)	34	65	22	240 1952 (77)
Bem4/4	7	FUCHS/BBC(M)/VW/SBB(MR)	34	65	22	240 1952 (77)

MOB Class ABDe8/8 No. 4004 'FRIBOURG' passing Chamby with the 16.20 Montreux to Zweisimmen on 30/07/88. It is climbing from Montreux to the first summit of the line in the Jaman Tunnel; this section includes the steepest adhesion worked gradient in Switzerland of 6%. *G.B. Wise*

La ABDe8/8 4004 «FRIBOURG» du MOB traverse Chamby avec un train Montreux–Zweisimmen. Le train monte vers le premier sommet de la ligne dans le tunnel de Jaman; cette section comporte la rampe la plus raide de Suisse exploitée en adhérence. 30/07/88. *G.B. Wise*

MARTIGNY ORSIÈRES (133) MO

A standard gauge light railway serving an area to the south of the Rhône Valley.
Une ligne à écartement normal qui dessert une région au sud de la vallée du Rhône.

Gauge/Ecartement: 1435 mm.
Electrical System/Courant: 15 kV 16⅔ Hz ac/monophasé.
Depots/Dépôts: Orsières, Martigny Croix.

ABDe4/4	5		ACMV/BBC	24	60	52	736	1955
ABDe4/4	6	ORSIÈRES	SIG/SWS/SAAS/BBC/MFO	6/47	100	64	1076	1965
ABDe4/4	7	MARTIGNY	SIG/SWS/SAAS/BBC/MFO	6/47	100	64	1076	1965
ABDe4/4	8	BAGNES	SIG/SWS/SAAS/BBC/MFO	6/47	100	64	1076	1965
ABDe4/4	9	SEMBRANCHER	SIG/SWS/SAAS/BBC/MFO	6/47	100	64	1076	1965
Tm2/2	512		DZ	-	34	21	96	1960
Tm2/2	514*		SLM/SAU	-	15	21	80	1928

* Originally SBB Em2/2 101/à l'origine Em2/2 101 des CFF.

MONTREUX OBERLAND BERNOIS (120, 321) MOB

The MOB is a lengthy metre gauge railway linking Montreux with Zweisimmen, where connections can be made for Interlaken. There is also a branch from Zweisimmen to Lenk. The climb out of Montreux is one of the world's steepest adhesion worked lines, and excellent views can be had over Lake Geneva. It is intended to convert the line from Zweisimmen to Interlaken (SEZ/BLS owned) to mixed gauge to enable through trains to operate to Luzern over the Brünig line.

Le MOB est une assez longue ligne entre Montreux et Zweisimmen, où il existe une correspondance pour Interlaken. De Zweisimmen il y a une deuxième ligne jusqu'à Lenk. La rampe en sortant de Montreux est une des plus raides du monde à être exploitée en adhérence et offre de magnifiques panoramas sur le lac Léman. Un projet existe pour convertir la ligne Zweisimmen–Interlaken (qui appartient aux SEZ et BLS) à écartement mixte afin de permettre des trains directs entre Zweisimmen et Lucerne par la ligne du Brünig.
Gauge/Ecartement: 1000 mm.
Electrical System/Courant: 850 V dc/continu.
Depots/Dépôts: Chernex, Montreux, Zweisimmen.

Tm2/2	1		OK	-	12	7	30	1938
Tm2/2	2		DZ	-	30	15.7	92	1953
ABDe4/4	11		SIG/ALIOTH		50	29	250	1904
BDe4/4	16		SIG/ALIOTH	28	35	27.6	192	1905
BDe4/4	18		SIG/ALIOTH	28	50	27.6	192	1905
BDe4/4	20		SIG/ALIOTH	28	35	27.6	192	1906
Xe4/4	22		SIG/ALIOTH	-	50	29.6	192	1906
BDe4/4	26		SIG/ALIOTH	21	50	33.5	336	1912
BDe4/4	27		SIG/BBC	14	50	36.2	388	1924
BDe4/4	28		SIG/BBC	14	50	36.2	388	1924
BDe4/4	36		SIG/BBC	40	65	26.7	368	1913
BDe4/4	37		SIG/MFO	40	60	25	218	1913
Be4/4	1001		ACMV/BBC/SWS/MFO	64	45	30.4	308	1955
Be4/4	1002		SWS/SAAS	56	60	29	176	1951
Be4/4	1003		SWS/SAAS/SLM/BBC	56	55	31	244	1958
Be4/4	1004		SWS/BBC	40	65	26.9	294	1948
DZe6/6	2001		SIG/BBC	-	65	62.8	738	1932
DZe6/6	2002		SIG/BBC	-	65	62.8	738	1933
Gm4/4	2003	MONTBOVON	MOY/POY/CFD	-	80	44	515	1976
Gm4/4	2004	ALBEUVE	MOY/POY/CFD	-	80	44	515	1982
BDe4/4	3001	ROUGEMONT	SIG/BBC	42	75	35.7	440	1944
BDe4/4	3002	CHÂTEAU D'OEX	SIG/BBC	42	75	35.7	440	1944
BDe4/4	3003		SIG/BBC	32	75	35.7	440	1944
BDe4/4	3004		SIG/BBC	32	75	35.7	440	1944
BDe4/4	3005		SIG/BBC	24	75	36	440	1946
BDe4/4	3006		SIG/BBC	24	75	36	440	1946
ABDe8/8	4001	SUISSE	SIG/BBC/SAAS	86	70	60	880	1968
ABDe8/8	4002	VAUD	SIG/BBC/SAAS	86	70	60	880	1968

MOB Class GDe4/4 No. 6001 'VEVEY' passes Chamby with the 15.00 Zweisimmen to Montreux 'Panoramic Express', formed of observation coaches, on 30/07/88. *G.B. Wise*

La GDe4/4 6001 «VEVEY» du MOB traverse Chamby avec le «Panorama Express» de Zweisimmen à Montreux, qui comporte des voitures panoramiques. 30/07/88. *G.B. Wise*

ABDe8/8	4003 BERN	SIG/BBC/SAAS	86	70	60	880	1968
ABDe8/8	4004 FRIBOURG	SIG/BBC/SAAS	86	70	60	880	1968
BDe4/4	5001 MONTREUX	SIG/SAAS	48	80	32	448	1976
BDe4/4	5002 ZWEISIMMEN	SIG/SAAS	48	80	32	448	1976
BDe4/4	5003 LENK	SIG/SAAS	48	80	32	448	1979
BDe4/4	5004 ST STEPHAN	SIG/SAAS	48	80	32	448	1979
GDe4/4	6001 VEVEY	SLM/BBC	-	90	48.2	1053	1983
GDe4/4	6002 ROSSINIÈRE	SLM/BBC	-	90	48.2	1053	1983
GDe4/4	6003 SAANEN	SLM/BBC	-	90	48.2	1053	1983
GDe4/4	6004 INTERLAKEN	SLM/BBC	-	90	48.2	1053	1983

On order: 3 Ge4/4 (convertible to dual voltage for through operation to Luzern).
En commande: 3 Ge4/4 (transformable en mode bi-courant pour des trains directs jusqu'à Lucerne)

MITTEL THURGAU BAHN (830) MThB

A standard gauge line in north east Switzerland linking Wil and Kreuzlingen, with through operation over the SBB to Konstanz in West Germany.

Une ligne à écartement normal entre Wil et Kreutzlingen dans le nord-est de la Suisse. Certains trains empruntent les voies CFF jusqu'à Constance en Allemagne Fédérale.

Gauge/Ecartement: 1435 mm.
Electrical System/Courant: 15 kV 16⅔ Hz ac/monophasé.
Depot/Dépôt: Weinfelden.

ABDe4/4	11	WIL	SIG/SWS/SAAS/BBC/MFO	12/39	100	64	1076	1965
ABDe4/4	12	WEINFELDEN	SIG/SWS/SAAS/BBC/MFO	12/39	100	64	1076	1965
ABDe4/4	13	KREUZLINGEN	SIG/SWS/SAAS/BBC/MFO	12/39	100	64	1076	1965
ABDe4/4	14	KONSTANZ	SIG/SWS/SAAS/BBC/MFO	12/39	100	64	1076	1965
ABDe4/4	15	BERG	SIG/SWS/SAAS/BBC/MFO	12/39	100	64	1076	1965
ABDe4/4	16		SIG/SWS/SAAS/BBC/MFO	12/31	100	64	1076	1966
Re4/4 II	21		SLM/BBC/MFO/SAAS	-	140	80	4650	1969
Em2/2	41	ROLFLI	STAD/BBC	-	60	30	315	1972
Tm2/2	51	SEPPLI	STAD/BBC	-	60	29	315	1966
Tm II	61		RACO/SAU	-	45	10	70	1969
Ee3/3	16318*		SLM/BBC	-	40	45	428	1928

* ex SBB 16318/ex 16318 des CFF.

NYON–ST CERGUE–MOREZ (155) NStCM

Once an international line linking Nyon on Lake Geneva with Morez in France, the French section was closed as long ago as 1958. Recently under threat of closure, the line has now been modernised with new rolling stock.

Autrefois une ligne internationale entre Nyon, sur les rives du lac Léman, et Morez en France. La section françcaise fut fermée en 1958. Après des menaces de fermeture, la ligne fut modernisée avec un nouveau matériel.

Gauge/Ecartement: 1000 mm.
Electrical System/Courant: 1500 V dc/continu.
Depots/Dépôts: Nyon Les Plantaz, St Cergue.

ABDe4/4	11	SWS/BBC	5/25	40	32.5	296	1918
Be4/4	201	ACMV/BBC/SAAS	40	65	33	752	1985
Be4/4	202	ACMV/BBC/SAAS	40	65	33	752	1985
Be4/4	203	ACMV/BBC/SAAS	40	65	33	752	1985
Be4/4	204	ACMV/BBC/SAAS	40	65	33	752	1985
Be4/4	205	ACMV/BBC/SAAS	40	65	33	752	1986
BDe4/4	211	ACMV/ABB		65	33	752	on order/
BDe4/4	212	ACMV/ABB		65	33	752	en commande
Tm2/2	251*	BEIL	-	50	22.1	149	1984

* Can be fitted with rotary snowplough when classification becomes Xtm2/2.
* Peut être doté d'un chasse-neige rotatif. Classification devient Xtm2/2.

▼OC Class BDe4/4 No. 13 between turns waits at Orbe on 30/07/88. *G.B. Wise*

▼▼Old and new at Orbe. OC Class De2/2 No. 32 restored as Fe2/2 (left) stands next to Class Ee2/2 No. 1 on 30/07/88. *G.B. Wise*

▲▲La BDe4/4 13 du OC attend à Orbe entre deux services. 30/07/88. *G.B. Wise*

▲Du vieux et du nouveau à Orbe. La De2/2 32 du OC, restaurée sous la classification Fe2/2 (à gauche) cotoie la Ee2/2 1. 30/07/88. *G.B. Wise*

ORBE CHAVORNAY (211) OC

A short branch line north of Lausanne which is the only Swiss private standard gauge adhesion line with dc electrification. The two elderly railcars which operated all passenger services have now been replaced by a new 4-wheel car built by Stadler.

Une courte ligne au nord de Lausanne qui est la seule ligne privée à voie normale électrifiée en courant continu en Suisse. Les deux vieilles automotrices qui furent utilisées pour tous les trains voyageurs ont été remplacées par une nouvelle automotrice à 2 essieux construite par Stadler.

Gauge/Ecartement: 1435 mm.
Electrical System/Courant: 700 V dc/continu.
Depots/Dépôts: Orbe, Les Granges.

Ee2/2	1	SIG/MFO	-	55	40	456	1970
Ee2/2	2	SIG/MFO	-	55	40	456	1970
Em3/3	3	HEN	-	50	60	550	1985
BDe4/4	12	SWS/MFO	60	50	29.5	130	1915
BDe4/4	13	SWS/MFO	60	50	29.5	130	1920
Be2/2	14	STAD/ABB	40	80	20	160	1990
De2/2	32	SWS/MFO	-	45	15.4	106	1902
De2/2	33	SWS/MFO	-	45	18	88	1921

OENSINGEN BALSTHAL BAHN (412) OeBB

A short branch line connecting with the SBB at Oensingen and using a motley selection of mostly second hand stock.

Une courte ligne, en correspondance avec les CFF à Oensingen, avec une sélection hétéroclite de matériel.

Gauge/Ecartement: 1435 mm.
Electrical System/Courant: 15 kV 16⅔ Hz ac/monophasé.
Depot/Dépôt: Balsthal.

Ce2/2	102	SLM/SAAS	-	60	28	257	1944
Ce2/2	103	SLM/SAAS	-	60	28	257	1947
Be2/4	201 (ex BLS 721)	SIG/BLS/BBC	60	90	34	220	1935
RBe2/4	202 (ex SBB 1007)	SLM/BBC/MFO/SAAS	67	125	38	394	1938
BDe4/12	204 *	MAN/ME/AEG/BBC/SSW	206	120	125	920	1935
De6/6	15301 (ex SBB 15301)	SLM/BBC	-	50	73	862	1926

* Ex DB 425.120 + 825.020 + 425.420.

OSST (ex-SNB) Class BDe4/4 No. 312 stands in the sidings at Langenthal on 14/04/ 86. *G.B. Wise*

La BDe4/4 312 du OSST (anciennement du SNB) est vue à Langenthal. 14/04/ 86. *G.B. Wise*

OSST (ex–BTI) Class Be4/4 No. 505 leaves Biel on the 11.50 to Täuffelen about to run for a short distance along the street before regaining its dedicated right of way on 14/04/86. *G.B. Wise*

La Be4/4 505 du OSST (anciennement du BTI) quitte Bienne avec un train pour Täufflen. Le train va s'engager sur une section de voie établie sur route avant de regagner le site propre. 14/04/86. *G.B. Wise*

OBERAARGAU SOLOTHURN SEELAND TRANSPORT OSST

This is the new group name for three light railways to the north and west of Bern, these being:

Le OSST est le nouveau nom sous lequel sont regroupés trois compagnies du nord et de l'ouest de Berne, soit:

BIEL–TÄUFFELEN–INS (261) BTI
REGIONALVERKEHR OBERAARGAU (413) RVO
SOLOTHURN NIEDERBIPP BAHN (413). SNB

The RVO was the OJB (Oberaargau Jura Bahn) until July 1990.
Le RVO fut appelé le OJB (Oberaargau Jura Bahn) jusqu'en 7/90).

There is now a common numbering system, and it is planned to replace most of the existing stock with tramway-type cars.

Avec le regroupement, on a introduit un système commun de numérotation. Il existe un projet pour le remplacement de la plupart du matériel existant par des véhicules de type tramway.

Gauge/Ecartement: 1000 mm.
Electrical System/Courant: 1200 V dc/continu.
Depots/Dépôts: Langenthal (RVO), Täufflen (BTI), Wiedlisbach (SNB).

Be4/4	101		SWS/MFO/BBC	52	60	32	368	1966
Be4/4	102		SWS/MFO/BBC	52	60	32	368	1966
Be4/4	103		SWS/OJB/SAAS	52	60	32	308	1973
Be4/4	108	MELCHNAU	SWS/OJB/MFO/SAAS	40	60	26	308	1913 (69)
Be4/4	109		SWS/SAAS	58	55	28	280	1963
Bre4/4	116		RING/ALIOTH	30	50	23.2	216	1907
De4/4	121		STAD/SIG/ABB	–	65	45	1040	1987
De4/4	122		SIG/BBC	–	50	24	206	1917
Ge4/4	126		SIG/BBC	–	35	20	206	1917
Xe4/4	131		SWS/MFO	–	45	26	216	1913
Xe2/2	132		SIG/BBC	–	50	15	104	1917
Tm	141		RACO/DZ	–	75	19	177	1985
Tm	142		RACO/PER	–	28	5.3	41	1933
Be4/4	301		SWS/MFO/BBC	52	60	32	368	1966
Be4/4	302		SWS/MFO/BBC	52	60	32	368	1966
Be4/4	303	SOLOTHURN	SWS/BBC	52	60	32	368	1971
Be4/4	304	WIEDLISBACH	SWS/MFO/BBC	52	60	32	368	1978
BDe4/4	311		SWS/MFO/SAAS	46	60	25.5	308	1918
BDe4/4	312		SWS/MFO	46	45	25	216	1918
De4/4	321		SZB/MFO	–	50	30.1	264	1957
Be4/4	501		SWS/MFO	48	65	33.7	368	1965
Be4/4	502		SWS/MFO	48	65	33.7	368	1965
Be4/4	503		SWS/MFO	48	65	33.7	368	1965
Be4/4	504		SWS/MFO	48	65	33.7	368	1970
Be4/4	505		SWS/MFO	48	65	33.7	368	1970
BDe4/4	511		SWS/MFO	40	60	34.1	264	1924
BDe4/4	512		SWS/MFO	46	60	33.4	264	1916
Tm	541		RACO/DZ	–	75	19	177	1985
Tm	542		RACO/ZÜR	–	45	4.8	22	1929

Note/Nota: 101–142 RVO, 301–321 SNB, 501–542 BTI.

PILATUS BAHN (473) PB

The world's steepest rack railway, requiring the "Locher" rack system, comprising a horizontal rack rail, the railcars having two pinions, one on each side of the rack.

Le chemin de fer à crémaillère le plus raide du monde qui nécessite un système de crémaillères latéraux dit «Locher». Les véhicules ont deux roues à pignon, une sur chaque côté de la crémaillère.

Gauge/Ecartement: 800 mm **Electrical System/Courant:** 1550 V dc/continu.
Depot/Dépôt: Alpnachstad.

Bhe1/2	21	SLM/MFO	40	12	9.65	155	1937
Bhe1/2	22	SLM/MFO	40	12	9.65	155	1937
Bhe1/2	23	SLM/MFO	40	12	9.65	155	1937
Bhe1/2	24	SLM/MFO	40	12	9.65	155	1937
Bhe1/2	25	SLM/MFO	40	12	9.65	155	1937
Bhe1/2	26	SLM/MFO	40	12	9.65	155	1937
Bhe1/2	27	SLM/MFO	40	12	9.65	155	1937
Bhe1/2	28	SLM/MFO	40	12	9.65	155	1937
Bhe1/2	29	SLM/MFO	40	12	9.6	155	1962
Bhe1/2	30	SLM/MFO	40	12	10.5	175	1968
Ohe1/2	31	SLM/MFO	–	12	8.3	155	1954
Xhm1/2	32	SLM/STAD/BBC	–	12	11.3	320	1981

Note: Only one underframe exists for cars 29 & 31, the bodies being exchanged as required. Hence, only one of these two cars can be in use at any one time.

Nota: Il n'existe qu'un chassis pour les voitures 29 et 31! Les caisses sont montées sur le chassis en alternance. En conséquence, seule une des ces deux voitures peut être utilisée à la fois.

PONT BRASSUS BAHN (201) PBr

A somewhat remote line in the west of the country, the PBr has always been operated by the SBB and its predecessors. The PBr never owned any motive power until tractor 101 was purchased from the SBB in 1982. Services have always run through to Vallorbe, but from 1989 these have been extended to Lausanne using railcars 2184–5, numbered in the SBB list and operated by them, but financed by the local Canton and lettered for the PBr (Vallée de Joux).

Une ligne assez isolée dans l'ouest du pays. Le PBr a toujours été exploité par les CFF et ses prédécesseurs. Le PBr ne fut pas propriétaire de matériel jusqu'en 1982, année où la compagnie a racheté le locotracteur 101 aux CFF. Les services du PBr sont toujours allés sur les voies CFF jusqu'à Vallorbe mais furent prolongés jusqu'à Lausannne en 1989 en utilisant les automotrices 2184 à 5. Celles-ci appartiennent aux et sont exploitées par les CFF mais furent financées par le canton; elles portent le sigle PBr et sont marquées «Vallée de Joux».

Gauge/Ecartement: 1435 mm.
Electrical System/Courant: 15 kV 16⅔ Hz ac/monophasé.
Depot/Dépôt: Le Brassus.

Te2/2	101	(ex SBB 957)	SLM/MFO	–	45	12	90	1946

POST TELEPHON TELEGRAPH PTT

Not a private railway, the Swiss Post Office is included since it uses shunting locos at a number of locations, often involving operation into SBB stations. Locations of locos are shown in the last column.

Ce n'est pas un chemin de fer privé, mais les PTT suisses sont inclu puisqu'ils ont des machines de manoeuvres à plusieurs endroits (voir la dernière colonne) qui sont parfois vues dans les gares CFF.

Te III	3	SLM/SAAS	60	28	250	1952	Lausanne
Ee3/3	4	SLM/BBC/MFO/SAAS	45	45	502	1962	Luzern/Lucerne
Te III	5	SLM/MFO	60	28	245	1965	Lausanne
Em3/3	6	HEN	60	45	375	1965	Zürich Mülligen
Ee3/3	7	SLM/BBC	40	45	428	1928	Zürich Mülligen
Ee3/3	8	SLM/BBC	60	48	660	1985	Zürich Mülligen
Ee3/3	9	SLM/BBC	60	48	660	1985	Zürich Mülligen
Ee3/3	10	SLM/BBC	60	48	660	1985	Daniken
Ee3/3	11	SLM/BBC	60	48	660	1985	Bern/Berne
Tm	12	SCH	23	14	81	1958	Ostermundigen
Tm	13	UNIMOG/MERC	20	6.8	92	1978	Kriens

REGIONALVERKEHR BERN–SOLOTHURN (293, 294, 295, 420) RBS

Once two separate railways, under common management for many years, the former SZB

(Solothurn Zollikofon Bern) and VBW (Vereinigte Bern Worb Bahnen) were merged as the RBS in 1985. The railway provides frequent suburban services from Bern, and at one time all routes entered the town over the urban tram tracks. A new line, terminating in an underground station below BernHB was opened in 1965, and is used by all Solothurn line trains, plus those on the ex VBW route from Worb via Bolligen. The other ex VBW route to Worb via Muri still enters Bern over the urban tram tracks, and terminates at the inconveniently located Helvetiaplatz. Due to the width and weight of the existing rolling stock, the cars could not continue further. Therefore, new tramway type cars have been purchased for this route, which will be extended into Bern centre once bridge strengthening is complete.

Auparavant deux compagnies distinctes mais gérées en commun pendant plusieurs années, l'ancien SZB (Solothurn Zollikofen Bern) et VBW (Vereinigte Bern Worb Bahnen) fusionnèrent en 1985 pour devenir le RBS. Ce réseau exploite des services de banlieue fréquents à partir de Berne. Dans le passé toutes les routes sont entrées dans Berne sur les voies du tramway urbain, mais en 1965 une nouvelle ligne finissant dans une station souterraine sous la gare centrale de Berne fut ouverte. La ligne est utilisée par tous les trains de la ligne de Soleure et ceux de l'ancienne ligne VBW de Worb via Bollingen. L'ancienne ligne VBW de Worb via Muri est toujours reliée au tramway urbain et les trains arrivent au terminus mal situé de Helvetiaplatz. Etant donné leur poids et leur largeur, les anciennes voitures VBW ne peuvent pas continuer au delà. Le RBS a donc acheté des voitures de type tramway pour cette route dont les services seront prolongés jusqu'au centre de Berne dès que des travaux de renforcement de ponts seront finis.

Gauge/Ecartement: 1000 mm.
Electrical System/Courant: 1250 V dc/continu (Bern–Muri–Worb 800 V dc/continu).
Depots/Dépôts: Solothurn, Worblaufen, Worb (2 depots), Boll–Utzigen.

BDre4/4	1		SWS/MFO	36	75	36.4	512	1916
BDre4/4	3		SWS/MFO	36	75	35.5	512	1929
BDre4/4	4		SWS/MFO	44	75	34.6	512	1950
BDe4/4	5		SWS/MFO	40	75	34.6	512	1950
BDe4/4	6		SWS/MFO	40	75	34.6	512	1950
BDre4/4	21		SWS/MFO	40	75	34	512	1955
BDre4/4	22		SWS/MFO	40	75	34	512	1955
BDre4/4	23		SWS/MFO	40	75	34	512	1955
BDe4/4	24		SWS/MFO	36	75	33.3	264	1916
Be4/8	41		SIG/BBC	136	75	48.7	326	1974
Be4/8	42		SIG/BBC	136	75	48.7	326	1974
Be4/8	43		SIG/BBC	136	75	48.7	326	1974
Be4/8	44		SIG/BBC	136	75	48.7	326	1974
Be4/8	45		SIG/BBC	136	75	48.7	326	1974
Be4/8	46		SIG/BBC	136	75	48.7	326	1974
Be4/8	48		SIG/BBC	136	75	48.7	326	1974
Be4/8	49		SIG/BBC	136	75	48.7	326	1974
Be4/8	50		SIG/BBC	136	75	48.7	326	1974
Be4/8	51		SIG/BBC	136	75	48.7	326	1974
Be4/8	52		SIG/BBC	136	75	48.7	326	1974
Be4/8	53		SIG/BBC	136	75	48.7	326	1978
Be4/8	54		SIG/BBC	136	75	48.7	326	1978
Be4/8	55		SIG/BBC	136	75	48.7	326	1978
Be4/8	56		SIG/BBC	136	75	48.7	326	1978
Be4/8	57		SIG/BBC	136	75	48.7	326	1978
Be4/8	58		SIG/BBC	136	75	48.7	326	1978
Be4/8	59		SIG/BBC	136	75	48.7	326	1978
Be4/8	60		SIG/BBC	136	75	48.7	326	1978
Be4/8	61		SIG/BBC	136	75	48.7	326	1978
Be4/4	74	*	SWS/MFO	36	65	28	240	1961
Be4/8	81	*		–				1987
Be4/8	82	*		–				1987
Be4/8	83	*		–				1987
Be4/8	84	*		–				1987
Be4/8	85	*		–				1987
Be4/8	86	*		–				1987
Be4/8	87	*		–				1987
Be4/8	88	*		–				1987
Be4/8	89	*		–				1988

De4/4	101	SZB/MFO	–	50	34	264	1961
De4/4	102	SZB/MFO	–	50	34.7	264	1965
De4/4	103	SZB/BBC/AEG	–	40	40	548	1973
De4/4	105 †	SIG/SZB/MFO	–	50	32	412	1924
Ge4/4	111 †	AEG	–	35	34	470	1927
Ge4/4	112 †	AEG	–	35	34	470	1927
Gem4/4	121	SIG/MFO/DZ	–	45	23	132/96	1912
Gem4/4	122	SWS/MFO/SSW/DZ	–	50	38	264	1916
Xm1/2	151	LÜTHI/VBW/VW	–	40	3.5	25	1925
Tm	162	RACO/DZ	–	30	3.2	37	1932

* 800 V dc cars/voitures utilisées sous 800 V continu.
† dual voltage/matériel bi-courant.

On order/en commande: 8 ABe4/8 & 3 Be4/8 from/de SIG/ABB (90 km/h, 600 kW).

RORSCHACH HEIDEN BAHN (857) RHB

A short rack and adhesion line running into the hills above Rorschach, with through running over the SBB to Rorschach Hafen.

Une courte ligne avec section à crémaillère qui monte les collines au-dessus de Rorschach. Les trains utilisent les voies CFF jusqu'à Rorschach Hafen.

Gauge/Ecartement: 1435 mm.
Electrical System/Courant: 15 kV 16⅔ Hz ac/monophasé.
Depots/Dépôts: Heiden, Rorschach.

DZeh2/4	21	SLM/MFO	–	25	42.8	420	1930
DZeh2/4	22	SLM/MFO	–	25	42.8	420	1930
ABDeh2/4	23	SLM/BBC	7/50	25	42.3	550	1953
ABDeh2/4	24	SLM/BBC	7/50	25	42.3	550	1967

RHEINECK WALZENHAUSEN (858) RhW

Once a tramway with a connecting funicular, the whole line was converted to rack and adhesion operation in 1958. This is one of the smallest Swiss railways, less than 2 km long with just one item of motive power.

A l'origine un tramway avec prolongement en funiculaire, la ligne fut transformée en 1958 pour une exploitation à crémaillère et en adhérence. C'est un des plus petits chemins de fer suisses – moins de 2km de voie et une seule voiture!

Gauge/Ecartement: 1200 mm.
Electrical System/Courant: 600 V dc/continu.
Depot: Ruderbach (but car normally stables overnight in Walzenhausen station).
Dépôt: Ruderbach (mais la voiture reste dans la gare de Walzenhausen chaque nuit).

BDeh1/2	1	SLM/FFA/BBC	28	30/20	14.7	215	1958

REGIONAL DE VAL DE TRAVERS (221) RVT

A secondary line in the west of the country, through services running over the SBB to Neuchâtel. The Fleurier to St Sulpice branch is freight only, but does see occasional use for steam specials.

Une ligne secondaire à l'ouest du pays avec services directs sur voies CFF jusqu'à Neuchâtel. La ligne Fleurier à St Sulpice n'a qu'un service marchandises mais voit parfois des trains spéciaux à vapeur.

Gauge/Ecartement: 1435 mm.
Electrical System/Courant: 15 kV 16⅔ Hz ac/monophasé.
Depot/Dépôt: Fleurier.

Be4/4	1		ACMV/SAAS	–	75	45	690	1951
Tm	12		RACO/DZ	–	75	19	177	1983
ABDe2/4	101		SWS/BBC	59	75	40	412	1944
ABDe2/4	102		SWS/BBC	59	75	40	412	1945
RABDe4/4	104	MÔTIERS NE	SIG/SWS/BBC	15/28	125	70	1700	1983
RABDe4/4	105	FLEURIER	SIG/SWS/BBC	15/28	125	70	1700	1983

RBDe4/4	106	COUVET	SWS/BBC	1985
RBDe4/4	107			on order/ en commande

S.A. DES TRANSPORTS EMOSSON BARBARINE (1143) SATEB

A most unusual line, originally built to provide access to a hydro-electric scheme. Connecting with the MC at Le Châtelard–Giétroz, there is a funicular to Château d'Eau and a narrow gauge line from here to Emosson. From Emosson a battery operated rack monorail continues to Barrage.

Une ligne très insolite qui fut construite pour donner accès à un barrage hydro-électrique. A partir de la gare du Châtelard Giétroz il y a un funiculaire jusqu'à Château d'Eau, puis une ligne à voie étroite jusqu'à Emosson. D'Emosson il y a un monorail à crémaillère avec véhicules à accumulateurs jusqu'au Barrage.

Gauge/Ecartement: 600 mm.
Electrical System/Courant: not electrified/non-électrifié.
Depot/Dépôt: Château d'Eau.

Tm2/2	4	LISTER	–	7.4	3.6	12	1940
Ta2/2	5	SSW	–	12	6	30	1952
Ta2/2	6	SSW	–	12	6	30	1952
Ta2/2	7	SSW	–	12	6	30	1952
Ta2/2	8	SSW	–	12	6	30	1952

SCHWEIZERISCHE SUDOSTBAHN (670, 671, 672) SOB

This line running from Arth Goldau on the Gotthard line to Rapperswil provides the middle section of the Luzern to Romanshorn route, over which a through service is operated jointly with the SBB and BT. There are also branches to Einsiedeln and Wädenswil and a surprisingly frequent service is operated.

Cette ligne entre Arth Goldau, sur la ligne du Gothard, et Rapperswil forme la section médiane de la route Lucerne–Romanshorn, sur laquelle un service direct est exploité par les CFF et le BT. Il y a aussi des branches jusqu'à Einsiedeln et Wädenswil avec des services très fréquents.

Gauge/Ecartement: 1435 mm.
Electrical System/Courant: 15 kV 16⅔ Hz ac/monophasé.
Depot/Dépôt: Samstagern.

ABe4/4	5		SLM/SWS/BBC/MFO/SAAS	53	80	44	745	1939
ABDe2/4	9	(ex BT 44)	SLM/SWP/SAAS	56	80	62	600	1952
ABe4/4	11	BURGHALDEN	SLM/SWS/BBC/MFO/SAAS	50	80	46.5	745	1940
ABe4/4	12	SAMSTAGERN	SLM/SWS/BBC/MFO/SAAS	50	80	46.5	745	1940
ABe4/4	13	RICHTERSWIL	SLM/SIG/BBC/MFO/SAAS	50	80	46.5	745	1940
ABe4/4	14	GRÜNFELD	SLM/SIG/BBC/MFO/SAAS	50	80	46.5	745	1940
De4/4	21	(ex SBB 603)	SLM/SIG/BBC/MFO/SAAS	–	90	47	1000	1940
De4/4	22	(ex SBB 602)	SLM/SIG/BBC/MFO/SAAS	–	90	47	1000	1940
Te2/2	31		SLM/SAAS	–	60	28.5	260	1943
Tm2/2	32	SCHNARCHLI	JUNG/DBZ	–	14	12	30	1958
Tm2/2	33	WILEN	STAD/CAT	–	60	37.7	565	1983
Tm2/2	34*	MANDARINLI	JUNG/KAEL	–				1960
Re4/4 III	41		SLM/BBC/MFO/SAAS	–	125	80	4650	1967
Re4/4 III	42†	ARTH GOLDAU	SLM/BBC/MFO/SAAS	–	125	80	4650	1971
Re4/4 III	43†	ROTHENTHURM	SLM/BBC/MFO/SAAS	–	125	80	4650	1971
Re4/4 III	44†	PFÄFFIKON	SLM/BBC/MFO/SAAS	–	125	80	4650	1971
Te2/2	52§		SLM/MFO	–	45	12	90	1950
BDe4/4	80	EINSIEDELN	SIG/BBC	32	110	71.5	1595	1959
BDe4/4	81	WÄDENSWIL	SIG/BBC	32	110	72	2135	1959
BDe4/4	82	RAPPERSWIL	SIG/BBC	32	110	72	2135	1966
BDe4/4	83	STEINERBERG	SIG/BBC	32	110	72	2135	1978
BDe4/4	84	SATTEL	SIG/BBC	32	110	72	2135	1979
BDe4/4	85	FEUSISBERG	SIG/BBC	32	110	72	2135	1979
BDe4/4	86	WOLLERAU	SIG/BBC	32	110	72	2135	1979
BDe4/4	87	FREIENBACH	SIG/BBC	32	110	72	2135	1979

* ex DB 323 812. † ex SBB 11352/3/1. § ex SBB 959.

▼SOB Class Re4/4 ^{III} No. 42 'ARTH GOLDAU' stands at Einsiedeln before working the 16.23 to Wädenswil. This locomotive was originally SBB No. 11352. *G.B. Wise*

▼▼SPB Class He2/2 No. 14 in red and cream livery stands at Schynige Platte in September 1988. *Paul Russenberger*

▲▲La Re4/4 ^{III} 42 «ARTH GOLDAU» du SOB est vue à Einsiedeln avant de remorquer un train pour Wäldenswil. Cette locomotive est l'ancienne 11352 des CFF. *G.B. Wise*

▲La He2/2 14 du SPB dans la livrée rouge et créme est vue à Schynige Platte en Septembre 1988. *Paul Russenberger*

SCHYNIGE PLATTE BAHN (314) SPB

Another member of the BOB group, this pure rack mountain line connects with the BOB at Wilderswil near Interlaken. It appears to the 'poor relation' of the group, since all trains are operated by elderly 4-wheel electric locomotives dating from the time of electrification, some being second hand from the WAB. Its rolling stock is lettered 'BOB'.

Encore un membre du groupe BOB, cette ligne de montagne entièrement à crémaillère fait correspondance avec le BOB à Wilderswil près d'Interlaken. Il semble être le parent pauvre du groupe puisque tous les trains sont remorqués par des locomotives électriques anciennes qui datent de l'électrification de la ligne. D'autres furent transférées du WAB. Tout le matériel porte le sigle «BOB».

Gauge/Ecartement: 800 mm.
Electrical System/Courant: 1500 V dc/continu.
Depot/Dépôt: Wilderswil.

He2/2	11		SLM/BBC	–	12	16.3	220	1914
He2/2	12		SLM/BBC	–	12	16.3	220	1914
He2/2	13		SLM/BBC	–	12	16.3	220	1914
He2/2	14		SLM/BBC	–	12	16.3	220	1914
He2/2	15		SLM/ALIOTH	–	12	16	220	1910
He2/2	16		SLM/ALIOTH	–	12	16	220	1910
He2/2	17		SLM/ALIOTH	–	12	16	220	1910
He2/2	18		SLM/ALIOTH	–	12	16	220	1910
He2/2	19		SLM/ALIOTH	–	12	16	220	1911
He2/2	20		SLM/ALIOTH	–	12	16	220	1911

SURSEE TRIENGEN ST

A branch off the SBB Luzern to Olten line, the ST lost its passenger service in 1971. Now freight only, the occasional steam special is operated.

Une branche de la ligne CFF de Lucerne à Olten. Le ST a perdu son service voyageurs en 1971 et n'a maintenant que des trains de marchandises bien qu'il y ait un train à vapeur spécial occasionellement.

Gauge/Ecartement: 1435 mm.
Electrical System/Courant: not electrified.
Depot/Dépôt: Triengen.

Em2/2	1	LISI	SIG/BBC/SAU	–	65	39	243	1965
Em2/2	2		SLM/MAN	–	60	30	280	1976

SENSETALBAHN (257) STB

A branch line linking the SBB at Flamatt to the BN at Gümmenen via the town of Laupen. Most of the stock is second hand. A recent development is a through Bern to Laupen service, using SBB RBDe4/4 railcars with intermediate trailers owned by the STB.

Une ligne qui donne une liaison entre les CFF à Flamatt et le BN à Gümmenen via la ville de Laupen. La plupart du matériel fut acheté d'occasion. Recemment un service direct fut introduit entre Laupen et Berne avec utilisation des RBDe4/4 des CFF avec des remorques intermédiaires appartenant au STB.

Gauge/Ecartement: 1435 mm.
Electrical System/Courant: 15 kV 16⅔ Hz ac/monophasé.
Depot/Dépôt: Laupen.

Tm2/2	11		STAD/BBC/SAU	–	55	23.5	185	1969
Em3/3	12*		MAK/MTU	–	60	48	485	1956
BDe4/6	102	LAUPEN	SIG/SAAS	128	110	82	708	1938
BDe4/6	103	NEUENEGG	SIG/SAAS	128	110	82	708	1938
Be4/4	106		SLM/SIG/BBC/MFO/SAAS	64	80	44	736	1939
Be4/4	107		SLM/SIG/BBC/MFO/SAAS	64	80	44	736	1939

* ex DB 260 106.

TB Class BDe4/8 No. 24 at St. Gallen Bohl on a St. Gallen to Trogen working on 19/04/86. *G.B. Wise*

La BDe4/8 24 du TB à St. Gall Bohl avec un train pour Trogen. 19/04/86. *G.B. Wise*

SIHLTAL ZÜRICH UETLIBERG (712, 713) SZU

Formerly two separate lines, merged in 1973. The Sihltalbahn provides a suburban service from Zürich to Langnau and Sihlbrugg and is electrified on high voltage ac. The Uetlibergbahn climbs up the hills above Zürich to a terminus at Uetliberg and is electrified on dc. To enable trains from both lines to use the common section from Zürich HB to Giesshübel, the dc wires are offset to one side, resulting in the tracks on this section having two sets of overhead wires, and giving the dc stock an odd appearance with off-centre pantographs. From May 1990, the line has been extended from the inconveniently located Selnau terminus to a new underground terminus at the Hauptbahnhof using platforms built for the never constructed U-Bahn.

Deux lignes distinctes qui ont fusionné en 1973. Le Sihltalbahn est électrifié en monophasé et exploite des services de banlieue de Zurich à Lagnau et Sihlbrugg. Le Uetlibergbahn est électrifié en continu et monte dans les collines à l'ouest de Zurich. Sur la section commune entre Zurich et Giesshübel, il y a deux fils de contact, le fils portant le courant continu étant décentré. Le matériel alimenté en continu a donc une apparence inhabituelle dûe au pantographe décentré. A partir de mai 1990 la ligne a été prolongée du terminus mal situé de Selnau à un nouveau terminus sous la gare centrale de Zurich utilisant les quais prévus pour le métro qui ne fut jamais construit.

Gauge/Ecartement: 1435 mm.
Electrical System/Courant: 15 kV 16⅔ Hz ac/monophasé and/et 1200 V dc/continu*
Depots/Dépôts: Giesshübel, Sihlwald.

Em3/3	6	LEU	SLM/SAAS/BBC	–	65	49	445	1962
Em2/2	7	MUTZ	SIG/BBC/SAU	–	55	39	245	1961
Tm2/2	8	GIRAFF	RACO/DZ	–	35	10	75	1975
Tm2/2	10	(ex SBB 536)	RACO/MB	–	45	7.5	35	1949
BDe4/4	11	*	SWS/MFO	40	50	26	330	1939
BDe4/4	12	*	SWS/MFO	40	50	28	330	1950
BDe4/4	13	*	SWS/MFO	48	50	28	330	1960
BDe4/4	14	*	SWS/MFO	48	50	28	330	1960
Be4/4	21		SLM/SE	64	70	39.8	544	on order
Be2/2	22	*	SWS/MFO	24	35	17.5	150	1923
Be4/4	23		SLM/SE	64	70	39.8	544	on order/
Be4/4	24		SLM/SE	64	70	39.8	544	en commande
Be4/4	25		SLM/SE	64	70	39.8	544	on order/
Be4/4	26		SLM/SE	64	70	39.8	544	en commande
Be4/4	27		SLM/SE	64	70	39.8	544	on order/
Be4/4	28		SLM/SE	64	70	39.8	544	en commande
Be8/8	31	*ZÜRICH	SWS/SE	162	60	60.4	850	1978
Be8/8	32	*UITIKON	SWS/SE	162	60	60.4	850	1978
De3/4	41		SIG/MFO	–	50	48	495	1926
Be4/4	42	(ex BT 13)	SLM/SAAS	–	80	66	1180	1931
Re4/4	46		SLM/ABB	–	130	68	3200	1987
Re4/4	47		SLM/ABB	–	130	68	3200	1987
De4/4	51	(ex SBB 601)	SLM/BBC/MFO/SAAS	–	90	47	1000	1940
BDe2/4	84	†	SWS/MFO	50	50	43	330	1924
BDe4/4	91		SWS/MFO	53	70	44	520	1955
BDe4/4	92	HORGEN	SWS/MFO	56	70	52.4	645	1968
BDe4/4	93	THALWIL	SWS/MFO	56	70	52.4	645	1968
BDe4/4	94	LANGNAU A/A	SWS/MFO	56	70	53	645	1971
BDe4/4	95	ADLISWIL	SWS/MFO	56	70	53	645	1971
BDe4/4	96	ZÜRICH	SWS/MFO	56	70	53	645	1971

† restored as FCe2/4 84/restaurée comme FCe2/4 84
On order/En commande: 8 Be4/4 from/de SLM/SE (800 kW, 64 seats/places).

TROGENER BAHN (859) TB

Originally an interurban tramway running from St. Gallen to Trogen, the TB has been upgraded to a light railway, mostly with roadside running, although there is still street running in St. Gallen.

A l'origine un tramway interurbain entre St Gall et Trogen, le TB a été transformé en chemin de fer établi en accotement de chaussée. Il existe toujours une section établie sur route dans la ville de St Gall.

WAB Class BDhe4/4 No. 103 at Grindelwald Grund on 29/06/90. This pure rack railcar has the incorrect painted classification 'BDeh4/4' which indicates rack and adhesion. *E.H. Sawford*

La BDhe4/4 103 du WAB à Grindelwald Grund. Cette automotrice purement à crémaillère porte la mauvaise classification «BDeh4/4» qui indique l'utilisation à crémaillère et en adhérence. 29/06/90. *E.H. Sawford*

Gauge/Ecartement: 1000 mm.
Electrical System/Courant: 1000 V dc/continu.
Depot/Dépôt: Speicher.

BDe4/4	6	SWP/MFO	30	65	27	385	1952
BDe4/4	7	SWP/MFO	30	65	27	385	1952
BDe4/4	8	SWP/MFO	30	65	27	385	1953
BDe4/8	21	FFA/BBC	72	65	39	405	1975
BDe4/8	22	FFA/BBC	72	65	39	405	1975
BDe4/8	23	FFA/BBC	72	65	39	405	1975
BDe4/8	24	FFA/BBC	72	65	39	405	1977
BDe4/8	25	FFA/BBC	72	65	39	405	1977
Xrotm2/2	72	RACO/BEIL/DZ	–	30	15	150	1974

VITZNAU RIGI BAHN (603) VRB

The VRB was the very first Swiss mountain rack line opened in 1871. The lower station connects with the steamers on Lake Lucerne, and the top section parallels the Arth Rigi Bahn.

Le VRB fut la toute première ligne à crémaillère en Suisse, ouverte en 1871. La station inférieure donne correspondance avec les bateaux sur le lac des Quatres Cantons et la section supérieure est parallèle au Arth Rigi Bahn.

Gauge/Ecartement: 1435 mm.
Electrical System/Courant: 1500 V dc/continu.
Depot/Dépôt: Vitznau.

Bhe2/4	1*	SLM/BBC	64	19	16.7	335	1937
Bhe2/4	2	SLM/BBC	64	19	16.7	335	1937
Bhe2/4	3	SLM/BBC	64	19	16.7	335	1937
Bhe2/4	4	SLM/BBC	64	19	18.2	335	1953
Bhe4/4	5	SLM/SIG/BBC	62	30	35	870	1965
He2/2	18	SLM/BBC	–	18	13.6	335	1938
Bhe4/4	21	SLM/BBC	74		30.5	824	1986
Bhe4/4	22	SLM/BBC	74		30.5	824	1986
Ta2/2	1*	RACO/STAD/MFO/BBC	–	8	7.5	7	1982
Xrotm	1*						1974

* Number duplicated/numéro dupliqué.

WENGERNALPBAHN (311, 312) WAB

Another member of the BOB group, this railway operates the middle section of the route to the Jungfrau, connecting the BOB at Lauterbrunnen and Grindelwald to the JB at Kliene Scheidegg. No through operation is possible due to the different gauges.

Autre membre du groupe BOB, cette compagnie exploite la section centrale de la route au Jungfrau. Il y a correspondance avec le BOB à Lauterbrunnen et Grindelwald et avec le JB à Kleine Scheidegg. Il n'y a pa de trains directs à cause des écartements différents.

Gauge/Ecartement: 800 mm.
Electrical System/Courant: 1500 V dc/continu.
Depots/Dépôts: Lauterbrunnen, Grindelwald Grund.

Xrote	11	SLM/MFO	–	11	14	138	1928
Xrote	12	SLM/MFO	–	11	14	228	1945
He2/2	51	SLM/ALIOTH	–	12	16	220	1909
He2/2	52	SLM/ALIOTH	–	12	16	220	1909
He2/2	53	SLM/ALIOTH	–	12	16	220	1909
He2/2	54	SLM/ALIOTH	–	12	16	220	1909
He2/2	61	SLM/ALIOTH	–	12	16	220	1912
He2/2	62	SLM/ALIOTH	–	12	16	220	1912
He2/2	63	SLM/ALIOTH	–	12	16	220	1912
He2/2	64	SLM/BBC	–	12	16.5	236	1926
He2/2	65	SLM/MFO	–	12	17	236	1929
BDhe4/4	101	SLM/BBC	52	25	23.5	440	1947
BDhe4/4	102	SLM/BBC	52	25	23.5	440	1947
BDhe4/4	103	SLM/BBC	52	25	23.5	440	1948

BDhe4/4	104	SLM/BBC	52	25	23.5	440	1951
BDhe4/4	105	SLM/BBC	52	25	23.5	440	1951
BDhe4/4	106	SLM/BBC	52	25	23.5	440	1954
BDhe4/4	107	SLM/BBC	52	25	23.5	440	1954
BDhe4/4	108	SLM/BBC	52	25	23.5	440	1958
BDhe4/4	109	SLM/BBC	52	25	23.5	440	1958
BDhe4/4	110	SLM/BBC	52	25	23.5	440	1960
BDhe4/4	111	SLM/BBC	52	25	23.5	440	1960
BDhe4/4	112	SLM/BBC	52	25	23.5	440	1963
BDhe4/4	113	SLM/BBC	52	25	23.5	440	1963
BDhe4/4	114	SLM/BBC	52	25	23.5	440	1963
BDhe4/4	115	SLM/BBC	52	25	23.5	440	1963
BDhe4/4	116	SLM/BBC	52	25	23.5	440	1963
BDhe4/4	117	SLM/BBC	52	25	23.5	440	1964
BDhe4/4	118	SLM/BBC	52	25	23.5	440	1964
BDhe4/4	119	SLM/SIG/BBC/SAAS	48	25	25.7	440	1970
BDhe4/4	120	SLM/SIG/BBC/SAAS	48	25	25.7	440	1970
BDhe4/4	121	SLM/SIG/BBC/SAAS	48	25	25.7	440	1970
BDhe4/4	122	SLM/SIG/BBC/SAAS	48	25	25.7	440	1970
BDhe4/4	123	SLM/SIG/BBC/SAAS	48	25	25.7	440	1970
BDhe4/4	124	SLM/SIG/BBC/SAAS	48	25	25.7	440	1970
BDhe4/8	131	SLM/ABB	64	28/16.5	42.4	804	1988
BDhe4/8	132	SLM/ABB	64	28/16.5	42.4	804	1988
BDhe4/8	133	SLM/ABB	64	28/16.5	42.4	804	1988
BDhe4/8	134	SLM/ABB	64	28/16.5	42.4	804	1988

WALDENBURGERBAHN (502) WB

Unique for Switzerland in being 750 mm gauge, the WB is a mainly roadside light railway with some street running. New stock has been purchased recently to enable an improved service to be introduced.

Unique en Suisse à cause de son écartement de 750mm, le WB est établi en accotement de chaussée sauf quelques sections de voie établie sur route. Du nouveau matériel a été acheté récemment afin de permettre une amélioration du service.

Gauge/Ecartement: 750 mm.
Electrical System/Courant: 1500 V dc/continu.
Depot/Dépôt: Waldenburg.

BDe4/4	1	SWP/BBC	36	55	26	368	1953
BDe4/4	2	SWP/BBC	36	55	26	368	1953
BDe4/4	3	SWP/BBC	36	55	26	368	1953
BDe4/4	11	SWP/SIG/BBC	–				1985
BDe4/4	12	SWP/SIG/BBC	–				1986
BDe4/4	13	SWP/SIG/BBC	–				1986
BDe4/4	14	SWP/SIG/BBC	–				1986

WYNENTAL UND SUHRENTALBAHN (643,644) WSB

Once two separate unconnected lines, a new station alongside the SBB one connected to both lines was opened in 1967. The lines are mainly a mixture of roadside and street running.

Auparavant deux lignes distinctes qui furent interconnectées en 1967 avec la construction d'une nouvelle station à côté de la gare CFF d'Aarau. Les deux lignes sont principalement établies en accotement de chaussée ou sur route.

Gauge/Ecartement: 1000 mm.
Electrical System/Courant: 750 V dc/continu.
Depots/Dépôts: Aarau, Schöftland.

Tm	1		ROBEL/DZ	–	63	7.5	67	1969
De4/4	6		SWS/BBC	–	65	27.5	286	1947
Be4/4	7		SWS/BBC	48	75	27.5	326	1954
Be4/4	8		SWS/BBC	48	75	27.5	326	1954
Be4/4	9	HIRSCHTHAL	SWS/BBC	48	80	29	448	1966
Be4/4	10	HOLZIKEN	SWS/BBC	48	80	29	448	1966

Be4/4	11	DÜRRENÄSCH	SWS/BBC	48	80	29	448	1966
Be4/4	12	ZETZWIL	SWS/BBC	48	80	29	448	1966
Be4/4	13	LEIMBACH	SWS/BBC	48	80	29	448	1966
Be4/4	14	BURG	SWS/BBC	48	80	29	448	1966
Be4/4	15	AARAU	SWS/BBC	52	80	31	442	1979
Be4/4	16	SUHR	SWS/BBC	52	80	31	442	1979
Be4/4	17	GRÄNICHEN	SWS/BBC	52	80	31	442	1979
Be4/4	19	UNTERKULM	SWS/BBC	52	80	31	442	1979
Be4/4	20	OBERKULM	SWS/BBC	52	80	31	442	1979
Be4/4	21	GONTENSCHWIL	SWS/BBC	52	80	31	442	1979
Be4/4	22	REINACH	SWS/BBC	52	80	31	442	1979
Be4/4	23	MENZIKEN	SWS/BBC	52	80	31	442	1979
Be4/4	24	UNTERENTFELDEN	SWS/BBC	52	80	31	442	1979
Be4/4	25	OBERENTFELDEN	SWS/BBC	52	80	31	442	1979
Be4/4	26	MUHEN	SWS/BBC	52	80	31	442	1979
Be4/4	27	SCHÖFTLAND	SWS/BBC	52	80	31	442	1979
De4/4	42		SWS/SSW/BBC	–	50	27.5	280	1904
De4/4	43		SWS/SE/BBC	–	60	46	536	1974
De4/4	44		SWS/SE/BBC	–	60	46	536	1974
De4/4	45		SWS/SE/BBC	–	60	46	536	1974
Te2/2	47		SWS/MFO/WSB	–	55	13.9	108	1954
Te2/2	48		SWS/MFO/WSB	–	55	13.9	108	1955
Te2/2	49		SWS/MFO/WSB	–	55	13.9	108	1957
Te2/2	50		SWS/VBZ/MFO	–	40	15.4	108	1915
ASe4/4	116		SWS/BBC	33	65	28.3	286	1901
Xe4/4	117		SWS/BBC	–	65	26	248	1919

On order/en commande: 7 Be4/8.

YVERDON–ST CROIX (212) YSC

A light railway running into the mountains near the French border. New stock delivered a few years ago seems to have averted a closure threat.

Une ligne d'intérêt local qui déssert une région montagneuse près de la frontière française. Avec la livraison de nouveau matériel, des menaces de fermeture semblent s'éloigner maintenant.

Gauge/Ecartement: 1000 mm.
Electrical System/Courant: 15 kV 16⅔ Hz ac/monophasé.
Depots/Dépôts: Yverdon, St Croix.

Be4/4	1	YVERDON	ACMV/HESS/BBC	40	75	44.5	780	1981
Be4/4	2	BAULMES	ACMV/HESS/BBC	40	75	44.5	780	1981
Be4/4	3	ST CROIX	ACMV/HESS/BBC	40	75	44.5	780	1981
Be4/4	4		SIG/BBC	50	65	37	440	1945
Be4/4	5		SIG/BBC	50	65	37	440	1945
Be2/4	11		SIG/BBC	36	65	28.7	220	1946
Be2/4	12		SIG/BBC	36	65	28.7	220	1947
Ge4/4	21		SIG/YSC/BBC	–	55	39	516	1950
Tm	22		SCH	–	40	54	48	1971
Tm2/2				–			310	on order/ en commande

PRESERVED LOCOMOTIVES/ LOCOMOTIVES PRESERVEES

In this section, all preserved locomotives and railcars from Swiss public railways are shown. In the case of steam locomotives, all known surviving locomotives from these railways are shown, since many of those not actually preserved will no doubt be the subject of future preservation attempts. Not detailed are industrial locomotives, trams, and items imported for preservation from countries outside Switzerland. The current status of the motive power is indicated as follows:

IA Industrial use, still active.
M Museum, on display (not active).
MA Museum, active.
MR Museum, under repair.
MS Museum, stored.
P Plinthed.
S Stored.

Cette section regroupe toutes les locomotives et automotrices préservées des chemins de fer publiques suisses. Dans le cas des machines à vapeur, toutes les machines survivantes sont indiquées même celles toujours en service, puisque beaucoup de celles-ci seront sans doûte préservées dans l'avenir. Les locomotives industrielles, les tramways et le matériel importé d'autres pays ne sont pas inclus. L'état actuel du matériel est indiqué comme suit:

IA Machine en service, en utilisation industrielle.
M Machine en musée ou sur ligne musée, en exposition mais pas en service.
MA Machine en musée ou sur ligne musée, en service.
MR Machine en musée ou sur ligne musée, en réparation.
MS Machine en musée ou sur ligne musée, garée hors service.
P Machine préservée sur socle.
S Machine garée hors service.

Steam Locomotives & Railcars
Locomotives et Automoteurs à vapeur.

The system for describing steam locomotives used here is the one which is in general use in Germany. Firstly, letters and numbers are used to describe the wheel arrangement as follows:

Driven axles are denoted by letters where Aê1, Bê2, Cê3 etc.
Non-driven axles are denoted by numbers.

This is then followed by 'h' for superheated locos (from the German 'heizdampf'), or 'n' for saturated locos (from the German 'nassdampf').

The number of cylinders follow, then codes for various features, i.e.

v compound.
z rack locomotive with 1 pinion.
zz rack locomotive with 2 pinions.
t tank locomotive.

e.g.: 1C1h2t is a superheated 2–6–2 tank locomotive with 2 cylinders.

La classification des locomotives à vapeur utilisée ici suit le système allemand. D'abord des chiffres et des lettres sont employés selon la disposition des essieux comme suit:

Une lettre correspond au nombre d'essieux moteurs – Aê1, Bê2, Cê3 etc.
Un chiffre correspond au nombre d'essieux porteurs.

Cette classification est suivie de la lettre 'h'pour les locomotives surchauffées ('h' de l'allemand 'heizdampf'), ou 'n' pour une locomotive saturée ('n' de l'Allemand 'nassdampf').

Ces lettres sont suivies du nombres de cylindres et, si necessaire, d'un code:

v compound.
z machine à crémaillère à 1 pignon.

zz machine à crémaillère à 2 pignons.
t locomotive-tender.

Par example: 1C1h2t est une locomotive-tender 131 surchauffée à 2 cylindres.

Rly. *Cie.*	*Gauge* *Ecart.*	*Class* *Série*	*No.* *No*	*Details* *Classification*	*Status* *Etat*	*Date* *Date*	*Location* *Lieu*
SBB	1000	G3/3	109 (BAM 6)	Cn2t	M	1901	Chaulin
SBB	1000	G3/4	203	1Ch2t	S	1912	Volos (Greece/Grèce)
SBB	1000	G3/4	204	1Ch2t	S	1912	Pirgos (Greece/Grèce)
SBB	1000	G3/4	205	1Ch2t	S	1912	Pirgos (Greece/Grèce)
SBB	1000	G3/4	208	1Ch2t	MA	1913	Meiringen
SBB	1000	A3/5	705	2Ch4v	MA	1904	VHS (Biel/Bienne)
SBB	1000	HG3/3	1055	Czn4vt	S	1906	Volos (Greece/Grèce)
SBB	1000	HG3/3	1058	Czn4vt	S	1908	Volos (Greece/Grèce)
SBB	1000	HG3/3	1063	Czn4vt	M	1909	VHS
SBB	1000	HG3/3	1067	Czn4vt	MA	1910	Meiringen
SBB	1000	HG3/3	1068	Czn4vt	P	1926	Meiringen
SBB	1435	B3/4	1367	1Ch2	M	1916	VHS
SBB	1435	C5/6	2958	1Eh4v	P	1915	Olten
SBB	1435	C5/6	2965	1Eh4v	M	1916	VHS
SBB	1435	C5/6	2969	1Eh4v	P	1916	Winterthur/Winterthour
SBB	1435	C5/6	2978	1Eh4v	MA	1917	St Sulpice (VHS)
SBB	1435	Eb2/4	5469	2Bn2t	MA	1891	Basel/Bâle (VHS)
SBB	1435	Eb3/5	5810	1C1h2t	S	1911	Fribourg
SBB	1435	Eb3/5	5811	1C1h2t	S	1911	Glarus
SBB	1435	Eb3/5	5819	1C1h2t	MA	1912	Zürich
SBB	1435	Eb3/5	5886 (BT 6)	1C1h2t	P	1910	Degersheim
SBB	1435	Eb3/5	5889 (BT 9)	1C1h2t	MA	1910	Herisau
SBB	1435	Ed2x2/2	7696 (SCB 196)	BBn4vt	M	1893	VHS
SBB	1435	E3/3	8410	Cn2t	S	1901	Zürich
SBB	1435	E3/3	8463	Cn2t	S	1904	Bodio
SBB	1435	E3/3	8474	Cn2t	MS	1907	Koblenz/Coblence
SBB	1435	E3/3	8476	Cn2t	MS	1907	Uetikon
SBB	1435	E3/3	8479 (ST 5)	Cn2t	MA	1907	Triengen
SBB	1435	E3/3	8481	Cn2t	IA	1907	Rheinfelden
SBB	1435	E3/3	8483	Cn2t	MS	1907	Haltingen (Germany/Allemagne)
SBB	1435	E3/3	8485	Cn2t	MS	1907	Koblenz/Coblence
SBB	1435	E3/3	8487	Cn2t	P	1909	Buchs
SBB	1435	E3/3	8491	Cn2t	MA	1909	Kriens
SBB	1435	E3/3	8492	Cn2t	MA	1909	Stabio
SBB	1435	E3/3	8494	Cn2t	MA	1909	Le Pont
SBB	1435	E3/3	8500	Cn2t	MS	1910	Haltingen (Germany/Allemagne)
SBB	1435	E3/3	8501	Cn2t	MA	1910	Samstagern
SBB	1435	E3/3	8507	Cn2t	P	1910	Sierre
SBB	1435	E3/3	8511	Cn2t	MA	1911	St Sulpice
SBB	1435	E3/3	8512	Cn2t	M	1911	VHS
SBB	1435	E3/3	8516	Cn2t	MA	1911	Zürich
SBB	1435	E3/3	8518	Cn2t	MA	1913	Bauma
SBB	1435	E3/3	8522	Cn2t	MA	1913	St Sulpice
SBB	1435	E3/3	8523	Cn2t	MA	1915	Le Pont
SBB	1435	E3/3	8527	Cn2t	P	1915	Kaufdorf
SBB	1435	E3/3	8532	Cn2t	MA	1915	Basel/Bâle (VHS)
SBB	1435	E3/3	8551	Cn2t	P	1894	Kleinhuningen (Basel/Bâle)
SBB	1435	E3/3	8554	Cn2t	P	1894	Dietikon
SBB	1435	E3/3	8573	Cn2t	MA	1890	Bern/Berne
SBB	1435	E3/3	8575	Cn2t	MA	1890	Laupen
SBB	1435	E3/3	8651 (KLB 1)	Cn2t	MA	1909	Balsthal
BLS	1435	E2/2	72 (Bodelibahn 3)	Bn2t	MA	1874	Spiez
BLS	1435	E3/3	77	Cn2t	M	1901	Thun/Thoune

BSB	1435	Ed3/4	51	1Cn2t	P	1906 Scharzenburg
EB	1435	Ed3/3	3	Cn2t	M	1881 VHS
EBT	1435	Ed4/5	8	1Dh2t	MA	1914 Burgdorf
FO	1000	HG3/4	1 (VHX 31-201)	1Czzh4vt	M	1913 Oberwald§
FO	1000	HG3/4	2 (VHX 31-202)	1Czzh4vt	S	1913 Song Pha (Vietnam)
FO	1000	HG3/4	3	1Czzh4vt	MA	1913 Chaulin
FO	1000	HG3/4	4	1Czzh4vt	MS	1913 Münster
FO	1000	HG3/4	8 (VHX 31-203)	1Czzh4vt	S	1914 Oberwald
FO	1000	HG3/4	9 (VHX 31-204)	1Czzh4vt	S	1914 Da Lat (Vietnam)
FW	1000	G3/3	2	Cn2t	P	1887 Wil
GB	1000	E2/2	11	Bn2t	M	1881 VHS
GGB	800	HII/3	8	B1zzh2t	MA	1892 Ribas de Freser (Spain/Espagne)
HWB	1435	E3/3	5	Ch2t	M	1936 VHS
HWB	1435	E3/3	8	Cn2t	IA	1898 Choindez
LEB	1000	G3/3	5	Cn2t	MA	1890 Chaulin
LEB	1000	G3/3	8	Cn2t	MA	1910 Eschallens
LHB	1435	Ed3/4	11	1Ch2t	MA	1908 Huttwil
MG	800	HII/3	2	B1zzn2t	MA	1890 Capolago
MThB	1435	Ed3/5	3	1C1h2t	MA	1912 Weinfelden
NOB	1435	D1	1*	1A1n2	M	1947 VHS
OeBB	1435	E3/3	2	Cn2t	MA	1899 Balsthal
PB	800	Bhm	9	railcar	M	1889 VHS
PB	800	Bhm	10	railcar	M	1900 München (Germany/Allemagne)
RdB	1000	G3/3	1	Cn2t	MA	1890 Chaulin
RdB	1000	G3/3	2	Cn2t	P	1890 Les Brenets
RdB	1000	G3/3	3	Cn2t	P	1892 Le Locle
RhB	1000	G3/4	1	1Cn2t	MA	1889 Chaulin†
RhB	1000	G3/4	11	1Cn2t	MA	1902 Zweilütschinen
RhB	1000	G3/4	14	1Cn2t	MA	1902 Herisau
RhB	1000	G4/5	107	1Dh2	MA	1906 Landquart
RhB	1000	G4/5	108	1Dh2	MA	1906 Landquart
RhB	1000	G4/5	118 (RSR 340)	1Dh2	P	1912 Chiengmai (Thailand/e)
RhB	1000	G4/5	122 (RSR 338)	1Dh2	P	1913 Makkasan (Thailand/e)
RhB	1435	Xrotd	9212	rotary	M	1913 Chaulin
RSG	1435	Ed3/4	2	1Ch2t	MR	1903 Wil
SCB	1435	Ec2/5	28	B3n2t	MA	1858 VHS
SiTB	1435	E3/3	2	Cn2t	MA	1893 Bouveret
SiTB	1435	E3/3	3	Cn2t	P	1897 Horgen
SiTB	1435	E3/3	4	Cn2t	P	1897 Adliswil
SiTB	1435	E3/3	5	Cn2t	MA	1899 Zürich Giesshubel
SMB	1435	Ed3/4	1	1Cn2t	MR	1907 Kreuzlingen
SMB	1435	Ed3/4	2	1Cn2t	MA	1907 Huttwil
SMB	1435	Ec4/5	11	1Dh2t	P	1911 Oberdorf
SOB	1435	E3/3	4	Cn2t	P	1887 Wadenswil
SOB	1435	E2/2	51 (KLB 2)	Bn2t	M	1891 Rorschach
SPB	800	HII/3	5	B1zzh2t	MA	1894 Wilderswil
STB	1435	Ed3/3	3	Cn2t	P	1884 Wildegg
UeBB	1435	CZm1/2	31	railcar	MA	1907 Zürich
UeBB	1435	E3/3	401	Ch2t	MA	1901 Bauma
VRB	1435	HI/2	7	1Azn2t	M	1873 VHS
VRB	1435	HII/3	16	B1zzh2t	MA	1923 Vitznau
VRB	1435	HII/3	17	B1zzh2t	MA	1925 Vitznau
VZ	1000	HG2/3	6	B1zzh4vt	MA	1902 Oberwald
VZ	1000	HG2/3	7	B1zzh4vt	MA	1906 Visp/Viege
WB	750	G3/3	5	Cn2t	MA	1902 Waldenburg
WB	750	G3/3	6	Cn2t	M	1912 VHS
YSC	1000	G4/4	4	Dh2t	S	1911 Volos (Greece/Grèce)

* Replica of 1847 loco/Copie d'une locomotive de 1847.
† At Landquart in 1989/à Landquart en 1989.
§ On loan to VHS in early 1991/Cette machine fut prêtée au VHS au début de 1991.

Diesel & Electric Locomotives and Railcars
Locomotives électriques et diesel, automotrices et autorails.

SBB	1435	Ae3/6 I	10601	P	1921	Baden
SBB	1435	Ae8/14	11852	MS	1940	Erstfeld
SBB	1435	Be4/6	12332	M	1922	VHS
SBB	1435	Be4/6	12339	MS	1923	Voghera (Italy/Italie)
SBB	1435	Be6/8 II	13254	M	1920	VHS
SBB	1435	Be6/8 II	13257	MS	1920	Linz (Austria/Autriche)
SBB	1435	Be6/8 III	13302	MA	1925	Rapperswil
SBB	1435	Ce4/4	13501 (SW 1)	M	1904	VHS
SBB	1435	Ce4/4	13502 (SW 2)	M	1904	VHS
SBB	1435	Ce6/8 I	14201	M	1920	VHS
SBB	1435	Ce6/8 II	14267	M	1921	Frankfurt (Germany/Allemagne)
SBB	1435	Ce6/8 II	14270	P	1921	Erstfeld
SBB	1435	Ce6/8 II	14276	MS	1922	Stabio
SBB	1435	Ce6/8 II	14282	M	1922	Sinsheim (Germany/Allemagne)
SBB	1435	Tm	464	M	1931	VHS
SBB	1435	Tm	873	MA	1925	Langenthal
SBB	1435	RCe2/4	203	M	1936	VHS
SBB	1435	RAe4/8	1021	MS	1939	Renens
SBB	1435	Fe4/4	18518 (1678)	M	1928	VHS
AG	1000	CFeh3/3	1 (SGA 16)	M	1911	VHS†
BA	1000	ABDe2/4	3	P	1911	Acquarossa
BLS	1435	Be5/7	151	M	1912	VHS
BN	1435	Ce2/4	727	M	1935	VHS
BOB	1000	HGe3/3	26	P	1915	Bern/Berne
BT	1435	Be4/4	13	M	1932	VHS
BT	1435	Be4/4	15	MA	1932	Bauma
BT	1435	Be4/4	16	MA	1932	Bauma
BTB	1435	De2/2	1	M	1899	München (Germany/Allemagne)
BTB	1435	De2/2	2	M	1899	VHS
EZB	1435	Ce4/6	307	MA	1920	Spiez
GBS	1435	Ce4/4	312 (SZU 42)	MA	1920	Samstagern
FO	1000	CFmh2/2	21	M	1927	VHS
JB	1000	He2/2	1	M	1898	VHS
LEB	1000	Te2/2	2	MA	1896	Chaulin
LJB	1000	Ce2/2	12	MA	1907	Chaulin
LLB	1000	BCFeh4/4	10	MA	1914	Chaulin
MCM	1000	BCFeh4/4	6	MA	1909	Chaulin
MIB	1000	Ta2/2	3	M	1931	Bruchhausen Vilsen (Germany/Allemagne)
MIB	1000	CFa2/2	4	M	1939	VHS
MIB	1000	CFa2/2	5	P	1949	Innertkirchen
NStCM	1000	ABDe4/4	1	MA	1916	La Mure (France)
NStCM	1000	ABDe4/4	2	P	1936	La Cure
NStCM	1000	ABDe4/4	5	MA	1916	La Mure (France)
OC	1435	CFe2/2	11	M	1894	VHS
RhB	1000	Ge4/4	181	MA	1916	Chaulin
RhB	1000	Ge4/4	182	MA	1928	La Mure (France)
RhB	1000	Ge2/4	205	P	1913	Winterthur/Winterthour
RhB	1000	Ge2/4	207	M	1913	VHS
RhB	1000	Ge4/6	391	M	1913	Berlin
RhB	1000	Ge6/6	402	M	1921	VHS
RhB	1000	Ge6/6	406	P	1921	Zürich Oerlikon
RhB	1000	Ge6/6	407	P	1922	Zürich
RhB	1000	ABDe4/4	453	P	1907	Mesocco
RVT	1435	BCm2/5	9	M	1914	VHS
SeTB	1000	BDe2/2	4	MA	1928	Chaulin
StEB	1000	HGe2/2	1	M	1898	VHS
TB	1000	CFe4/4	1	P	1903	Meilen§
VBW	1000	Be4/4	30	MA	1910	Worb

† Incorrectly restored as AG 3.
§ Incorrectly restored as WM 3.

† restaurée sous la mauvaise appellation AG 3.
§ restaurée sous la mauvaise appellation WM 3.

Additional Abbreviations/abbréviations supplémentaires

AG Altstätten Gais
BA Biasca Acquarossa
BSB Bern/Berne Schwarzenburg Bahn
BTB Burgdorf Thun/Thoune Bahn
EB Emmental Bahn
EZB Erlenbach Zweisimmen Bahn
GB Gotthard Bahn
HWB Huttwil Wolhusen Bahn
LHB Langenthal Huttwil Bahn
LJB Langenthal Jura Bahn
LLB Leuk Leukerbad Bahn
MCM Monthey Champéry Morgins
NOB Nordostbahn
RdB Régional des Brenets
RSG Régional Saignelégier Glovelier
RSR Royal Siamese Railway
SCB Schweizerischen Central Bahn
SeTB Sernftalbahn
SiTB Sihltalbahn
STB Seetalbahn (not Sensetalbahn, which is now the STB/pas le Sensetalbahn qui est maintenant le STB)
StEB Stansstad Engelberg Bahn
SW Seebach Wettingen
UeBB Uerikon Bauma Bahn
VHS Verkehrshaus der Schweiz (Lucerne Transport Museum/Musée des transports de Lucerne)
VHX Vietnam Hoa Xa
VZ Visp/Viege Zermatt
WM Wetzikon Meilen

MUSEUMS AND MUSEUM LINES

There are few museum lines as such in Switzerland, due to the fact that very few lines have been closed by either the SBB or the various private railways. However, a number of steam locomotives belonging to the Luzern Transport Museum are in working order and these run public excursions on certain weekends, often in association with special events. As detailed in the SBB section, a number of old electric locomotives have been retained as official museum locomotives, and these have limited regular diagrams on freight trains. They are also used on specials, and appear at open days etc. Several of the private railways have retained steam locomotives, or older examples of modern traction, and these either operate at weekends, or are available for private hire.

The National Transport Museum is located at Luzern, and is well worth a visit. It covers all aspects of communications, not just railways. The best known museum line operated by enthusiasts is the Blonay–Chamby near Montreux, but there are a number of other operations, often over the lines of private railways.

The Swiss National Tourist Office produces an annual booklet 'Steam in Switzerland' detailing all regular steam operations. Some of these are also detailed in the SBB timetable.

Also of interest are the paddle steamers operating on the Brienzersee, Lac Leman (Lake Geneva), Vierwaldstättersee (Lake Lucerne) and Zürichsee. These are also detailed in the SBB timetable.

It should be noted that all the above operations are summer only, usually from May to September.

The list below of museum operations is arranged into alphabetical order of cantons.

AARGAU

Brugg

The 'Mikado 1244' Club operate ex SNCF 141R 1244 on occasional public excursions over SBB main lines.

Rheinfelden

Not really a museum operation, but the Feldschlossen Brewery near the station still uses steam for shunting, nowadays mainly for publicity. A set of coaches is available to take parties from the SBB station to the brewery.
2 steam.

Schinznach Bad

A 600 mm gauge line operating at weekends around a nursery.
4 steam, 7 diesel.

APPENZELL

Herisau

The Appenzellerbahnen have one steam locomotive available for charter.

Herisau

The Bodensee Toggenburg Bahn has one steam locomotive available for charter.

BASEL LAND

Waldenburg

The Waldenburgerbahn has one steam locomotive used on public excursions on the 3rd Sunday of the month.

BERN

Brienz

As detailed under the Brienz Rothorn Bahn, this railway still uses steam in regular service.

Burgdorf

The Emmental Burgdorf Thun Bahn has one steam locomotive used on occasional public excursions.

Huttwil

Eurovapor have two steam locomotives based at the VHB Depot used on occasional public excursions.

Laupen

The Sensetalbahn has 3 steam locomotives used on public excursions on the 1st Sunday of the month.

Meiringen

Two steam locomotives are based at the SBB Depot, and used on occasional excursions on the SBB metre gauge line to Interlaken.

Spiez

The Bern Lötschberg Simplon Bahn has one steam locomotive used on occasional public excursions.

Wilderswil

The Schynige Platte Bahn has one steam locomotive available for charter.

Worblaufen

Eurovapor have one metre gauge steam locomotive based here, and used on private excursions over the Regionalverkehr Bern Solothurn between Worblaufen and Worb Dorf or Solothurn on the 2nd Sunday of the month.

Zweilütschinen

The Berner Oberland Bahnen have one steam locomotive available for charter.

GRAUBUNDEN

Landquart

The Rhätische Bahn has 3 steam locomotives used on occasional public excursions.

LUZERN

Luzern

The National Transport Museum (Verkehrshaus) is located on the north side of Lake Lucerne, about 2 km from the station (take a No. 2 trolleybus). Some of the exhibits are changed from time to time, so not all are on display.
13 steam, 15 electrics, 1 diesel, 8 railcars, 4 trams.

Triengen

The Sursee Triengen Bahn has two steam locomotives available for charter.

Vitznau

The Vitznau Rigi Bahn has 2 steam locomotives used on public excursions on the 1st & 3rd Sundays of the month.

NEUCHÂTEL

St Sulpice

The 'Vapeur Val de Travers' Society operate steam services on certain weekends over the normally freight only St Sulpice to Fleurier section of the Régional Val de Travers.

SOLOTHURN

Balsthal

The Oensingen Balsthal Bahn has 2 steam locomotives used on public excursions on the last Sunday of the month.

THURGAU

Sulgen

Eurovapor have ex DB 23.058 based here for use on occasional excursions over main lines.

Weinfelden

The Mittel Thurgau Bahn has one steam locomotive used on occasional public excursions.

TICINO

Capolago

The Ferrovia Monte Generoso has one steam locomotive used on occasional public excursions.

VALAIS

Oberwald

The Furka Bergstrecke Society is restoring the section of the Furka Oberalp Bahn over the Furka Pass, abandoned when the Furka Base Tunnel was opened. One steam locomotive has been restored, and others have been repatriated from Vietnam!
1 steam, 1 diesel.

Visp

The Brig Visp Zermatt Bahn has one steam locomotive available for charter.

VAUD

Bouveret

'Trains de Rive Bleu' operate steam trains at weekends between Bouveret and Evian les Bains (France) on the recently closed line along the south side of Lake Geneva.

Chaulin

The Blonay Chamby metre gauge line is undoubtedly Switzerland's premier enthusiast-operated line, with excellent views over Lake Geneva. Operates at weekends using both steam and electric traction. Some of the stock is stored at other locations. Occasional excursions operated on the nearby Gruyère Fribourg Morat line.
13 steam, 3 electrics, 4 railcars, 10 trams.

Eschallens

The Lausanne Eschallens Bercher Bahn has one steam used on occasional public excursions.

Le Pont

The Compagnie du Trains à Vapeur de la Vallée de Joux has 2 steam locomotives used on occasional public excursions over the Pont Brassus Bahn.

ZÜRICH

Bauma

The Dampfverein Zürcher Oberland (DVZO) run steam trains over the normally freight-only SBB line between Bauma and Hinwil on the 1st and 3rd Sunday of the month. The locomotives are kept at various locations.
4 steam, 2 electrics.

Samstagern

Oswald Steam have a museum adjacent to the Sudostbahn station, and steam charters can be operated over the SOB. The museum is open on request, and a 610 mm gauge steam locomotive is available for hire on a 'self drive' basis!
7 steam, 1 diesel.

Zürich Giesshubel

The Sihltal Zürich Uetliberg Bahn has one steam locomotive available for charter.

MUSEES ET LIGNES «MUSEES»

Il y a peu de lignes «musées» en Suisse puisque très peu de lignes ont été fermées par les CFF ou par les compagnies privées. Cependant, quelques locomotives à vapeur qui appartiennent au Musée des Transports de Lucerne sont en état de marche et utilisées sur des trains spéciaux certains weekends de l'année, souvent lors d'évènements spécifiques. Comme nous l'avons signalé déjà dans la section sur les CFF, plusieurs locomotives électriques anciennes ont été retenues comme locomotives «historiques» et celles-ci ont des roulements limités sur des trains de marchandises. Elles sont également utilisées pour des trains spéciaux et sont présentes lors d'occasions particulières telles que journées portes ouvertes, etc. Plusieurs compagnies privées ont gardé des machines à vapeur ou d'anciennes machines électriques. Celles-ci sont utilisées les weekends ou sont disponibles pour des trains charters.

Le Musée National des Transports est situé à Lucerne et vaut bien la visite. Tout comme les chemins de fer, tous les moyens de communications y sont représentés. La ligne musée la plus connue est exploitée par des amateurs à Blonay-Chamby près de Montreux, mais il existe bien d'autres services touristiques, parfois sur les lignes des compagnies privées.

L'Office National de Tourisme Suisse publie chaque année une brochure (seulement en anglais) «Steam In Switzerland» qui donne les détails des services réguliers à vapeur. Certains sont signalés aussi dans l'indicateur CFF.

Les bateaux vapeur à roues qui sont utilisés sur le lac de Brienz, le lac Léman, le lac des Quatre Cantons et le lac de Zurich sont aussi intéressants. Ceux-ci sont aussi indiqués dans l'indicateur CFF.

Il faut remarquer que tous les services ci-dessus sont exploités en été seulement, en général entre mai et septembre.

La liste de services touristiques ci-dessous est présentée dans l'ordre alphabétique des cantons.

AARGAU

Brougg

Le 'Mikado 1244' utilise la 141R 1244 (ex SNCF) sur des trains speciaux sur les principales lignes des CFF de temps à autre.

Rapperswil

Le club «Mikado 1244» exploite l'ancienne 141 R 1244 de la SNCF sur des trains spéciaux occasionels sur les lignes principales des CFF.

Rheinfelden

Pas vraiment un service touristique, la brasserie près de la gare de Feldschlossen utilise toujours des machines à vapeur pour des manoeuvres, principalement pour la publicité. Une rame de voitures est disponible pour amener des groupes de la gare à la brasserie.
2 vapeur

Schinznach Bad

Une ligne à écartement de 600mm qui est exploitée le weekend autour d'une jardinerie.
4 vapeur, 7 diesel

APPENZELL

Herisau

Le AB a une locomotive à vapeur disponible pour des trains charters.

Herisau

Le BT a une locomotive à vapeur disponible pour des trains charters.

BASEL LAND

Waldenburg

Le Waldenburgbahn a une machine à vapeur utilisée pour des trains spéciaux le troisième dimanche du mois.

BERNE

Brienz

Comme indiqué ci-dessus, le BRB utilise des machines à vapeur en service régulier.

Burgdorf

Le EBT a une machine à vapeur utilisée de temps à autre sur des trains spéciaux.

Huttwil

Eurovapor a deux machines à vapeur basées au dépôt du VHB qui sont utilisées parfois sur des trains spéciaux.

Laupen

Le STB a 3 machines à vapeur qui sont utilisées sur des trains spéciaux le premier dimanche de chaque mois.

Meiringen

Deux machines à vapeur sont basées au dépôt CFF et sont utilisées parfois sur des trains spéciaux sur la ligne du Brünig.

Spiez

Le BLS a une machine à vapeur qui est utilisée parfois sur des trains spéciaux.

Wilderswil

Le SPB a une machine à vapeur disponible pour des trains charters.

Worblaufen

Eurovapor a une locomotive à vapeur à voie métrique basée à Worblaufen. Elle est utilisée pour des trains spéciaux sur le RBS entre Worblaufen et Worb Dorf ou Soleure le deuxième dimanche du mois.

Zweilütschinen

Le BOB a une locomotive à vapeur disponible pour des trains charters.

GRAUBUNDEN

Landquart

Le RhB a 3 machines à vapeur utilisées sur des trains spéciaux occasionels.

LUZERN

Lucerne

Le Musée National des Transports (Verkehrshaus) se situe sur la rive nord du lac des Quatre Cantons à environ 2 km de la gare (empruntez le trolleybus de la ligne 2). Certains matériels ne sont exposés que de temps à autre.
13 vapeurs, 15 électriques, 1 diesel, 8 automotrices, 4 tramways.

Triengen

Le Sursee Triengen Bahn a deux locomotives à vapeur disponible pour des trains charters.

Vitznau

Le VRB a 3 machines à vapeur utilisées sur des trains spéciaux les 1re et 3me dimanches du mois.

NEUCHATEL

St Sulpice

Le club «Vapeur Val de Travers» exploite des trains à vapeur certains weekends sur la section St Sulpice–Fleurier du RVT qui est normalement réservée aux marchandises. 6 vapeurs.

SOLOTHURN

Balsthal

Le OeBB a 2 machines à vapeur utilisées sur des trains spéciaux le dernier dimanche du mois.

THURGAU

Sulgen

Eurovapor a l'ancienne 23.058 du DB, utilisée ici pour des trains spéciaux occasionels sur des lignes principales.

Weinfelden

Le MThB a une machine à vapeur utilisée sur des trains spéciaux occasionels.

TICINO

Capolago

Le MG a une machine à vapeur utilisée sur des trains spéciaux occasionels.

VALAIS

Oberwald

Le club Furka Bergstrecke est en train de restaurer la section du FO sur le col du Furka qui fut abondonnée à l'ouverture du tunnel de base du Furka. Une machine à vapeur a été restaurée et d'autres a été rapatriées du Vietnam! 1 vapeur, 1 diesel.

Viege (Visp)

Le BVZ a une locomotive à vapeur disponible pour des trains charters.

VAUD

Bouveret

Le club «Trains de Rive Bleue» exploite des trains à vapeur les weekends entre Bouveret et Evian-les-Bains (France) sur la ligne de la rive sud du Lac Leman qui était récemment fermée au trafic.

Chaulin

La ligne à voie métrique de Blonay Chambay, qui offre d'excellents panoramas sur le lac Léman, est sans doûte la plus importante ligne exploitée par des amateurs en Suisse. Elle est exploitée les weekends avec des locomotives à vapeur et électriques. Une partie du matériel est garée sur d'autres sites. Des trains occasionels sont exploités sur le GFM qui est tout près.

Eschallens

Le LEB a une machine à vapeur utilisée sur des trains spéciaux occasionels.

Le Pont

Le Compagnie des Trains à Vapeur de la Vallée de Joux a 2 machines à vapeur utilisées sur des trains spéciaux occasionels sur le PBr.

ZÜRICH

Bauma

Le Dampfverein Zürcher Oberland (DVZO) exploite des trains à vapeur sur la ligne de marchandises CFF entre Bauma et Hinwil les 1re et 3me dimanches du mois. Les locomotives sont garées à plusieurs endroits.
4 vapeurs, 2 électriques.

Samstagern

Oswald Steam ont un musée près de la gare et les trains charters peuvent être exploités sur le SOB. Le musée s'ouvre sur demande et on peut louer une machine à vapeur à écartement de 610mm qu'on peut conduire soi-même! 7 vapeurs, 1 diesel.

Zürich Giesshubel

Le SZU a une locomotive à vapeur disponible pour des trains charters.